CompTIA

SECURITY+™

EXAM SY0–601

STUDY
SUPPLEMENT

Lowry Global Media LLC

Disclaimer
This book is not affiliated with or endorsed by CompTIA, Inc., or any representatives thereof.

ISBN: 978-1-950961-67-2

Contents

Introduction

At a minimum, you need to be able to speak the language Security; when Security comes up in conversation you need to be able to speak intelligently on the subject (this is the bare minimum). Aditionally, when in planning meetings (you know there are going to be a LOT of these) you need to be able to compare and contrast different approaches and implementations of Security.

This is the book to get you where you need to be. Just 133 pages, in an easy to read format, so you can get up to speed.

This book contains the perfect balance of subject matter and depth to provide you with the additional perspective you need to broaden your experience so you can speak the language of security and get ready for the Security+ exam.

Open source software is created by the community we belong to; IT professionals that want to do more and contribute. Just like open source software, this book has been created from open sources; a compilation of information for your benefit to help you speak the language of security and get ready for the Security+ exam.

Enjoy,

Mark "Shue" Schumacher
President
Lowry Global Media LLC

Social Engineering

In the context of information security, **social engineering** is the psychological manipulation of people into performing actions or divulging confidential information. This differs from social engineering within the social sciences, which does not concern the divulging of confidential information. A type of confidence trick for the purpose of information gathering, fraud, or system access, it differs from a traditional "con" in that it is often one of many steps in a more complex fraud scheme.[1]

It has also been defined as "any act that influences a person to take an action that may or may not be in their best interests."[2]

Information security culture

Employee behavior can have a big impact on information security in organizations. Cultural concepts can help different segments of the organization work effectively or work against effectiveness towards information security within an organization. "Exploring the Relationship between Organizational Culture and Information Security Culture" provides the following definition of information security culture: "ISC is the totality of patterns of behavior in an organization that contribute to the protection of information of all kinds."[3]

Andersson and Reimers (2014) found that employees often do not see themselves as part of the organization Information Security "effort" and often take actions that ignore organizational information security best interests.[4] Research shows Information security culture needs to be improved continuously. In "Information Security Culture from Analysis to Change," authors commented that "it's a never ending process, a cycle of evaluation and change or maintenance." They suggest that to manage information security culture, five steps should be taken: Pre-evaluation, strategic planning, operative planning, implementation, and post-evaluation.[5]

- Pre-Evaluation: to identify the awareness of information security within employees and to analyse current security policy.
- Strategic Planning: to come up with a better awareness-program, we need to set clear targets. Clustering people is helpful to achieve it.
- Operative Planning: set a good security culture based on internal communication, management-buy-in, and security awareness and training program.[5]
- Implementation: four stages should be used to implement the information security culture. They are commitment of the management, communication with organizational members, courses for all organizational members, and commitment of the employees.[5]

Techniques and terms

All social engineering techniques are based on specific attributes of human decision-making known as cognitive biases.[6] These biases, sometimes called "bugs in the human hardware", are exploited in various combinations to create attack techniques, some of which are listed below. The attacks used in social engineering can be used to steal employees' confidential information. The most common type of social engineering happens over the phone. Other examples of social engineering attacks are criminals posing as exterminators, fire marshals and technicians to go unnoticed as they steal company secrets.

One example of social engineering is an individual who walks into a building and posts an official-looking announcement to the company bulletin that says the number for the help desk has changed. So, when employees call for help the individual asks them for their passwords and IDs thereby gaining the ability to access the company's private information. Another example of social engineering would be that the hacker contacts the target on a social networking site and starts a conversation with the target. Gradually the hacker gains the trust of the target and then uses that trust to get access to sensitive information like password or bank account details.[7]

Social engineering relies heavily on the six principles of influence established by Robert Cialdini. Cialdini's theory of influence is based on six key principles: reciprocity, commitment and consistency, social proof, authority, liking, scarcity.

Six key principles

1. Reciprocity – People tend to return a favor, thus the pervasiveness of free samples in marketing. In his conferences, he often uses the example of Ethiopia providing thousands of dollars in humanitarian aid to Mexico just after the 1985 earthquake, despite Ethiopia suffering from a crippling famine and civil war at the time. Ethiopia had been reciprocating the diplomatic support Mexico provided when Italy invaded Ethiopia in 1935. The good cop/bad cop strategy is also based on this principle.
2. Commitment and consistency – If people commit, orally or in writing, to an idea or goal, they are more likely to honor that commitment because they have stated that that idea or goal fits their self-image. Even if the original incentive or motivation is removed after they have already agreed, they will continue to honor the agreement. Cialdini notes Chinese brainwashing of American prisoners of war to rewrite their self-image and gain automatic unenforced compliance. Another example is marketers who make the user close popups by saying "I'll sign up later" or "No thanks, I prefer not making money".
3. Social proof – People will do things that they see other people are doing. For example, in one experiment, one or more confederates would look up into the sky; bystanders would then look up into the sky to see what they were missing. At one point this experiment was aborted, as so many people were looking up that they stopped traffic. See conformity, and the Asch conformity experiments.
4. Authority – People will tend to obey authority figures, even if they are asked to perform objectionable acts. Cialdini cites incidents such as the Milgram experiments in the early 1960s and the My Lai massacre.
5. Liking – People are easily persuaded by other people whom they like. Cialdini cites the marketing of Tupperware in what might now be called viral marketing. People were more likely to buy if they liked the person selling it to them. Some of the many biases favoring more attractive people are discussed. See physical attractiveness stereotype.
6. Scarcity – Perceived scarcity will generate demand. For example, saying offers are available for a "limited time only" encourages sales.

Four social engineering vectors

Vishing

Vishing, otherwise known as "voice phishing", is the criminal practice of using social engineering over a telephone system to gain access to private personal and financial information from the public for the purpose of financial reward. It is also employed by attackers for reconnaissance purposes to gather more detailed intelligence on a target organization.

Phishing

Phishing is a technique of fraudulently obtaining private information. Typically, the phisher sends an e-mail that appears to come from a legitimate business—a bank, or credit card company—requesting "verification" of information and warning of some dire consequence if it is not provided. The e-mail usually contains a link to a fraudulent web page that seems legitimate—with company logos and content—and has a form requesting everything from a home address to an ATM card's PIN or a credit card number. For example, in 2003, there was a phishing scam in which users received emails supposedly from eBay claiming that the user's account was about to be suspended unless a link provided was clicked to update a credit card (information that the genuine eBay already had). By mimicking a legitimate organization's HTML code and logos, it is relatively simple to make a fake Website look authentic. The scam tricked some people into thinking that eBay was requiring them to update their account information by clicking on the link provided. By indiscriminately spamming extremely large groups of people, the "phisher" counted on gaining sensitive financial information from the small percentage (yet large number) of recipients who already have eBay accounts and also fall prey to the scam.

Smishing

The act of using SMS text messaging to lure victims into a specific course of action. Like phishing it can be clicking on a malicious link or divulging information.

Impersonation

Pretending or pretexting to be another person with the goal of gaining access physically to a system or building. Impersonation is used in the "SIM swap scam" fraud.

Other concepts

Pretexting

Pretexting (adj. **pretextual**) is the act of creating and using an invented scenario (the pretext) to engage a targeted victim in a manner that increases the chance the victim will divulge information or perform actions that would be unlikely in ordinary circumstances.[8] An elaborate lie, it most often involves some prior research or setup and the use of this information for impersonation (*e.g.*, date of birth, Social Security number, last bill amount) to establish legitimacy in the mind of the target.[9]

This technique can be used to fool a business into disclosing customer information as well as by private investigators to obtain telephone records, utility records, banking records and other information directly from company service representatives.[10] The information can then be used to establish even greater legitimacy under tougher questioning with a manager, *e.g.*, to make account changes, get specific balances, etc.

Pretexting can also be used to impersonate co-workers, police, bank, tax authorities, clergy, insurance investigators—or any other individual who could have perceived authority or right-to-know in the mind of the targeted victim. The pretexter must simply prepare answers to questions that might be asked by the victim. In some cases, all that is needed is a voice that sounds authoritative, an earnest tone, and an ability to think on one's feet to create a pretextual scenario.

Vishing

Phone phishing (or "vishing") uses a rogue interactive voice response (IVR) system to recreate a legitimate-sounding copy of a bank or other institution's IVR system. The victim is prompted (typically via a phishing e-mail) to call in to the "bank" via a (ideally toll free) number provided in order to "verify" information. A typical "vishing" system will reject log-ins continually, ensuring the victim enters PINs or passwords multiple times, often disclosing several different passwords. More advanced systems transfer the victim to the attacker/defrauder, who poses as a customer service agent or security expert for further questioning of the victim.

Spear phishing

Although similar to "phishing", spear phishing is a technique that fraudulently obtains private information by sending highly customized emails to few end users. It is the main difference between phishing attacks because phishing campaigns focus on sending out high volumes of generalized emails with the expectation that only a few people will respond. On the other hand, spear phishing emails require the attacker to perform additional research on their targets in order to "trick" end users into performing requested activities. The success rate of spear-phishing attacks is considerably higher than phishing attacks with people opening roughly 3% of phishing emails when compared to roughly 70% of potential attempts. Furthermore, when users actually open the emails phishing emails have a relatively modest 5% success rate to have the link or attachment clicked when compared to a spear-phishing attack's 50% success rate.[11]

Spear Phishing success is heavily dependent on the amount and quality of OSINT (Open Source Intelligence) that the attacker can obtain. Social media account activity is one example of a source of OSINT.

Water holing

Water holing is a targeted social engineering strategy that capitalizes on the trust users have in websites they regularly visit. The victim feels safe to do things they would not do in a different situation. A wary person might, for example, purposefully avoid clicking a link in an unsolicited email, but the same person would not hesitate to follow a link on a website they often visit. So, the attacker prepares a trap for the unwary prey at a favored watering hole. This strategy has been successfully used to gain access to some (supposedly) very secure systems.[12]

The attacker may set out by identifying a group or individuals to target. The preparation involves gathering information about websites the targets often visit from the secure system. The information gathering confirms that the targets visit the websites and that the system allows such visits. The attacker then tests these websites for vulnerabilities to inject code that may infect a visitor's system with malware. The injected code trap and malware may be tailored to the specific target group and the specific systems they use. In time, one or more members of the target group will get infected and the attacker can gain access to the secure system.

Baiting

Baiting is like the real-world Trojan horse that uses physical media and relies on the curiosity or greed of the victim.[13] In this attack, attackers leave malware-infected floppy disks, CD-ROMs, or USB flash drives in locations people will find them (bathrooms, elevators, sidewalks, parking lots, etc.), give them legitimate and curiosity-piquing labels, and waits for victims.

For example, an attacker may create a disk featuring a corporate logo, available from the target's website, and label it "Executive Salary Summary Q2 2012". The attacker then leaves the disk on the floor of an elevator or somewhere in the lobby of the target company. An unknowing employee may find it and insert the disk into a computer to satisfy their curiosity, or a good Samaritan may find it and return it to the company. In any case, just inserting the disk into a computer installs malware, giving attackers access to the victim's PC and, perhaps, the target company's internal computer network.

Unless computer controls block infections, insertion compromises PCs "auto-running" media. Hostile devices can also be used.[14] For instance, a "lucky winner" is sent a free digital audio player compromising any computer it is plugged to. A "**road apple**" (the colloquial term for horse manure, suggesting the device's undesirable nature) is any removable media with malicious software left in opportunistic or conspicuous places. It may be a CD, DVD, or USB flash drive, among other media. Curious people take it and plug it into a computer, infecting the host and any attached networks. Again, hackers may give them enticing labels, such as "Employee Salaries" or "Confidential".[15]

One study done in 2016 had researchers drop 297 USB drives around the campus of the University of Illinois. The drives contained files on them that linked to webpages owned by the researchers. The researchers were able to see how many of the drives had files on them opened, but not how many were inserted into a computer without having a file opened. Of the 297 drives that were dropped, 290 (98%) of them were picked up and 135 (45%) of them "called home".[16]

Quid pro quo

Quid pro quo means *something for something*:

- An attacker calls random numbers at a company, claiming to be calling back from technical support. Eventually this person will hit someone with a legitimate problem, grateful that someone is calling back to help them. The attacker will "help" solve the problem and, in the process, have the user type commands that give the attacker access or launch malware.
- In a 2003 information security survey, 91% of office workers gave researchers what they claimed was their password in answer to a survey question in exchange for a cheap pen.[17] Similar surveys in later years obtained similar results using chocolates and other cheap lures, although they made no attempt to validate the passwords.[18]

Tailgating

An attacker, seeking entry to a restricted area secured by unattended, electronic access control, e.g. by RFID card, simply walks in behind a person who has legitimate access. Following common courtesy, the legitimate person will usually hold the door open for the attacker or the attackers themselves may ask the employee to hold it open for them. The legitimate person may fail to ask for identification for any of several reasons, or may accept an assertion that the attacker has forgotten or lost the appropriate identity token. The attacker may also fake the action of presenting an identity token.

Other types

Common confidence tricksters or fraudsters also could be considered "social engineers" in the wider sense, in that they deliberately deceive and manipulate people, exploiting human weaknesses to obtain personal benefit. They may, for example, use social engineering techniques as part of an IT fraud.

A very recent[*when?*] type of social engineering technique includes spoofing or hacking IDs of people having popular e-mail IDs such as Yahoo!, Gmail, Hotmail, etc. Among the many motivations for deception are:

- Phishing credit-card account numbers and their passwords.
- Cracking private e-mails and chat histories, and manipulating them by using common editing techniques before using them to extort money and creating distrust among individuals.
- Cracking websites of companies or organizations and destroying their reputation.
- Computer virus hoaxes
- Convincing users to run malicious code within the web browser via self-XSS attack to allow access to their web account

Countermeasures

Organizations reduce their security risks by:

Training to Employees Training employees in security protocols relevant to their position. (e.g., in situations such as tailgating, if a person's identity cannot be verified, then employees must be trained to politely refuse.)

Standard Framework Establishing frameworks of trust on an employee/personnel level (i.e., specify and train personnel when/where/why/how sensitive information should be handled)

Scrutinizing Information Identifying which information is sensitive and evaluating its exposure to social engineering and breakdowns in security systems (building, computer system, etc.)

Security Protocols Establishing security protocols, policies, and procedures for handling sensitive information.

Event Test Performing unannounced, periodic tests of the security framework.

Inoculation Preventing social engineering and other fraudulent tricks or traps by instilling a resistance to persuasion attempts through exposure to similar or related attempts.[19]

Review Reviewing the above steps regularly: no solutions to information integrity are perfect.[20]

Waste Management Using a waste management service that has dumpsters with locks on them, with keys to them limited only to the waste management company and the cleaning staff. Locating the dumpster either in view of employees so that trying to access it carries a risk of being seen or caught, or behind a locked gate or fence where the person must trespass before they can attempt to access the dumpster.[21]

The lifecycle of social engineering

1. **Information gathering**-Information gathering is the first and for the most step that requires much patience and keenly watching habits of the victim. This step gathering data about the victim's interests, personal information. It determines the success rate of the overall attack.
2. **Engaging with victim**-After gathering required amount of information, the attacker opens a conversation with the victim smoothly without the victim finding anything inappropriate.
3. **Attacking**-This step generally occurs after a long period of engaging with the target and during this information from the target is retrieved by using social engineering. In phase, the attacker gets the results from the target.

4. **Closing interaction**-This is the last step which includes slowly shutting down the communication by the attacker without arising any suspicion in the victim. In this way, the motive is fulfilled as well as the victim rarely comes to know the attack even happened.[22]

Preventive measures

Taking some precautions reduce the risk of being a victim to social engineering frauds. The precautions that can be made are as follows:-

* Be aware of offers that seem "Too good to be true ".
* Avoid clicking on attachments from unknown sources.
* Not giving out personal information to anyone via email, phone, or text messages.
* Use of spam filter software such as Spam box.
* Avoid befriending people that you do not know in real life.
* Teach kids to contact a trusted adult in case they are being bullied over the internet (cyberbullying) or feel threatened by anything online.[41]

Malware

Malware (a portmanteau for **malicious software**) is any software intentionally designed to cause damage to a computer, server, client, or computer network[1][2] (by contrast, software that causes *unintentional* harm due to some deficiency is typically described as a software bug).[3] A wide variety of malware types exist, including computer viruses, worms, Trojan horses, ransomware, spyware, adware, rogue software, and scareware.

Programs are also considered malware if they secretly act against the interests of the computer user. For example, at one point Sony music Compact discs silently installed a rootkit on purchasers' computers with the intention of preventing illicit copying, but which also reported on users' listening habits, and unintentionally created extra security vulnerabilities.[4]

A range of antivirus software, firewalls and other strategies are used to help protect against the introduction of malware, to help detect it if it is already present, and to recover from malware-associated malicious activity and attacks.[5]

Purposes

Malware is sometimes used broadly against government or corporate websites to gather guarded information,[9] or to disrupt their operation in general. However, malware can be used against individuals to gain information such as personal identification numbers or details, bank or credit card numbers, and passwords.

Since the rise of widespread broadband Internet access, malicious software has more frequently been designed for profit. Since 2003, the majority of widespread viruses and worms have been designed to take control of users' computers for illicit purposes.[10] Infected "zombie computers" can be used to send email spam, to host contraband data such as child pornography,[11] or to engage in distributed denial-of-service attacks as a form of extortion.[12]

Programs designed to monitor users' web browsing, display unsolicited advertisements, or redirect affiliate marketing revenues are called spyware. Spyware programs do not spread like viruses; instead they are generally installed by exploiting security holes. They can also be hidden and packaged together with unrelated user-installed software.[13] The Sony BMG rootkit was intended to prevent illicit copying; but also reported on users' listening habits, and unintentionally created extra security vulnerabilities.[4]

Ransomware affects an infected computer system in some way, and demands payment to bring it back to its normal state. There are two variations of ransomware, being crypto ransomware and locker ransomware. [14] With the locker ransomware just locking down a computer system without encrypting its contents. Whereas the traditional ransomware is one that locks down a system and encrypts its contents. For example, programs such as CryptoLocker encrypt files securely, and only decrypt them on payment of a substantial sum of money.[15]

Some malware is used to generate money by click fraud, making it appear that the computer user has clicked an advertising link on a site, generating a payment from the advertiser. It was estimated in 2012 that about 60 to 70% of all active malware used some kind of click fraud, and 22% of all ad-clicks were fraudulent.[16]

In addition to criminal money-making, malware can be used for sabotage, often for political motives. Stuxnet, for example, was designed to disrupt very specific industrial equipment. There have been politically motivated attacks which spread over and shut down large computer networks, including massive deletion of files and corruption of master boot records, described as "computer killing." Such attacks were made on Sony Pictures Entertainment (25 November 2014, using malware known as Shamoon or W32.Disttrack) and Saudi Aramco (August 2012).[17][18]

Infectious malware

The best-known types of malware, viruses and worms, are known for the manner in which they spread, rather than any specific types of behavior. A computer virus is software that embeds itself in some other executable software (including the operating system itself) on the target system without the user's knowledge and consent and when it is run, the virus is spread to other executables. On the other hand, a *worm* is a stand-alone malware software that *actively* transmits itself over a network to infect other computers. These definitions lead to the observation that a virus requires the user to run an infected software or operating system for the virus to spread, whereas a worm spreads itself.[19]

Concealment

These categories are not mutually exclusive, so malware may use multiple techniques.[20] This section only applies to malware designed to operate undetected, not sabotage and ransomware.

Viruses

A computer virus is software usually hidden within another seemingly innocuous program that can produce copies of itself and insert them into other programs or files, and that usually performs a harmful action (such as destroying data).[21] An example of this is a PE infection, a technique, usually used to spread malware, that inserts extra data or executable code into PE files.[22]

Screen-locking ransomware

'Lock-screens', or screen lockers is a type of "cyber police" ransomware that blocks screens on Windows or Android devices with a false accusation in harvesting illegal content, trying to scare the victims into paying up a fee.[23] Jisut and SLocker impact Android devices more than other lock-screens, with Jisut making up nearly 60 percent of all Android ransomware detections.[24]

Trojan horses

A Trojan horse is a harmful program that misrepresents itself to masquerade as a regular, benign program or utility in order to persuade a victim to install it. A Trojan horse usually carries a hidden destructive function that is activated when the application is started. The term is derived from the Ancient Greek story of the Trojan horse used to invade the city of Troy by stealth.[25][26][27][28][29]

Trojan horses are generally spread by some form of social engineering, for example, where a user is duped into executing an e-mail attachment disguised to be unsuspicious, (e.g., a routine form to be filled in), or by drive-by download. Although their payload can be anything, many modern forms act as a backdoor, contacting a controller (phoning home) which can then have unauthorized access to the affected computer, potentially installing additional software such as a keylogger to steal confidential information, cryptomining software or adware to generate revenue to the operator of the trojan.[30] While Trojan horses and backdoors are not easily detectable by themselves, computers may appear to run slower, emit more heat or fan noise due to heavy processor or network usage, as may occur when cryptomining software is installed.

Unlike computer viruses and worms, Trojan horses generally do not attempt to inject themselves into other files or otherwise propagate themselves.[31]

In spring 2017 Mac users were hit by the new version of Proton Remote Access Trojan (RAT)[32] trained to extract password data from various sources, such as browser auto-fill data, the Mac-OS keychain, and password vaults.[33]

Rootkits

Once malicious software is installed on a system, it is essential that it stays concealed, to avoid detection. Software packages known as *rootkits* allow this concealment, by modifying the host's operating system so that the malware is hidden from the user. Rootkits can prevent a harmful process from being visible in the system's list of processes, or keep its files from being read.[34]

Some types of harmful software contain routines to evade identification and/or removal attempts, not merely to hide themselves. An early example of this behavior is recorded in the Jargon File tale of a pair of programs infesting a Xerox CP-V time sharing system:

> Each ghost-job would detect the fact that the other had been killed, and would start a new copy of the recently stopped program within a few milliseconds. The only way to kill both ghosts was to kill them simultaneously (very difficult) or to deliberately crash the system.[35]

Backdoors

A backdoor is a method of bypassing normal authentication procedures, usually over a connection to a network such as the Internet. Once a system has been compromised, one or more backdoors may be installed in order to allow access in the future,[36] invisibly to the user.

The idea has often been suggested that computer manufacturers preinstall backdoors on their systems to provide technical support for customers, but this has never been reliably verified. It was reported in 2014 that US government agencies had been diverting computers purchased by those considered "targets" to secret workshops where software or hardware permitting remote access by the agency was installed, considered to be among the most productive operations to obtain access to networks around the world.[37] Backdoors may be installed by Trojan horses, worms, implants, or other methods.[38][39]

Evasion

Since the beginning of 2015, a sizable portion of malware has been utilizing a combination of many techniques designed to avoid detection and analysis.[40] From the more common, to the least common:

1. evasion of analysis and detection by fingerprinting the environment when executed.[41]
2. confusing automated tools' detection methods. This allows malware to avoid detection by technologies such as signature-based antivirus software by changing the server used by the malware.[42]
3. timing-based evasion. This is when malware runs at certain times or following certain actions taken by the user, so it executes during certain vulnerable periods, such as during the boot process, while remaining dormant the rest of the time.
4. obfuscating internal data so that automated tools do not detect the malware.[43]

An increasingly common technique (2015) is adware that uses stolen certificates to disable anti-malware and virus protection; technical remedies are available to deal with the adware.[44]

Nowadays, one of the most sophisticated and stealthy ways of evasion is to use information hiding techniques, namely stegomalware. A survey on stegomalware was published by Cabaj et al. in 2018.[45]

Another type of evasion technique is Fileless malware or Advanced Volatile Threats (AVTs). Fileless malware does not require a file to operate. It runs within memory and utilizes existing system tools to carry out malicious acts. Because there are no files on the system, there are no executable files for antivirus and forensic tools to analyze, making such malware nearly impossible to detect. The only way to detect fileless malware is to catch it operating in real time. Recently these type attacks have become more frequent with a 432% increase in 2017 and makeup 35% of the attacks in 2018. Such attacks are not easy to perform but are becoming more prevalent with the help of exploit-kits. [46][47]

Vulnerability

- In this context, and throughout, what is called the "system" under attack may be anything from a single application, through a complete computer and operating system, to a large network.
- Various factors make a system more vulnerable to malware:

Security defects in software

Malware exploits security defects (security bugs or vulnerabilities) in the design of the operating system, in applications (such as browsers, e.g. older versions of Microsoft Internet Explorer supported by Windows

XP[48]), or in vulnerable versions of browser plugins such as Adobe Flash Player, Adobe Acrobat or Reader, or Java SE.[49][50] Sometimes even installing new versions of such plugins does not automatically uninstall old versions. Security advisories from plug-in providers announce security-related updates.[51] Common vulnerabilities are assigned CVE IDs and listed in the US National Vulnerability Database. Secunia PSI[52] is an example of software, free for personal use, that will check a PC for vulnerable out-of-date software, and attempt to update it.

Malware authors target bugs, or loopholes, to exploit. A common method is exploitation of a buffer overrun vulnerability, where software designed to store data in a specified region of memory does not prevent more data than the buffer can accommodate being supplied. Malware may provide data that overflows the buffer, with malicious executable code or data after the end; when this payload is accessed it does what the attacker, not the legitimate software, determines.

Insecure design or user error

Early PCs had to be booted from floppy disks. When built-in hard drives became common, the operating system was normally started from them, but it was possible to boot from another boot device if available, such as a floppy disk, CD-ROM, DVD-ROM, USB flash drive or network. It was common to configure the computer to boot from one of these devices when available. Normally none would be available; the user would intentionally insert, say, a CD into the optical drive to boot the computer in some special way, for example, to install an operating system. Even without booting, computers can be configured to execute software on some media as soon as they become available, e.g. to autorun a CD or USB device when inserted.

Malware distributors would trick the user into booting or running from an infected device or medium. For example, a virus could make an infected computer add autorunnable code to any USB stick plugged into it. Anyone who then attached the stick to another computer set to autorun from USB would in turn become infected, and also pass on the infection in the same way.[53] More generally, any device that plugs into a USB port - even lights, fans, speakers, toys, or peripherals such as a digital microscope - can be used to spread malware. Devices can be infected during manufacturing or supply if quality control is inadequate. [53]

This form of infection can largely be avoided by setting up computers by default to boot from the internal hard drive, if available, and not to autorun from devices.[53] Intentional booting from another device is always possible by pressing certain keys during boot.

Older email software would automatically open HTML email containing potentially malicious JavaScript code. Users may also execute disguised malicious email attachments. The *2018 Data Breach Investigations Report* by Verizon, cited by CSO Online, states that emails are the primary method of malware delivery, accounting for 92% of malware delivery around the world.[54][55]

Over-privileged users and over-privileged code

In computing, privilege refers to how much a user or program is allowed to modify a system. In poorly designed computer systems, both users and programs can be assigned more privileges than they should have, and malware can take advantage of this. The two ways that malware does this is through overprivileged users and overprivileged code.[*citation needed*]

Some systems allow all users to modify their internal structures, and such users today would be considered over-privileged users. This was the standard operating procedure for early microcomputer and home computer systems, where there was no distinction between an *administrator* or *root*, and a regular user of the system. In some systems, non-administrator users are over-privileged by design, in the sense that they are allowed to modify internal structures of the system. In some environments, users are over-privileged because they have been inappropriately granted administrator or equivalent status.[*citation needed*]

Some systems allow code executed by a user to access all rights of that user, which is known as over-privileged code. This was also standard operating procedure for early microcomputer and home computer systems. Malware, running as over-privileged code, can use this privilege to subvert the system. Almost all currently popular operating systems, and also many scripting applications allow code too many privileges, usually in the sense that when a user executes code, the system allows that code all rights of that user. This makes users vulnerable to malware in the form of e-mail attachments, which may or may not be disguised. [*citation needed*]

Use of the same operating system

- Homogeneity can be a vulnerability. For example, when all computers in a network run the same operating system, upon exploiting one, one worm can exploit them all:[56] In particular, Microsoft Windows or Mac OS X have such a large share of the market that an exploited vulnerability concentrating on either operating system could subvert a large number of systems. Introducing diversity purely for the sake of robustness, such as adding Linux computers, could increase short-term costs for training and maintenance. However, as long as all the nodes are not part of the same directory service for authentication, having a few diverse nodes could deter total shutdown of the network and allow those nodes to help with recovery of the infected nodes. Such separate, functional redundancy could avoid the cost of a total shutdown, at the cost of increased complexity and reduced usability in terms of single sign-on authentication.[*citation needed*]

Anti-malware strategies

As malware attacks become more frequent, attention has begun to shift from viruses and spyware protection, to malware protection, and programs that have been specifically developed to combat malware. (Other preventive and recovery measures, such as backup and recovery methods, are mentioned in the computer virus article).

Anti-virus and anti-malware software

A specific component of anti-virus and anti-malware software, commonly referred to as an on-access or real-time scanner, hooks deep into the operating system's core or kernel and functions in a manner similar to how certain malware itself would attempt to operate, though with the user's informed permission for protecting the system. Any time the operating system accesses a file, the on-access scanner checks if the file is a 'legitimate' file or not. If the file is identified as malware by the scanner, the access operation will be stopped, the file will be dealt with by the scanner in a pre-defined way (how the anti-virus program was configured during/post installation), and the user will be notified.[*citation needed*] This may have a considerable performance impact on the operating system, though the degree of impact is dependent on how well the scanner was programmed. The goal is to stop any operations the malware may attempt on the system before they occur, including activities which might exploit bugs or trigger unexpected operating system behavior.

Anti-malware programs can combat malware in two ways:

1. They can provide real time protection against the installation of malware software on a computer.

This type of malware protection works the same way as that of antivirus protection in that the anti-malware software scans all incoming network data for malware and blocks any threats it comes across.

2. Anti-malware software programs can be used solely for detection and removal of malware software that has already been installed onto a computer. This type of anti-malware software scans the contents of the Windows registry, operating system files, and installed programs on a computer and will provide a list of any threats found, allowing the user to choose which files to delete or keep, or to compare this list to a list of known malware components, removing files that match.[57]

Real-time protection from malware works identically to real-time antivirus protection: the software scans disk files at download time, and blocks the activity of components known to represent malware. In some cases, it may also intercept attempts to install start-up items or to modify browser settings. Because many malware components are installed as a result of browser exploits or user error, using security software (some of which are anti-malware, though many are not) to "sandbox" browsers (essentially isolate the browser from the computer and hence any malware induced change) can also be effective in helping to restrict any damage done.[58]

Examples of Microsoft Windows antivirus and anti-malware software include the optional Microsoft Security Essentials[59] (for Windows XP, Vista, and Windows 7) for real-time protection, the Windows Malicious Software Removal Tool[60] (now included with Windows (Security) Updates on "Patch Tuesday", the second Tuesday of each month), and Windows Defender (an optional download in the case of Windows XP, incorporating MSE functionality in the case of Windows 8 and later).[61] Additionally, several capable antivirus software programs are available for free download from the Internet (usually restricted to non-commercial use).[62] Tests found some free programs to be competitive with commercial ones.[62][63][64] Microsoft's System File Checker can be used to check for and repair corrupted system files.

Some viruses disable System Restore and other important Windows tools such as Task Manager and Command Prompt. Many such viruses can be removed by rebooting the computer, entering Windows safe mode with networking,[65] and then using system tools or Microsoft Safety Scanner.[66]

Hardware implants can be of any type, so there can be no general way to detect them.

Website security scans

As malware also harms the compromised websites (by breaking reputation, blacklisting in search engines, etc.), some websites offer vulnerability scanning.[67][68][69][70] Such scans check the website, detect malware[71], may note outdated software, and may report known security issues.

"Air gap" isolation or "parallel network"

As a last resort, computers can be protected from malware, and infected computers can be prevented from disseminating trusted information, by imposing an "air gap" (i.e. completely disconnecting them from all other networks). However, malware can still cross the air gap in some situations. For example, removable media can carry malware across the gap.[*citation needed*]

"AirHopper",[72] "BitWhisper",[73] "GSMem" [74] and "Fansmitter" [75] are four techniques introduced by researchers that can leak data from air-gapped computers using electromagnetic, thermal and acoustic emissions.

Grayware

Grayware is a term applied to unwanted applications or files that are not classified as malware, but can worsen the performance of computers and may cause security risks.[76]

It describes applications that behave in an annoying or undesirable manner, and yet are less serious or troublesome than malware. Grayware encompasses spyware, adware, fraudulent dialers, joke programs, remote access tools and other unwanted programs that may harm the performance of computers or cause inconvenience. The term came into use around 2004.[77]

Another term, potentially unwanted program (PUP) or potentially unwanted application (PUA),[78] refers to applications that would be considered unwanted despite often having been downloaded by the user, possibly after failing to read a download agreement. PUPs include spyware, adware, and fraudulent dialers. Many security products classify unauthorised key generators as grayware, although they frequently carry true malware in addition to their ostensible purpose.

Software maker Malwarebytes lists several criteria for classifying a program as a PUP.[79] Some types of adware (using stolen certificates) turn off anti-malware and virus protection; technical remedies are available.[44]

History of viruses and worms

Before Internet access became widespread, viruses spread on personal computers by infecting executable programs or boot sectors of floppy disks. By inserting a copy of itself into the machine code instructions in these programs or boot sectors, a virus causes itself to be run whenever the program is run or the disk is booted. Early computer viruses were written for the Apple II and Macintosh, but they became more widespread with the dominance of the IBM PC and MS-DOS system. The first IBM PC virus in the "wild" was a boot sector virus dubbed (c)Brain,[80] created in 1986 by the Farooq Alvi brothers in Pakistan.[81] Executable-infecting viruses are dependent on users exchanging software or boot-able floppies and thumb drives so they spread rapidly in computer hobbyist circles.[citation needed]

The first worms, network-borne infectious programs, originated not on personal computers, but on multitasking Unix systems. The first well-known worm was the Internet Worm of 1988, which infected SunOS and VAX BSD systems. Unlike a virus, this worm did not insert itself into other programs. Instead, it exploited security holes (vulnerabilities) in network server programs and started itself running as a separate process.[82] This same behavior is used by today's worms as well.[83][84]

With the rise of the Microsoft Windows platform in the 1990s, and the flexible macros of its applications, it became possible to write infectious code in the macro language of Microsoft Word and similar programs. These *macro viruses* infect documents and templates rather than applications (executables), but rely on the fact that macros in a Word document are a form of executable code.[85]

Academic research

The notion of a self-reproducing computer program can be traced back to initial theories about the operation of complex automata.[86] John von Neumann showed that in theory a program could reproduce itself. This constituted a plausibility result in computability theory. Fred Cohen experimented with computer viruses and confirmed Neumann's postulate and investigated other properties of malware such as detectability and self-obfuscation using rudimentary encryption. His 1987 doctoral dissertation was on the subject of computer viruses.[87] The combination of cryptographic technology as part of the payload of the virus, exploiting it for attack purposes was initialized and investigated from the mid 1990s, and includes initial ransomware and evasion ideas.[88]

Security Testing

Security testing is a process intended to reveal flaws in the security mechanisms of an information system that protect data and maintain functionality as intended.[1] Due to the logical limitations of security testing, passing security testing is not an indication that no flaws exist or that the system adequately satisfies the security requirements.

Typical security requirements may include specific elements of confidentiality, integrity, authentication, availability, authorization and non-repudiation.[2] Actual security requirements tested depend on the security requirements implemented by the system. Security testing as a term has a number of different meanings and can be completed in a number of different ways. As such a Security Taxonomy helps us to understand these different approaches and meanings by providing a base level to work from.

Confidentiality

- A security measure which protects against the disclosure of information to parties other than the intended recipient is by no means the only way of ensuring the security.

Integrity

Integrity of information refers to protecting information from being modified by unauthorized parties

- A measure intended to allow the receiver to determine that the information provided by a system is correct.
- Integrity schemes often use some of the same underlying technologies as confidentiality schemes, but they usually involve adding information to a communication, to form the basis of an algorithmic check, rather than the encoding all of the communication.
- To check if the correct information is transferred from one application to other.

Authentication

This might involve confirming the identity of a person, tracing the origins of an artifact, ensuring that a product is what its packaging and labeling claims to be, or assuring that a computer program is a trusted one.

Authorization

- The process of determining that a requester is allowed to receive a service or perform an operation.

- Access control is an example of authorization.

Availability

- Assuring information and communications services will be ready for use when expected.
- Information must be kept available to authorized persons when they need it.

Non-repudiation

- In reference to digital security, non-repudiation means to ensure that a transferred message has been sent and received by the parties claiming to have sent and received the message. Non-repudiation is a way to guarantee that the sender of a message cannot later deny having sent the message and that the recipient cannot deny having received the message.

Taxonomy

Common terms used for the delivery of security testing:

- **Discovery** - The purpose of this stage is to identify systems within scope and the services in use. It is not intended to discover vulnerabilities, but version detection may highlight deprecated versions of software / firmware and thus indicate potential vulnerabilities.
- **Vulnerability Scan** - Following the discovery stage this looks for known security issues by using automated tools to match conditions with known vulnerabilities. The reported risk level is set automatically by the tool with no manual verification or interpretation by the test vendor. This can be supplemented with credential based scanning that looks to remove some common false positives by using supplied credentials to authenticate with a service (such as local windows accounts).
- **Vulnerability Assessment** - This uses discovery and vulnerability scanning to identify security vulnerabilities and places the findings into the context of the environment under test. An example would be removing common false positives from the report and deciding risk levels that should be applied to each report finding to improve business understanding and context.
- **Security Assessment** - Builds upon Vulnerability Assessment by adding manual verification to confirm exposure, but does not include the exploitation of vulnerabilities to gain further access. Verification could be in the form of authorized access to a system to confirm system settings and involve examining logs, system responses, error messages, codes, etc. A Security Assessment is looking to gain a broad coverage of the systems under test but not the depth of exposure that a specific vulnerability could lead to.
- **Penetration Test** - Penetration test simulates an attack by a malicious party. Building on the previous stages and involves exploitation of found vulnerabilities to gain further access. Using this approach will result in an understanding of the ability of an attacker to gain access to confidential information, affect data integrity or availability of a service and the respective impact. Each test is approached using a consistent and complete methodology in a way that allows the tester to use their problem solving abilities, the output from a range of tools and their own knowledge of networking and systems to find vulnerabilities that would/ could not be identified by automated tools. This approach looks at the depth of attack as compared to the Security Assessment approach that looks at the broader coverage.
- **Security Audit** - Driven by an Audit / Risk function to look at a specific control or compliance issue. Characterized by a narrow scope, this type of engagement could make use of any of the

earlier approaches discussed (vulnerability assessment, security assessment, penetration test).

- **Security Review** - Verification that industry or internal security standards have been applied to system components or product. This is typically completed through gap analysis and utilizes build / code reviews or by reviewing design documents and architecture diagrams. This activity does not utilize any of the earlier approaches (Vulnerability Assessment, Security Assessment, Penetration Test, Security Audit)

Tools

- CSA - Container and Infrastructure Security Analysis
- DAST - Dynamic Application Security Testing
- DLP - Data Loss Prevention
- IAST - Interactive Application Security Testing
- IDS/IPS - Intrusion Detection and/or Intrusion Prevention
- OSS - Open Source Software Scanning
- RASP - Runtime Application Self Protection
- SAST - Static Application Security Testing
- SCA - Software Composition Analysis
- WAF - Web Application Firewall

Vulnerability

In computer security, a **vulnerability** is a weakness which can be exploited by a threat actor, such as an attacker, to cross privilege boundaries (i.e. perform unauthorized actions) within a computer system. To exploit a vulnerability, an attacker must have at least one applicable tool or technique that can connect to a system weakness. In this frame, vulnerabilities are also known as the attack surface.

Vulnerability management is the cyclical practice that varies in theory but contains common processes which include: discover all assets, prioritize assets, assess or perform a complete vulnerability scan, report on results, remediate vulnerabilities, verify remediation - repeat. This practice generally refers to software vulnerabilities in computing systems.[1]

A security risk is often incorrectly classified as a vulnerability. The use of vulnerability with the same meaning of risk can lead to confusion. The risk is the potential of a significant impact resulting from the exploit of a vulnerability. Then there are vulnerabilities without risk: for example when the affected asset has no value. A vulnerability with one or more known instances of working and fully implemented attacks is classified as an exploitable vulnerability—a vulnerability for which an exploit exists. The window of vulnerability is the time from when the security hole was introduced or manifested in deployed software, to when access was removed, a security fix was available/deployed, or the attacker was disabled—see zero-day attack.

Security bug (security defect) is a narrower concept. There are vulnerabilities that are not related to software: hardware, site, personnel vulnerabilities are examples of vulnerabilities that are not software security bugs.

Constructs in programming languages that are difficult to use properly can manifest large numbers of vulnerabilities.

Definitions

ISO 27005 defines **vulnerability** as:[2]

> *A weakness of an asset or group of assets that can be exploited by one or more threats,* where an *asset is anything that has value to the organization, its business operations and their continuity, including information resources that support the organization's mission*[3]

IETF RFC 4949 **vulnerability** as:[4]

> *A flaw or weakness in a system's design, implementation, or operation and management that could be exploited to violate the system's security policy*

The Committee on National Security Systems of United States of America defined **vulnerability** in CNSS Instruction No. 4009 dated 26 April 2010 National Information Assurance Glossary:[5]

> *Vulnerability—Weakness in an information system, system security procedures, internal controls, or implementation that could be exploited by a threat source.*

Many NIST publications define **vulnerability** in IT context in different publications: FISMApedia[6] term[7] provide a list. Between them SP 800-30,[8] give a broader one:

> *A flaw or weakness in system security procedures, design, implementation, or internal controls that could be exercised (accidentally triggered or intentionally exploited) and result in a security breach or a violation of the system's security policy.*

ENISA defines **vulnerability** in[9] as:

> *The existence of a weakness, design, or implementation error that can lead to an unexpected, undesirable event [G.11] compromising the security of the computer system, network, application, or protocol involved.(ITSEC)*

The Open Group defines **vulnerability** in[10] as

> *The probability that threat capability exceeds the ability to resist the threat.*

Factor Analysis of Information Risk (FAIR) defines **vulnerability** as:[11]

> *The probability that an asset will be unable to resist the actions of a threat agent*

According FAIR vulnerability is related to Control Strength, i.e. the strength of a control as compared to a standard measure of force and the threat Capabilities, i.e. the probable level of force that a threat agent is capable of applying against an asset.

ISACA defines **vulnerability** in Risk It framework as:

> *A weakness in design, implementation, operation or internal control*

Data and Computer Security: Dictionary of standards concepts and terms, authors Dennis Longley and Michael Shain, Stockton Press, ISBN 0-935859-17-9, defines **vulnerability** as:

1) In computer security, a weakness in automated systems security procedures, administrative controls, Internet controls, etc., that could be exploited by a threat to gain unauthorized access to information or to disrupt critical processing. 2) In computer security, a weakness in the physical layout, organization, procedures, personnel, management, administration, hardware or software that may be exploited to cause harm to the ADP system or activity. 3) In computer security, any weakness or flaw existing in a system. The attack or harmful event, or the opportunity available to a threat agent to mount that attack.

Matt Bishop and Dave Bailey[12] give the following definition of computer **vulnerability**:

A computer system is composed of states describing the current configuration of the entities that make up the computer system. The system computes through the application of state transitions that change the state of the system. All states reachable from a given initial state using a set of state transitions fall into the class of authorized or unauthorized, as defined by a security policy. In this paper, the definitions of these classes and transitions is considered axiomatic. A vulnerable state is an authorized state from which an unauthorized state can be reached using authorized state transitions. A compromised state is the state so reached. An attack is a sequence of authorized state transitions which end in a compromised state. By definition, an attack begins in a vulnerable state. A vulnerability is a characterization of a vulnerable state which distinguishes it from all non-vulnerable states. If generic, the vulnerability may characterize many vulnerable states; if specific, it may characterize only one...

National Information Assurance Training and Education Center defines **vulnerability**:[13][14]

A weakness in automated system security procedures, administrative controls, internal controls, and so forth, that could be exploited by a threat to gain unauthorized access to information or disrupt critical processing. 2. A weakness in system security procedures, hardware design, internal controls, etc. , which could be exploited to gain unauthorized access to classified or sensitive information. 3. A weakness in the physical layout, organization, procedures, personnel, management, administration, hardware, or software that may be exploited to cause harm to the ADP system or activity. The presence of a vulnerability does not in itself cause harm; a vulnerability is merely a condition or set of conditions that may allow the ADP system or activity to be harmed by an attack. 4. An assertion primarily concerning entities of the internal environment (assets); we say that an asset (or class of assets) is vulnerable (in some way, possibly involving an agent or collection of agents); we write: V(i,e) where: e may be an empty set. 5. Susceptibility to various threats. 6. A set of properties of a specific internal entity that, in union with a set of properties of a specific external entity, implies a risk. 7. The characteristics of a system which cause it to suffer a definite degradation (incapability to perform the designated mission) as a result of having been subjected to a certain level of effects in an unnatural (manmade) hostile environment.

Vulnerability and risk factor models

A resource (either physical or logical) may have one or more vulnerabilities that can be exploited by a threat actor. The result can potentially compromise the confidentiality, integrity or availability of resources (not necessarily the vulnerable one) belonging to an organization and/or other parties involved (customers, suppliers). The so-called CIA triad is a cornerstone of Information Security.

An attack can be *active* when it attempts to alter system resources or affect their operation, compromising integrity or availability. A "*passive attack*" attempts to learn or make use of information from the system but does not affect system resources, compromising confidentiality.[4]

OWASP (see figure) depicts the same phenomenon in slightly different terms: a threat agent through an attack vector exploits a weakness (vulnerability) of the system and the related security controls, causing a technical impact on an IT resource (asset) connected to a business impact.

The overall picture represents the risk factors of the risk scenario.[15]

Information security management system

A set of policies concerned with the information security management system (ISMS), has been developed to manage, according to Risk management principles, the countermeasures to ensure a security strategy is set up following the rules and regulations applicable to a given organization. These countermeasures are also called Security controls, but when applied to the transmission of information, they are called security services.[16]

Classification

Vulnerabilities are classified according to the asset class they are related to:[2]

- hardware
  - susceptibility to humidity or dust
  - susceptibility to unprotected storage
  - age-based wear that causes failure
  - over-heating
- software
  - insufficient testing
  - insecure coding
  - lack of audit trail
  - design flaw
- network
  - unprotected communication lines (e.g. lack of cryptography)
  - insecure network architecture
- personnel
  - inadequate recruiting process
  - inadequate security awareness
  - insider threat
- physical site
  - area subject to natural disasters (e.g. flood, earthquake)
  - interruption to power source
- organizational
  - lack of regular audits
  - lack of continuity plans

- lack of security

Causes

- Complexity: Large, complex systems increase the probability of flaws and unintended access points. [17]
- Familiarity: Using common, well-known code, software, operating systems, and/or hardware increases the probability an attacker has or can find the knowledge and tools to exploit the flaw.[18]
- Connectivity: More physical connections, privileges, ports, protocols, and services and time each of those are accessible increase vulnerability.[11]
- Password management flaws: The computer user uses weak passwords that could be discovered by brute force.[19] The computer user stores the password on the computer where a program can access it. Users re-use passwords between many programs and websites.[17]

- Fundamental operating system design flaws: The operating system designer chooses to enforce suboptimal policies on user/program management. For example, operating systems with policies such as default permit grant every program and every user full access to the entire computer.[17] This operating system flaw allows viruses and malware to execute commands on behalf of the administrator.[20]
- Internet Website Browsing: Some internet websites may contain harmful Spyware or Adware that can be installed automatically on the computer systems. After visiting those websites, the computer systems become infected and personal information will be collected and passed on to third party individuals.[21]
- Software bugs: The programmer leaves an exploitable bug in a software program. The software bug may allow an attacker to misuse an application.[17]
- Unchecked user input: The program assumes that all user input is safe. Programs that do not check user input can allow unintended direct execution of commands or SQL statements (known as Buffer overflows, SQL injection or other non-validated inputs).[17]
- Not learning from past mistakes:[22][23] for example most vulnerabilities discovered in IPv4 protocol software were discovered in the new IPv6 implementations.[24]

The research has shown that the most vulnerable point in most information systems is the human user, operator, designer, or other human:[25] so humans should be considered in their different roles as asset, threat, information resources. Social engineering is an increasing security concern.

Vulnerability consequences

The impact of a security breach can be very high.[26] The fact that IT managers, or upper management, can (easily) know that IT systems and applications have vulnerabilities and do not perform any action to manage the IT risk is seen as a misconduct in most legislations. Privacy law forces managers to act to reduce the impact or likelihood of that security risk. Information technology security audit is a way to let other independent people certify that the IT environment is managed properly and lessen the responsibilities, at least having demonstrated the good faith. Penetration test is a form of verification of the weakness and countermeasures adopted by an organization: a White hat hacker tries to attack an organization's information technology assets, to find out how easy or difficult it is to compromise the IT security.[27] The proper way to professionally manage the IT risk is to adopt an Information Security Management System, such as ISO/IEC 27002 or Risk IT and follow them, according to the security strategy set forth by the upper management.[16]

One of the key concept of information security is the principle of defence in depth, i.e. to set up a multilayer defense system that can:[26]

- prevent the exploit
- detect and intercept the attack
- find out the threat agents and prosecute them

Intrusion detection system is an example of a class of systems used to detect attacks.

Physical security is a set of measures to physically protect an information asset: if somebody can get physical access to the information asset, it is widely accepted that an attacker can access any information on it or make the resource unavailable to its legitimate users.

Some sets of criteria to be satisfied by a computer, its operating system and applications in order to meet a good security level have been developed: ITSEC and Common criteria are two examples.

Vulnerability disclosure

Coordinated disclosure (some refer to it as 'responsible disclosure' but that is considered a biased term by others) of vulnerabilities is a topic of great debate. As reported by The Tech Herald in August 2010, "Google, Microsoft, TippingPoint, and Rapid7 have issued guidelines and statements addressing how they will deal with disclosure going forward."[28] The other method is typically called Full disclosure which is when all the details of a vulnerability is publicized, sometimes with the intent to put pressure on the software author to publish a fix more quickly. In January 2014 when Google revealed a Microsoft vulnerability before Microsoft released a patch to fix it, a Microsoft representative called for coordinated practices among software companies in revealing disclosures.[29]

Vulnerability inventory

Mitre Corporation maintains an incomplete list of publicly disclosed vulnerabilities in a system called Common Vulnerabilities and Exposures. This information is immediately shared with the National Institute of Standards and Technology (NIST), where each vulnerability is given a risk score using Common Vulnerability Scoring System (CVSS), Common Platform Enumeration (CPE) scheme, and Common Weakness Enumeration.

OWASP maintains a list of vulnerability classes with the aim of educating system designers and programmers, therefore reducing the likelihood of vulnerabilities being written unintentionally into the software.[30]

Vulnerability disclosure date

The time of disclosure of a vulnerability is defined differently in the security community and industry. It is most commonly referred to as "a kind of public disclosure of security information by a certain party". Usually, vulnerability information is discussed on a mailing list or published on a security web site and results in a security advisory afterward.

The **time of disclosure** is the first date a security vulnerability is described on a channel where the disclosed information on the vulnerability has to fulfill the following requirement:

- The information is freely available to the public
- The vulnerability information is published by a trusted and independent channel/source
- The vulnerability has undergone analysis by experts such that risk rating information is included upon disclosure

Identifying and removing vulnerabilities

Many software tools exist that can aid in the discovery (and sometimes removal) of vulnerabilities in a computer system. Though these tools can provide an auditor with a good overview of possible vulnerabilities present, they can not replace human judgment. Relying solely on scanners will yield false positives and a limited-scope view of the problems present in the system.

Vulnerabilities have been found in every major operating system [31] including Windows, macOS, various forms of Unix and Linux, OpenVMS, and others. The only way to reduce the chance of a vulnerability being used against a system is through constant vigilance, including careful system maintenance (e.g. applying software patches), best practices in deployment (e.g. the use of firewalls and access controls) and auditing (both during development and throughout the deployment lifecycle).

Examples of Where Vulnerabilities Manifest

Vulnerabilities are related to and can manifest in:

- physical environment of the system
- the personnel (i.e. employees, management)
- administration procedures and security policy
- business operation and service delivery
- hardware including peripheral devices [32] [33]
- software (i.e. on premises or in cloud)
- connectivity (i.e. communication equipment and facilities)

It is evident that a pure technical approach cannot always protect physical assets: one should have administrative procedure to let maintenance personnel to enter the facilities and people with adequate knowledge of the procedures, motivated to follow it with proper care. However, technical protections do not necessarily stop Social engineering (security) attacks.

Examples of vulnerabilities:

- an attacker finds and uses a buffer overflow weakness to install malware to then exfiltrate sensitive data;
- an attacker convinces a user to open an email message with attached malware;
- a flood damages one's computer systems installed at ground floor.

Software vulnerabilities

Common types of software flaws that lead to vulnerabilities include:

- Memory safety violations, such as:
  - Buffer overflows and over-reads
  - Dangling pointers
- Input validation errors, such as:

- Code injection
- Cross-site scripting in web applications
- Directory traversal
- E-mail injection
- Format string attacks
- HTTP header injection
- HTTP response splitting
- SQL injection
- Privilege-confusion bugs, such as:
  - Clickjacking
  - Cross-site request forgery in web applications
  - FTP bounce attack
- Privilege escalation
- Race conditions, such as:
  - Symlink races
  - Time-of-check-to-time-of-use bugs
- Side-channel attack
  - Timing attack
- User interface failures, such as:
  - Blaming the Victim prompting a user to make a security decision without giving the user enough information to answer it[34]
  - Race Conditions[35][36]
  - Warning fatigue[37] or user conditioning.

Some set of coding guidelines have been developed and a large number of static code analysers has been used to verify that the code follows the guidelines.

Computer Security

Computer security, **cybersecurity**[1] or **information technology security** (**IT security**) is the protection of computer systems and networks from the theft of or damage to their hardware, software, or electronic data, as well as from the disruption or misdirection of the services they provide.

The field is becoming more important due to increased reliance on computer systems, the Internet[2] and wireless network standards such as Bluetooth and Wi-Fi, and due to the growth of "smart" devices, including smartphones, televisions, and the various devices that constitute the "Internet of things". Owing to its complexity, both in terms of politics and technology, cybersecurity is also one of the major challenges in the contemporary world.[3]

Vulnerabilities and attacks

A vulnerability is a weakness in design, implementation, operation, or internal control. Most of the vulnerabilities that have been discovered are documented in the Common Vulnerabilities and Exposures (CVE) database. An *exploitable* vulnerability is one for which at least one working attack or "exploit" exists.[4] Vulnerabilities can be researched, reverse-engineered, hunted, or exploited using automated tools or customized scripts.[5][6] To secure a computer system, it is important to understand the attacks that can be made against it, and these threats can typically be classified into one of these categories below:

Backdoor

A backdoor in a computer system, a cryptosystem or an algorithm, is any secret method of bypassing normal authentication or security controls. They may exist for a number of reasons, including by original design or from poor configuration. They may have been added by an authorised party to allow some legitimate access, or by an attacker for malicious reasons; but regardless of the motives for their existence, they create a vulnerability. Backdoors can be very hard to detect, and detection of backdoors are usually discovered by someone who has access to application source code or intimate knowledge of the computer's Operating System.

Denial-of-service attack

Denial of service attacks (DoS) are designed to make a machine or network resource unavailable to its intended users.[7] Attackers can deny service to individual victims, such as by deliberately entering a wrong password enough consecutive times to cause the victim's account to be locked, or they may overload the capabilities of a machine or network and block all users at once. While a network attack from a single IP address can be blocked by adding a new firewall rule, many forms of Distributed denial of service (DDoS) attacks are possible, where the attack comes from a large number of points – and defending is much more difficult. Such attacks can originate from the zombie computers of a botnet or from a range of other possible techniques, including reflection and amplification attacks, where innocent systems are fooled into sending traffic to the victim.

Direct-access attacks

An unauthorized user gaining physical access to a computer is most likely able to directly copy data from it. They may also compromise security by making operating system modifications, installing software worms, keyloggers, covert listening devices or using wireless mice. Even when the system is protected by standard security measures, these may be able to be by-passed by booting another operating system or tool from a CD-ROM or other bootable media. Disk encryption and Trusted Platform Module are designed to prevent these attacks.

Eavesdropping

Eavesdropping is the act of surreptitiously listening to a private computer "conversation" (communication), typically between hosts on a network. For instance, programs such as Carnivore and NarusInSight have been used by the FBI and NSA to eavesdrop on the systems of internet service providers. Even machines that operate as a closed system (i.e., with no contact to the outside world) can be eavesdropped upon via monitoring the faint electromagnetic transmissions generated by the hardware; TEMPEST is a specification by the NSA referring to these attacks.

Multi-vector, polymorphic attacks

Surfacing in 2017, a new class of multi-vector,[8] polymorphic[9] cyber threats surfaced that combined several types of attacks and changed form to avoid cybersecurity controls as they spread. These threats have been classified as fifth-generation cyberattacks.[*citation needed*]

Phishing

Phishing is the attempt to acquire sensitive information such as usernames, passwords, and credit card details directly from users by deceiving the users.[10] Phishing is typically carried out by email spoofing or instant messaging, and it often directs users to enter details at a fake website whose "look" and "feel" are almost identical to the legitimate one. The fake website often asks for personal information, such as log-in details and passwords. This information can then be used to gain access to the individual's real account on the real website. Preying on a victim's trust, phishing can be classified as a form of social engineering. Attackers are using creative ways to gain access to real accounts. A common scam is for attackers to send fake electronic invoices[11] to individuals showing that they recently purchased music, apps, or other, and instructing them to click on a link if the purchases were not authorized.

Privilege escalation

Privilege escalation describes a situation where an attacker with some level of restricted access is able to, without authorization, elevate their privileges or access level. For example, a standard computer user may be able to exploit a vulnerability in the system to gain access to restricted data; or even become "root" and have full unrestricted access to a system.

Reverse engineering

Reverse engineering is the process by which a man-made object is deconstructed to reveal its designs, code, architecture, or to extract knowledge from the object; similar to scientific research, the only difference being that scientific research is about a natural phenomenon.[12]:3

Social engineering

Social engineering, insofar as computer security is concerned, aims to convince a user to disclose secrets such as passwords, card numbers, etc. by, for example, impersonating a bank, a contractor, or a customer. [13]

Social engineering, in the context of information security, is the psychological manipulation of people into performing actions or divulging confidential information.

A common scam involves fake CEO emails sent to accounting and finance departments. In early 2016, the FBI reported that the scam has cost US businesses more than $2 billion in about two years.[14]

In May 2016, the Milwaukee Bucks NBA team was the victim of this type of cyber scam with a perpetrator impersonating the team's president Peter Feigin, resulting in the handover of all the team's employees' 2015 W-2 tax forms.[15]

Spoofing

Spoofing is the act of masquerading as a valid entity through falsification of data (such as an IP address or username), in order to gain access to information or resources that one is otherwise unauthorized to obtain. [16][17] There are several types of spoofing, including:

- Email spoofing, where an attacker forges the sending (*From*, or source) address of an email.
- IP address spoofing, where an attacker alters the source IP address in a network packet to hide their identity or impersonate another computing system.
- MAC spoofing, where an attacker modifies the Media Access Control (MAC) address of their network interface to pose as a valid user on a network.
- Biometric spoofing, where an attacker produces a fake biometric sample to pose as another user.[18]

Tampering

Tampering describes a malicious modification or alteration of data. So-called Evil Maid attacks and security services planting of surveillance capability into routers are examples.[19]

Malware

Malicious software that installed in your computer without your consent can leak your personal information, can give control of your system to the attacker and delete your data permanently.[20]

Information security culture

Employee behavior can have a big impact on information security in organizations. Cultural concepts can help different segments of the organization work effectively or work against effectiveness towards information security within an organization. Information security culture is the "...totality of patterns of behavior in an organization that contributes to the protection of information of all kinds."[21]

Andersson and Reimers (2014) found that employees often do not see themselves as part of their organization's information security effort and often take actions that impede organizational changes.[22] Research shows information security culture needs to be improved continuously. In "Information Security Culture from Analysis to Change", authors commented, "It's a never-ending process, a cycle of evaluation and change or maintenance." To manage the information security culture, five steps should be taken: pre-evaluation, strategic planning, operative planning, implementation, and post-evaluation.[23]

- Pre-Evaluation: to identify the awareness of information security within employees and to analyze the current security policy.
- Strategic Planning: to come up with a better awareness program, clear targets need to be set. Assembling a team of skilled professionals is helpful to achieve it.
- Operative Planning: a good security culture can be established based on internal communication, management-buy-in, and security awareness and a training program.[23]
- Implementation: four stages should be used to implement the information security culture. They are:

1. Commitment of the management
2. Communication with organizational members
3. Courses for all organizational members
4. Commitment of the employees[23]

- Post-Evaluation: to assess the success of the planning and implementation, and to identify unresolved areas of concern.

Systems at risk

The growth in the number of computer systems and the increasing reliance upon them by individuals, businesses, industries, and governments means that there is an increasing number of systems at risk.

Financial systems

The computer systems of financial regulators and financial institutions like the U.S. Securities and Exchange Commission, SWIFT, investment banks, and commercial banks are prominent hacking targets for cybercriminals interested in manipulating markets and making illicit gains.[24] Web sites and apps that accept or store credit card numbers, brokerage accounts, and bank account information are also prominent hacking targets, because of the potential for immediate financial gain from transferring money, making purchases, or selling the information on the black market.[25] In-store payment systems and ATMs have also been tampered with in order to gather customer account data and PINs.

Utilities and industrial equipment

Computers control functions at many utilities, including coordination of telecommunications, the power grid, nuclear power plants, and valve opening and closing in water and gas networks. The Internet is a potential attack vector for such machines if connected, but the Stuxnet worm demonstrated that even equipment controlled by computers not connected to the Internet can be vulnerable. In 2014, the Computer Emergency Readiness Team, a division of the Department of Homeland Security, investigated 79 hacking incidents at energy companies.[26] Vulnerabilities in smart meters (many of which use local radio or cellular communications) can cause problems with billing fraud.[*citation needed*]

Aviation

The aviation industry is very reliant on a series of complex systems which could be attacked.[27] A simple power outage at one airport can cause repercussions worldwide,[28] much of the system relies on radio transmissions which could be disrupted,[29] and controlling aircraft over oceans is especially dangerous because radar surveillance only extends 175 to 225 miles offshore.[30] There is also potential for attack from within an aircraft.[31]

In Europe, with the (Pan-European Network Service)[32] and NewPENS,[33] and in the US with the NextGen program,[34] air navigation service providers are moving to create their own dedicated networks.

The consequences of a successful attack range from loss of confidentiality to loss of system integrity, air traffic control outages, loss of aircraft, and even loss of life.

Consumer devices

Desktop computers and laptops are commonly targeted to gather passwords or financial account information, or to construct a botnet to attack another target. Smartphones, tablet computers, smart watches, and other mobile devices such as quantified self devices like activity trackers have sensors such as cameras, microphones, GPS receivers, compasses, and accelerometers which could be exploited, and may collect personal information, including sensitive health information. WiFi, Bluetooth, and cell phone networks on any of these devices could be used as attack vectors, and sensors might be remotely activated after a successful breach.[35]

The increasing number of home automation devices such as the Nest thermostat are also potential targets.

[35]

Large corporations

Large corporations are common targets. In many cases attacks are aimed at financial gain through identity theft and involve data breaches. Examples include loss of millions of clients' credit card details by Home Depot,[36] Staples,[37] Target Corporation,[38] and the most recent breach of Equifax.[39]

Some cyberattacks are ordered by foreign governments, which engage in cyberwarfare with the intent to spread their propaganda, sabotage, or spy on their targets. Many people believe the Russian government played a major role in the US presidential election of 2016 by using Twitter and Facebook to affect the results of the election.[40]

Medical records have been targeted in general identify theft, health insurance fraud, and impersonating patients to obtain prescription drugs for recreational purposes or resale.[41] Although cyber threats continue to increase, 62% of all organizations did not increase security training for their business in 2015. [42]

Not all attacks are financially motivated, however: security firm HBGary Federal suffered a serious series of attacks in 2011 from hacktivist group Anonymous in retaliation for the firm's CEO claiming to have infiltrated their group,[43][44] and Sony Pictures was hacked in 2014 with the apparent dual motive of embarrassing the company through data leaks and crippling the company by wiping workstations and servers.[45][46]

Automobiles

Vehicles are increasingly computerized, with engine timing, cruise control, anti-lock brakes, seat belt tensioners, door locks, airbags and advanced driver-assistance systems on many models. Additionally, connected cars may use WiFi and Bluetooth to communicate with onboard consumer devices and the cell phone network.[47] Self-driving cars are expected to be even more complex.

All of these systems carry some security risk, and such issues have gained wide attention.[48][49][50] Simple examples of risk include a malicious compact disc being used as an attack vector,[51] and the car's onboard microphones being used for eavesdropping. However, if access is gained to a car's internal controller area network, the danger is much greater[47] – and in a widely publicized 2015 test, hackers remotely carjacked a vehicle from 10 miles away and drove it into a ditch.[52][53]

Manufacturers are reacting in a number of ways, with Tesla in 2016 pushing out some security fixes "over the air" into its cars' computer systems.[54]

In the area of autonomous vehicles, in September 2016 the United States Department of Transportation announced some initial safety standards, and called for states to come up with uniform policies.[55][56]

Government

Government and military computer systems are commonly attacked by activists[57][58][59] and foreign powers.[60][61][62][63] Local and regional government infrastructure such as traffic light controls, police and intelligence agency communications, personnel records, student records,[64] and financial systems are also potential targets as they are now all largely computerized. Passports and government ID cards that control access to facilities which use RFID can be vulnerable to cloning.

Internet of things and physical vulnerabilities

The Internet of things (IoT) is the network of physical objects such as devices, vehicles, and buildings that are embedded with electronics, software, sensors, and network connectivity that enables them to collect and exchange data[65] – and concerns have been raised that this is being developed without appropriate consideration of the security challenges involved.[66][67]

While the IoT creates opportunities for more direct integration of the physical world into computer-based systems,[68][69] it also provides opportunities for misuse. In particular, as the Internet of Things spreads widely, cyberattacks are likely to become an increasingly physical (rather than simply virtual) threat.[70] If a front door's lock is connected to the Internet, and can be locked/unlocked from a phone, then a criminal could enter the home at the press of a button from a stolen or hacked phone. People could stand to lose much more than their credit card numbers in a world controlled by IoT-enabled devices. Thieves have also used electronic means to circumvent non-Internet-connected hotel door locks.[71]

An attack that targets physical infrastructure and/or human lives is classified as a Cyber-kinetic attack. As IoT devices and appliances gain currency, cyber-kinetic attacks can become pervasive and significantly damaging.

Medical systems

Medical devices have either been successfully attacked or had potentially deadly vulnerabilities demonstrated, including both in-hospital diagnostic equipment[72] and implanted devices including pacemakers[73] and insulin pumps.[74] There are many reports of hospitals and hospital organizations getting hacked, including ransomware attacks,[75][76][77][78] Windows XP exploits,[79][80] viruses,[81][82] and data breaches of sensitive data stored on hospital servers.[83][76][84][85] On 28 December 2016 the US Food and Drug Administration released its recommendations for how medical device manufacturers should maintain the security of Internet-connected devices – but no structure for enforcement.[86][87]

Energy sector

In distributed generation systems, the risk of a cyber attack is real, according to *Daily Energy Insider*. An attack could cause a loss of power in a large area for a long period of time, and such an attack could have just as severe consequences as a natural disaster. The District of Columbia is considering creating a Distributed Energy Resources (DER) Authority within the city, with the goal being for customers to have more insight into their own energy use and giving the local electric utility, Pepco, the chance to better estimate energy demand. The D.C. proposal, however, would "allow third-party vendors to create numerous points of energy distribution, which could potentially create more opportunities for cyber attackers to threaten the electric grid."[88]

Impact of security breaches

Serious financial damage has been caused by security breaches, but because there is no standard model for estimating the cost of an incident, the only data available is that which is made public by the organizations involved. "Several computer security consulting firms produce estimates of total worldwide losses attributable to virus and worm attacks and to hostile digital acts in general. The 2003 loss estimates by these firms range from $13 billion (worms and viruses only) to $226 billion (for all forms of covert attacks). The reliability of these estimates is often challenged; the underlying methodology is basically anecdotal."[89] Security breaches continue to cost businesses billions of dollars but a survey revealed that

66% of security staffs do not believe senior leadership takes cyber precautions as a strategic priority. [*citation needed*]

However, reasonable estimates of the financial cost of security breaches can actually help organizations make rational investment decisions. According to the classic Gordon-Loeb Model analyzing the optimal investment level in information security, one can conclude that the amount a firm spends to protect information should generally be only a small fraction of the expected loss (i.e., the expected value of the loss resulting from a cyber/information security breach).[90]

Attacker motivation

As with physical security, the motivations for breaches of computer security vary between attackers. Some are thrill-seekers or vandals, some are activists, others are criminals looking for financial gain. State-sponsored attackers are now common and well resourced but started with amateurs such as Markus Hess who hacked for the KGB, as recounted by Clifford Stoll in *The Cuckoo's Egg*.

Additionally, recent attacker motivations can be traced back to extremist organizations seeking to gain political advantage or disrupt social agendas.[*citation needed*] The growth of the internet, mobile technologies, and inexpensive computing devices have led to a rise in capabilities but also to the risk to environments that are deemed as vital to operations. All critical targeted environments are susceptible to compromise and this has led to a series of proactive studies on how to migrate the risk by taking into consideration motivations by these types of actors. Several stark differences exist between the hacker motivation and that of nation state actors seeking to attack based an ideological preference.[91]

A standard part of threat modeling for any particular system is to identify what might motivate an attack on that system, and who might be motivated to breach it. The level and detail of precautions will vary depending on the system to be secured. A home personal computer, bank, and classified military network face very different threats, even when the underlying technologies in use are similar.[*citation needed*]

Computer protection (countermeasures)

In computer security a countermeasure is an action, device, procedure or technique that reduces a threat, a vulnerability, or an attack by eliminating or preventing it, by minimizing the harm it can cause, or by discovering and reporting it so that corrective action can be taken.[92][93][94]

Some common countermeasures are listed in the following sections:

Security by design

Security by design, or alternately secure by design, means that the software has been designed from the ground up to be secure. In this case, security is considered as a main feature.

Some of the techniques in this approach include:

- The principle of least privilege, where each part of the system has only the privileges that are needed for its function. That way even if an attacker gains access to that part, they have only limited access to the whole system.
- Automated theorem proving to prove the correctness of crucial software subsystems.
- Code reviews and unit testing, approaches to make modules more secure where formal correctness proofs are not possible.

- Defense in depth, where the design is such that more than one subsystem needs to be violated to compromise the integrity of the system and the information it holds.
- Default secure settings, and design to "fail secure" rather than "fail insecure" (see fail-safe for the equivalent in safety engineering). Ideally, a secure system should require a deliberate, conscious, knowledgeable and free decision on the part of legitimate authorities in order to make it insecure.
- Audit trails tracking system activity, so that when a security breach occurs, the mechanism and extent of the breach can be determined. Storing audit trails remotely, where they can only be appended to, can keep intruders from covering their tracks.
- Full disclosure of all vulnerabilities, to ensure that the "window of vulnerability" is kept as short as possible when bugs are discovered.

Security architecture

The Open Security Architecture organization defines IT security architecture as "the design artifacts that describe how the security controls (security countermeasures) are positioned, and how they relate to the overall information technology architecture. These controls serve the purpose to maintain the system's quality attributes: confidentiality, integrity, availability, accountability and assurance services".[95]

Techopedia defines security architecture as "a unified security design that addresses the necessities and potential risks involved in a certain scenario or environment. It also specifies when and where to apply security controls. The design process is generally reproducible." The key attributes of security architecture are:[96]

- the relationship of different components and how they depend on each other.
- the determination of controls based on risk assessment, good practice, finances, and legal matters.
- the standardization of controls.

Practicing security architecture provides the right foundation to systematically address business, IT and security concerns in an organization.

Security measures

A state of computer "security" is the conceptual ideal, attained by the use of the three processes: threat prevention, detection, and response. These processes are based on various policies and system components, which include the following:

- User account access controls and cryptography can protect systems files and data, respectively.
- Firewalls are by far the most common prevention systems from a network security perspective as they can (if properly configured) shield access to internal network services, and block certain kinds of attacks through packet filtering. Firewalls can be both hardware- or software-based.
- Intrusion Detection System (IDS) products are designed to detect network attacks in-progress and assist in post-attack forensics, while audit trails and logs serve a similar function for individual systems.
- "Response" is necessarily defined by the assessed security requirements of an individual system and may cover the range from simple upgrade of protections to notification of legal authorities, counter-attacks, and the like. In some special cases, the complete destruction of the compromised system is favored, as it may happen that not all the compromised resources are detected.

Today, computer security comprises mainly "preventive" measures, like firewalls or an exit procedure. A firewall can be defined as a way of filtering network data between a host or a network and another network, such as the Internet, and can be implemented as software running on the machine, hooking into the network stack (or, in the case of most UNIX-based operating systems such as Linux, built into the operating system kernel) to provide real-time filtering and blocking. Another implementation is a so-called "physical firewall", which consists of a separate machine filtering network traffic. Firewalls are common amongst machines that are permanently connected to the Internet.

Some organizations are turning to big data platforms, such as Apache Hadoop, to extend data accessibility and machine learning to detect advanced persistent threats.[97]

However, relatively few organizations maintain computer systems with effective detection systems, and fewer still have organized response mechanisms in place. As a result, as Reuters points out: "Companies for the first time report they are losing more through electronic theft of data than physical stealing of assets". [98] The primary obstacle to effective eradication of cybercrime could be traced to excessive reliance on firewalls and other automated "detection" systems. Yet it is basic evidence gathering by using packet capture appliances that puts criminals behind bars.[*citation needed*]

In order to ensure adequate security, the confidentiality, integrity and availability of a network, better known as the CIA triad, must be protected and is considered the foundation to information security.[99] To achieve those objectives, administrative, physical and technical security measures should be employed. The amount of security afforded to an asset can only be determined when its value is known.[100]

Vulnerability management

Vulnerability management is the cycle of identifying, and remediating or mitigating vulnerabilities,[101] especially in software and firmware. Vulnerability management is integral to computer security and network security.

Vulnerabilities can be discovered with a vulnerability scanner, which analyzes a computer system in search of known vulnerabilities,[102] such as open ports, insecure software configuration, and susceptibility to malware. In order for these tools to be effective, they must be kept up to date with every new update the vendors release. Typically, these updates will scan for the new vulnerabilities that were introduced recently.

Beyond vulnerability scanning, many organizations contract outside security auditors to run regular penetration tests against their systems to identify vulnerabilities. In some sectors, this is a contractual requirement.[103]

Reducing vulnerabilities

While formal verification of the correctness of computer systems is possible,[104][105] it is not yet common. Operating systems formally verified include seL4,[106] and SYSGO's PikeOS[107][108] – but these make up a very small percentage of the market.

Two factor authentication is a method for mitigating unauthorized access to a system or sensitive information. It requires "something you know"; a password or PIN, and "something you have"; a card, dongle, cellphone, or another piece of hardware. This increases security as an unauthorized person needs both of these to gain access.

Social engineering and direct computer access (physical) attacks can only be prevented by non-computer means, which can be difficult to enforce, relative to the sensitivity of the information. Training is often involved to help mitigate this risk, but even in highly disciplined environments (e.g. military organizations), social engineering attacks can still be difficult to foresee and prevent.

Inoculation, derived from inoculation theory, seeks to prevent social engineering and other fraudulent tricks or traps by instilling a resistance to persuasion attempts through exposure to similar or related attempts. [109]

It is possible to reduce an attacker's chances by keeping systems up to date with security patches and updates, using a security scanner[*definition needed*] and/or hiring people with expertise in security, though none of these guarantee the prevention of an attack. The effects of data loss/damage can be reduced by careful backing up and insurance.

Hardware protection mechanisms

While hardware may be a source of insecurity, such as with microchip vulnerabilities maliciously introduced during the manufacturing process,[110][111] hardware-based or assisted computer security also offers an alternative to software-only computer security. Using devices and methods such as dongles, trusted platform modules, intrusion-aware cases, drive locks, disabling USB ports, and mobile-enabled access may be considered more secure due to the physical access (or sophisticated backdoor access) required in order to be compromised. Each of these is covered in more detail below.

- USB dongles are typically used in software licensing schemes to unlock software capabilities, [*citation needed*] but they can also be seen as a way to prevent unauthorized access to a computer or other device's software. The dongle, or key, essentially creates a secure encrypted tunnel between the software application and the key. The principle is that an encryption scheme on the dongle, such as Advanced Encryption Standard (AES) provides a stronger measure of security since it is harder to hack and replicate the dongle than to simply copy the native software to another machine and use it. Another security application for dongles is to use them for accessing web-based content such as cloud software or Virtual Private Networks (VPNs).[112] In addition, a USB dongle can be configured to lock or unlock a computer.[113]
- Trusted platform modules (TPMs) secure devices by integrating cryptographic capabilities onto access devices, through the use of microprocessors, or so-called computers-on-a-chip. TPMs used in conjunction with server-side software offer a way to detect and authenticate hardware devices, preventing unauthorized network and data access.[114]
- Computer case intrusion detection refers to a device, typically a push-button switch, which detects when a computer case is opened. The firmware or BIOS is programmed to show an alert to the operator when the computer is booted up the next time.
- Drive locks are essentially software tools to encrypt hard drives, making them inaccessible to thieves.[115] Tools exist specifically for encrypting external drives as well.[116]
- Disabling USB ports is a security option for preventing unauthorized and malicious access to an otherwise secure computer. Infected USB dongles connected to a network from a computer inside the firewall are considered by the magazine Network World as the most common hardware threat facing computer networks.
- Disconnecting or disabling peripheral devices (like camera, GPS, removable storage etc.), that are not in use.[117]
- Mobile-enabled access devices are growing in popularity due to the ubiquitous nature of cell phones. Built-in capabilities such as Bluetooth, the newer Bluetooth low energy (LE), Near field communication (NFC) on non-iOS devices and biometric validation such as thumb print readers, as well as QR code reader software designed for mobile devices, offer new, secure ways for mobile phones to connect to access control systems. These control systems provide computer security and can also be used for controlling access to secure buildings.[118]

Secure operating systems

One use of the term "computer security" refers to technology that is used to implement secure operating systems. In the 1980s the United States Department of Defense (DoD) used the "Orange Book"[119] standards, but the current international standard ISO/IEC 15408, "Common Criteria" defines a number of progressively more stringent Evaluation Assurance Levels. Many common operating systems meet the EAL4 standard of being "Methodically Designed, Tested and Reviewed", but the formal verification required for the highest levels means that they are uncommon. An example of an EAL6 ("Semiformally Verified Design and Tested") system is Integrity-178B, which is used in the Airbus A380[120] and several military jets.[121]

Secure coding

In software engineering, secure coding aims to guard against the accidental introduction of security vulnerabilities. It is also possible to create software designed from the ground up to be secure. Such systems are "secure by design". Beyond this, formal verification aims to prove the correctness of the algorithms underlying a system;[122] important for cryptographic protocols for example.

Capabilities and access control lists

Within computer systems, two of many security models capable of enforcing privilege separation are access control lists (ACLs) and capability-based security. Using ACLs to confine programs has been proven to be insecure in many situations, such as if the host computer can be tricked into indirectly allowing restricted file access, an issue known as the confused deputy problem. It has also been shown that the promise of ACLs of giving access to an object to only one person can never be guaranteed in practice. Both of these problems are resolved by capabilities. This does not mean practical flaws exist in all ACL-based systems, but only that the designers of certain utilities must take responsibility to ensure that they do not introduce flaws.[123]

Capabilities have been mostly restricted to research operating systems, while commercial OSs still use ACLs. Capabilities can, however, also be implemented at the language level, leading to a style of programming that is essentially a refinement of standard object-oriented design. An open-source project in the area is the E language.

End user security training

The end-user is widely recognized as the weakest link in the security chain[124] and it is estimated that more than 90% of security incidents and breaches involve some kind of human error.[125][126] Among the most commonly recorded forms of errors and misjudgment are poor password management, sending emails containing sensitive data and attachments to the wrong recipient, the inability to recognize misleading URLs and to identify fake websites and dangerous email attachments. A common mistake that users make is saving their userid/password in their browsers to make it easier to log in to banking sites. This is a gift to attackers who have obtained access to a machine by some means. The risk may be mitigated by the use of two-factor authentication.[127]

As the human component of cyber risk is particularly relevant in determining the global cyber risk[*citation needed*][128] an organization is facing, security awareness training, at all levels, not only provides formal compliance with regulatory and industry mandates but is considered essential[129] in reducing cyber risk and protecting individuals and companies from the great majority of cyber threats.

The focus on the end-user represents a profound cultural change for many security practitioners, who have traditionally approached cybersecurity exclusively from a technical perspective, and moves along the lines suggested by major security centers[130] to develop a culture of cyber awareness within the organization, recognizing that a security-aware user provides an important line of defense against cyber attacks.

Digital hygiene

Related to end-user training, **digital hygiene** or **cyber hygiene** is a fundamental principle relating to information security and, as the analogy with personal hygiene shows, is the equivalent of establishing simple routine measures to minimize the risks from cyber threats. The assumption is that good cyber hygiene practices can give networked users another layer of protection, reducing the risk that one vulnerable node will be used to either mount attacks or compromise another node or network, especially from common cyberattacks.[131]

As opposed to a purely technology-based defense against threats, cyber hygiene mostly regards routine measures that are technically simple to implement and mostly dependent on discipline[132] or education. [133] It can be thought of as an abstract list of tips or measures that have been demonstrated as having a positive effect on personal and/or collective digital security. As such, these measures can be performed by laypeople, not just security experts.

Cyber hygiene relates to personal hygiene as computer viruses relate to biological viruses (or pathogens). However, while the term *computer virus* was coined almost simultaneously with the creation of the first working computer viruses,[134] the term *cyber hygiene* is a much later invention, perhaps as late as 2000[135] by Internet pioneer Vint Cerf. It has since been adopted by the Congress[136] and Senate of the United States,[137] the FBI,[138] EU institutions[131] and heads of state.[139]

Cyber hygiene should also not be mistaken for proactive cyber defence, a military term.[139]

Response to breaches

Responding forcefully to attempted security breaches (in the manner that one would for attempted physical security breaches) is often very difficult for a variety of reasons:

- Identifying attackers is difficult, as they are often in a different jurisdiction to the systems they attempt to breach and operate through proxies, temporary anonymous dial-up accounts, wireless connections, and other anonymizing procedures which make backtracing difficult and are often located in yet another jurisdiction. If they successfully breach security, they are often able to delete logs to cover their tracks.
- The sheer number of attempted attacks is so large that organizations cannot spend time pursuing each attacker (a typical home user with a permanent (e.g., cable modem) connection will be attacked at least several times per day, so more attractive targets could be presumed to see many more). Note, however, that most of the sheer bulk of these attacks are made by automated vulnerability scanners and computer worms.
- Law enforcement officers are often unfamiliar with information technology, and so lack the skills and interest in pursuing attackers. There are also budgetary constraints. It has been argued that the high cost of technology, such as DNA testing and improved forensics, mean less money for other kinds of law enforcement, so the overall rate of criminals not getting dealt with goes up as the cost of the technology increases. In addition, the identification of attackers across a network may require logs from various points in the network and in many countries, the release of these records to law enforcement (with the exception of being voluntarily surrendered by a network administrator or a

system administrator) requires a search warrant and, depending on the circumstances, the legal proceedings required can be drawn out to the point where the records are either regularly destroyed, or the information is no longer relevant.

- The United States government spends the largest amount of money every year on cybersecurity. The United States has a yearly budget of 28 billion dollars. Canada has the 2nd highest annual budget at 1 billion dollars. Australia has the third-highest budget with only 70 million dollars.[*citation needed*]

Types of security and privacy

- Access control
- Anti-keyloggers
- Anti-malware
- Anti-spyware
- Anti-subversion software
- Anti-tamper software
- Anti-theft
- Antivirus software
- Cryptographic software
- Computer-aided dispatch (CAD)
- Firewall
- Intrusion detection system (IDS)
- Intrusion prevention system (IPS)
- Log management software
- Parental control
- Records management
- Sandbox
- Security information management
- SIEM
- Software and operating system updating

Incident response planning

Incident response is an organized approach to addressing and managing the aftermath of a computer security incident or compromise with the goal of preventing a breach or thwarting a cyberattack. An incident that is not identified and managed at the time of intrusion typically escalates to a more damaging event such as a data breach or system failure. The intended outcome of a computer security incident response plan is to limit damage and reduce recovery time and costs. Responding to compromises quickly can mitigate exploited vulnerabilities, restore services and processes and minimize losses.[*citation needed*] Incident response planning allows an organization to establish a series of best practices to stop an intrusion before it causes damage. Typical incident response plans contain a set of written instructions that outline the organization's response to a cyberattack. Without a documented plan in place, an organization may not successfully detect an intrusion or compromise and stakeholders may not understand their roles, processes and procedures during an escalation, slowing the organization's response and resolution.

There are four key components of a computer security incident response plan:

1. **Preparation**: Preparing stakeholders on the procedures for handling computer security incidents or compromises
2. **Detection & Analysis**: Identifying and investigating suspicious activity to confirm a security incident, prioritizing the response based on impact and coordinating notification of the incident
3. **Containment, Eradication & Recovery**: Isolating affected systems to prevent escalation and limit impact, pinpointing the genesis of the incident, removing malware, affected systems and bad actors from the environment and restoring systems and data when a threat no longer remains
4. **Post Incident Activity**: Post mortem analysis of the incident, its root cause and the organization's response with the intent of improving the incident response plan and future response efforts[*citation needed*]

Terminology

The following terms used with regards to computer security are explained below:

- Access authorization restricts access to a computer to a group of users through the use of authentication systems. These systems can protect either the whole computer, such as through an interactive login screen, or individual services, such as a FTP server. There are many methods for identifying and authenticating users, such as passwords, identification cards, smart cards, and biometric systems.
- Anti-virus software consists of computer programs that attempt to identify, thwart, and eliminate computer viruses and other malicious software (malware).
- Applications are executable code, so general practice is to disallow users the power to install them; to install only those which are known to be reputable – and to reduce the attack surface by installing as few as possible. They are typically run with least privilege, with a robust process in place to identify, test and install any released security patches or updates for them.
- Authentication techniques can be used to ensure that communication end-points are who they say they are.
- Automated theorem proving and other verification tools can enable critical algorithms and code used in secure systems to be mathematically proven to meet their specifications.
- Backups are one or more copies kept of important computer files. Typically, multiple copies will be kept at different locations so that if a copy is stolen or damaged, other copies will still exist.
- Capability and access control list techniques can be used to ensure privilege separation and mandatory access control. Capabilities vs. ACLs discusses their use.
- Chain of trust techniques can be used to attempt to ensure that all software loaded has been certified as authentic by the system's designers.
- Confidentiality is the nondisclosure of information except to another authorized person.[228]
- Cryptographic techniques can be used to defend data in transit between systems, reducing the probability that data exchanged between systems can be intercepted or modified.
- Cyberwarfare is an Internet-based conflict that involves politically motivated attacks on information and information systems. Such attacks can, for example, disable official websites and networks, disrupt or disable essential services, steal or alter classified data, and cripple financial systems.
- Data integrity is the accuracy and consistency of stored data, indicated by an absence of any alteration in data between two updates of a data record.[229]

Cryptographic techniques involve transforming information, scrambling it, so it becomes unreadable during transmission. The intended recipient can unscramble the message; ideally, eavesdroppers cannot.

- Encryption is used to protect the confidentiality of a message. Cryptographically secure ciphers are designed to make any practical attempt of breaking them infeasible. Symmetric-key ciphers are suitable for bulk encryption using shared keys, and public-key encryption using digital certificates can provide a practical solution for the problem of securely communicating when no key is shared in advance.
- Endpoint security software aids networks in preventing malware infection and data theft at network entry points made vulnerable by the prevalence of potentially infected devices such as laptops, mobile devices, and USB drives.[230]
- Firewalls serve as a gatekeeper system between networks, allowing only traffic that matches defined rules. They often include detailed logging, and may include intrusion detection and intrusion prevention features. They are near-universal between company local area networks and the Internet, but can also be used internally to impose traffic rules between networks if network segmentation is configured.
- A hacker is someone who seeks to breach defenses and exploit weaknesses in a computer system or network.
- Honey pots are computers that are intentionally left vulnerable to attack by crackers. They can be used to catch crackers and to identify their techniques.
- Intrusion-detection systems are devices or software applications that monitor networks or systems for malicious activity or policy violations.
- A microkernel is an approach to operating system design which has only the near-minimum amount of code running at the most privileged level – and runs other elements of the operating system such as device drivers, protocol stacks and file systems, in the safer, less privileged user space.
- Pinging. The standard "ping" application can be used to test if an IP address is in use. If it is, attackers may then try a port scan to detect which services are exposed.
- A port scan is used to probe an IP address for open ports to identify accessible network services and applications.
- A Key logger is spyware silently captures and stores each keystroke that a user types on the computer's keyboard.
- Social engineering is the use of deception to manipulate individuals to breach security.
- Logic bombs is a type of malware added to a legitimate program that lies dormant until it is triggered by a specific event.

Information Security

Information security, sometimes shortened to **infosec**, is the practice of protecting information by mitigating information risks. It is part of information risk management. It typically involves preventing or at least reducing the probability of unauthorized/inappropriate access to data, or the unlawful use, disclosure, disruption, deletion, corruption, modification, inspection, recording or devaluation of information. It also involves actions intended to reduce the adverse impacts of such incidents. Protected information may take any form, e.g. electronic or physical, tangible (e.g. paperwork) or intangible (e.g. knowledge). Information security's primary focus is the balanced protection of the confidentiality, integrity and availability of data (also known as the CIA triad) while maintaining a focus on efficient policy implementation, all without hampering organization productivity. This is largely achieved through a structured risk management process that involves:

- Identifying information and related assets, plus potential threats, vulnerabilities and impacts;
- Evaluating the risks;
- Deciding how to address or treat the risks i.e. to avoid, mitigate, share or accept them;
- Where risk mitigation is required, selecting or designing appropriate security controls and implementing them;
- Monitoring the activities, making adjustments as necessary to address any issues, changes and improvement opportunities.

To standardize this discipline, academics and professionals collaborate to offer guidance, policies, and industry standards on password, antivirus software, firewall, encryption software, legal liability, security awareness and training, and so forth. This standardization may be further driven by a wide variety of laws and regulations that affect how data is accessed, processed, stored, transferred and destroyed. However, the implementation of any standards and guidance within an entity may have limited effect if a culture of continual improvement isn't adopted.

Definition

Information Systems are composed in three main portions, hardware, software and communications with the purpose to help identify and apply information security industry standards, as mechanisms of protection and prevention, at three levels or layers: physical, personal and organizational. Essentially, procedures or policies are implemented to tell administrators, users and operators how to use products to ensure information security within the organizations.[1]

Various definitions of information security are suggested below, summarized from different sources:

1. "Preservation of confidentiality, integrity and availability of information. Note: In addition, other properties, such as authenticity, accountability, non-repudiation and reliability can also be involved." (ISO/IEC 27000:2009)[2]
2. "The protection of information and information systems from unauthorized access, use, disclosure, disruption, modification, or destruction in order to provide confidentiality, integrity, and availability." (CNSS, 2010)[3]
3. "Ensures that only authorized users (confidentiality) have access to accurate and complete information (integrity) when required (availability)." (ISACA, 2008)[4]
4. "Information Security is the process of protecting the intellectual property of an organisation." (Pipkin, 2000)[5]
5. "...information security is a risk management discipline, whose job is to manage the cost of information risk to the business." (McDermott and Geer, 2001)[6]
6. "A well-informed sense of assurance that information risks and controls are in balance." (Anderson, J., 2003)[7]
7. "Information security is the protection of information and minimizes the risk of exposing information to unauthorized parties." (Venter and Eloff, 2003)[8]
8. "Information Security is a multidisciplinary area of study and professional activity which is concerned with the development and implementation of security mechanisms of all available types (technical, organizational, human-oriented and legal) in order to keep information in all its locations (within and outside the organization's perimeter) and, consequently, information systems, where information is created, processed, stored, transmitted and destroyed, free from threats.Threats to

information and information systems may be categorized and a corresponding security goal may be defined for each category of threats. A set of security goals, identified as a result of a threat analysis, should be revised periodically to ensure its adequacy and conformance with the evolving environment. The currently relevant set of security goals may include: *confidentiality, integrity, availability, privacy, authenticity & trustworthiness, non-repudiation, accountability and auditability.*" (Cherdantseva and Hilton, 2013)[1]

9. Information and information resource security using telecommunication system or devices means protecting information, information systems or books from unauthorized access, damage, theft, or destruction (Kurose and Ross, 2010).

Overview

At the core of information security is information assurance, the act of maintaining the confidentiality, integrity and availability (CIA) of information, ensuring that information is not compromised in any way when critical issues arise.[9] These issues include but are not limited to natural disasters, computer/server malfunction, and physical theft. While paper-based business operations are still prevalent, requiring their own set of information security practices, enterprise digital initiatives are increasingly being emphasized, [10][11] with information assurance now typically being dealt with by information technology (IT) security specialists. These specialists apply information security to technology (most often some form of computer system). It is worthwhile to note that a computer does not necessarily mean a home desktop. A computer is any device with a processor and some memory. Such devices can range from non-networked standalone devices as simple as calculators, to networked mobile computing devices such as smartphones and tablet computers. IT security specialists are almost always found in any major enterprise/establishment due to the nature and value of the data within larger businesses. They are responsible for keeping all of the technology within the company secure from malicious cyber attacks that often attempt to acquire critical private information or gain control of the internal systems.

The field of information security has grown and evolved significantly in recent years. It offers many areas for specialization, including securing networks and allied infrastructure, securing applications and databases, security testing, information systems auditing, business continuity planning, electronic record discovery, and digital forensics. Information security professionals are very stable in their employment. As of 2013 more than 80 percent of professionals had no change in employer or employment over a period of a year, and the number of professionals is projected to continuously grow more than 11 percent annually from 2014 to 2019.[12]

Threats

Information security threats come in many different forms. Some of the most common threats today are software attacks, theft of intellectual property, identity theft, theft of equipment or information, sabotage, and information extortion. Most people have experienced software attacks of some sort. Viruses,[13] worms, phishing attacks and Trojan horses are a few common examples of software attacks. The theft of intellectual property has also been an extensive issue for many businesses in the information technology (IT) field. Identity theft is the attempt to act as someone else usually to obtain that person's personal information or to take advantage of their access to vital information through social engineering. Theft of equipment or information is becoming more prevalent today due to the fact that most devices today are mobile,[14] are prone to theft and have also become far more desirable as the amount of data capacity increases. Sabotage usually consists of the destruction of an organization's website in an attempt to cause loss of confidence on the part of its customers. Information extortion consists of theft of a company's property or information as an attempt to receive a payment in exchange for returning the information or property back to its owner, as with ransomware. There are many ways to help protect yourself from some of these attacks but one of the most functional precautions is conduct periodical user awareness. The number one threat to any organisation are users or internal employees, they are also called insider threats.

Governments, military, corporations, financial institutions, hospitals, non-profit organisations and private businesses amass a great deal of confidential information about their employees, customers, products, research and financial status. Should confidential information about a business' customers or finances or new product line fall into the hands of a competitor or a black hat hacker, a business and its customers could suffer widespread, irreparable financial loss, as well as damage to the company's reputation. From a business perspective, information security must be balanced against cost; the Gordon-Loeb Model provides a mathematical economic approach for addressing this concern.[15]

For the individual, information security has a significant effect on privacy, which is viewed very differently in various cultures.

Responses to threats

Possible responses to a security threat or risk are:[16]

- reduce/mitigate – implement safeguards and countermeasures to eliminate vulnerabilities or block threats
- assign/transfer – place the cost of the threat onto another entity or organization such as purchasing insurance or outsourcing
- accept – evaluate if the cost of the countermeasure outweighs the possible cost of loss due to the threat

History

Since the early days of communication, diplomats and military commanders understood that it was necessary to provide some mechanism to protect the confidentiality of correspondence and to have some means of detecting tampering. Julius Caesar is credited with the invention of the Caesar cipher c. 50 B.C., which was created in order to prevent his secret messages from being read should a message fall into the wrong hands. However, for the most part protection was achieved through the application of procedural handling controls.[17][18] Sensitive information was marked up to indicate that it should be protected and transported by trusted persons, guarded and stored in a secure environment or strong box. As postal services expanded, governments created official organizations to intercept, decipher, read and reseal letters (e.g., the U.K.'s Secret Office, founded in 1653[19]).

In the mid-nineteenth century more complex classification systems were developed to allow governments to manage their information according to the degree of sensitivity. For example, the British Government codified this, to some extent, with the publication of the Official Secrets Act in 1889.[20] Section 1 of the law concerned espionage and unlawful disclosures of information, while Section 2 dealt with breaches of official trust. A public interest defense was soon added to defend disclosures in the interest of the state.[21] A similar law was passed in India in 1889, The Indian Official Secrets Act, which was associated with the British colonial era and used to crackdown on newspapers that opposed the Raj's policies. A newer version was passed in 1923 that extended to all matters of confidential or secret information for governance.[22]

By the time of the First World War, multi-tier classification systems were used to communicate information to and from various fronts, which encouraged greater use of code making and breaking sections in diplomatic and military headquarters. Encoding became more sophisticated between the wars as machines were employed to scramble and unscramble information. The volume of information shared by the Allied countries during the Second World War necessitated formal alignment of classification systems and procedural controls. An arcane range of markings evolved to indicate who could handle documents (usually officers rather than enlisted troops) and where they should be stored as increasingly complex safes and storage facilities were developed. The Enigma Machine, which was employed by the Germans to encrypt the data of warfare and was successfully decrypted by Alan Turing, can be regarded as a striking example of creating and using secured information.[23] Procedures evolved to ensure documents were destroyed properly, and it was the failure to follow these procedures which led to some of the greatest intelligence coups of the war (e.g., the capture of U-570[23]).

The end of the twentieth century and the early years of the twenty-first century saw rapid advancements in telecommunications, computing hardware and software, and data encryption. The availability of smaller, more powerful and less expensive computing equipment made electronic data processing within the reach of small business and the home user.[*citation needed*] The establishment of Transfer Control Protocol/Internetwork Protocol (TCP/IP) in the early 1980s enabled different types of computers to communicate.[24] These computers quickly became interconnected through the internet.

The rapid growth and widespread use of electronic data processing and electronic business conducted through the internet, along with numerous occurrences of international terrorism, fueled the need for better methods of protecting the computers and the information they store, process and transmit.[25] The academic disciplines of computer security and information assurance emerged along with numerous professional organizations, all sharing the common goals of ensuring the security and reliability of information systems.

Basic principles

Key concepts

The CIA triad of confidentiality, integrity, and availability is at the heart of information security.[26] (The members of the classic InfoSec triad—confidentiality, integrity and availability—are interchangeably referred to in the literature as security attributes, properties, security goals, fundamental aspects, information criteria, critical information characteristics and basic building blocks.) However, debate continues about whether or not this CIA triad is sufficient to address rapidly changing technology and business requirements, with recommendations to consider expanding on the intersections between availability and confidentiality, as well as the relationship between security and privacy.[9] Other principles such as "accountability" have sometimes been proposed; it has been pointed out that issues such as non-repudiation do not fit well within the three core concepts.[27]

The triad seems to have first been mentioned in a NIST publication in 1977.[28]

In 1992 and revised in 2002, the OECD's *Guidelines for the Security of Information Systems and Networks*[29] proposed the nine generally accepted principles: awareness, responsibility, response, ethics, democracy, risk assessment, security design and implementation, security management, and reassessment. Building upon those, in 2004 the NIST's *Engineering Principles for Information Technology Security*[27] proposed 33 principles. From each of these derived guidelines and practices.

In 1998, Donn Parker proposed an alternative model for the classic CIA triad that he called the six atomic elements of information. The elements are confidentiality, possession, integrity, authenticity, availability, and utility. The merits of the Parkerian Hexad are a subject of debate amongst security professionals.[30]

In 2011, The Open Group published the information security management standard O-ISM3.[31] This standard proposed an operational definition of the key concepts of security, with elements called "security objectives", related to access control (9), availability (3), data quality (1), compliance and technical (4). In 2009, DoD Software Protection Initiative released the Three Tenets of Cybersecurity which are System Susceptibility, Access to the Flaw, and Capability to Exploit the Flaw.[32][33][34] Neither of these models are widely adopted.

Confidentiality

In information security, confidentiality "is the property, that information is not made available or disclosed to unauthorized individuals, entities, or processes."[35] While similar to "privacy," the two words aren't interchangeable. Rather, confidentiality is a component of privacy that implements to protect our data from unauthorized viewers. Examples of confidentiality of electronic data being compromised include laptop theft, password theft, or sensitive emails being sent to the incorrect individuals.[36]

Integrity

In information security, data integrity means maintaining and assuring the accuracy and completeness of data over its entire lifecycle.[37] This means that data cannot be modified in an unauthorized or undetected manner. This is not the same thing as referential integrity in databases, although it can be viewed as a special case of consistency as understood in the classic ACID model of transaction processing. Information security systems typically provide message integrity alongside confidentiality.

Availability

For any information system to serve its purpose, the information must be available when it is needed. This means the computing systems used to store and process the information, the security controls used to protect it, and the communication channels used to access it must be functioning correctly. High availability systems aim to remain available at all times, preventing service disruptions due to power outages, hardware failures, and system upgrades. Ensuring availability also involves preventing denial-of-service attacks, such as a flood of incoming messages to the target system, essentially forcing it to shut down.[38]

In the realm of information security, availability can often be viewed as one of the most important parts of a successful information security program. Ultimately end-users need to be able to perform job functions; by ensuring availability an organization is able to perform to the standards that an organization's stakeholders expect. This can involve topics such as proxy configurations, outside web access, the ability to access shared drives and the ability to send emails. Executives oftentimes do not understand the technical side of information security and look at availability as an easy fix, but this often requires collaboration from many different organizational teams, such as network operations, development operations, incident response and policy/change management. A successful information security team involves many different key roles to mesh and align for the CIA triad to be provided effectively.

Non-repudiation

In law, non-repudiation implies one's intention to fulfill their obligations to a contract. It also implies that one party of a transaction cannot deny having received a transaction, nor can the other party deny having sent a transaction.[39]

It is important to note that while technology such as cryptographic systems can assist in non-repudiation efforts, the concept is at its core a legal concept transcending the realm of technology. It is not, for instance, sufficient to show that the message matches a digital signature signed with the sender's private key, and thus only the sender could have sent the message, and nobody else could have altered it in transit (data integrity). The alleged sender could in return demonstrate that the digital signature algorithm is vulnerable or flawed, or allege or prove that his signing key has been compromised. The fault for these violations may or may not lie with the sender, and such assertions may or may not relieve the sender of liability, but the assertion would invalidate the claim that the signature necessarily proves authenticity and integrity. As such, the sender may repudiate the message (because authenticity and integrity are pre-requisites for non-repudiation).

Risk management

Broadly speaking, risk is the likelihood that something bad will happen that causes harm to an informational asset (or the loss of the asset). A vulnerability is a weakness that could be used to endanger or cause harm to an informational asset. A threat is anything (man-made or act of nature) that has the potential to cause harm. The likelihood that a threat will use a vulnerability to cause harm creates a risk. When a threat does use a vulnerability to inflict harm, it has an impact. In the context of information security, the impact is a loss of availability, integrity, and confidentiality, and possibly other losses (lost income, loss of life, loss of real property).[40]

The *Certified Information Systems Auditor (CISA) Review Manual 2006* defines **risk management** as "the process of identifying vulnerabilities and threats to the information resources used by an organization in achieving business objectives, and deciding what countermeasures, if any, to take in reducing risk to an acceptable level, based on the value of the information resource to the organization."[41]

There are two things in this definition that may need some clarification. First, the *process* of risk management is an ongoing, iterative process. It must be repeated indefinitely. The business environment is constantly changing and new threats and vulnerabilities emerge every day. Second, the choice of countermeasures (controls) used to manage risks must strike a balance between productivity, cost, effectiveness of the countermeasure, and the value of the informational asset being protected. Furthermore, these processes have limitations as security breaches are generally rare and emerge in a specific context which may not be easily duplicated. Thus, any process and countermeasure should itself be evaluated for vulnerabilities.[42] It is not possible to identify all risks, nor is it possible to eliminate all risk. The remaining risk is called "residual risk."

A risk assessment is carried out by a team of people who have knowledge of specific areas of the business. Membership of the team may vary over time as different parts of the business are assessed. The assessment may use a subjective qualitative analysis based on informed opinion, or where reliable dollar figures and historical information is available, the analysis may use quantitative analysis.

Research has shown that the most vulnerable point in most information systems is the human user, operator, designer, or other human.[43] The ISO/IEC 27002:2005 Code of practice for information security management recommends the following be examined during a risk assessment:

- security policy,
- organization of information security,
- asset management,
- human resources security,
- physical and environmental security,
- communications and operations management,
- access control,

- information systems acquisition, development and maintenance,
- information security incident management,
- business continuity management, and
- regulatory compliance.

In broad terms, the risk management process consists of:[44][45]

1. Identification of assets and estimating their value. Include: people, buildings, hardware, software, data (electronic, print, other), supplies.
2. Conduct a threat assessment. Include: Acts of nature, acts of war, accidents, malicious acts originating from inside or outside the organization.
3. Conduct a vulnerability assessment, and for each vulnerability, calculate the probability that it will be exploited. Evaluate policies, procedures, standards, training, physical security, quality control, technical security.
4. Calculate the impact that each threat would have on each asset. Use qualitative analysis or quantitative analysis.
5. Identify, select and implement appropriate controls. Provide a proportional response. Consider productivity, cost effectiveness, and value of the asset.
6. Evaluate the effectiveness of the control measures. Ensure the controls provide the required cost effective protection without discernible loss of productivity.

For any given risk, management can choose to accept the risk based upon the relative low value of the asset, the relative low frequency of occurrence, and the relative low impact on the business. Or, leadership may choose to mitigate the risk by selecting and implementing appropriate control measures to reduce the risk. In some cases, the risk can be transferred to another business by buying insurance or outsourcing to another business.[46] The reality of some risks may be disputed. In such cases leadership may choose to deny the risk.

Security controls

Selecting and implementing proper security controls will initially help an organization bring down risk to acceptable levels. Control selection should follow and should be based on the risk assessment. Controls can vary in nature, but fundamentally they are ways of protecting the confidentiality, integrity or availability of information. ISO/IEC 27001 has defined controls in different areas. Organizations can implement additional controls according to requirement of the organization.[47] ISO/IEC 27002 offers a guideline for organizational information security standards.

Administrative

Administrative controls consist of approved written policies, procedures, standards and guidelines. Administrative controls form the framework for running the business and managing people. They inform people on how the business is to be run and how day-to-day operations are to be conducted. Laws and regulations created by government bodies are also a type of administrative control because they inform the business. Some industry sectors have policies, procedures, standards and guidelines that must be followed – the Payment Card Industry Data Security Standard[48] (PCI DSS) required by Visa and MasterCard is such an example. Other examples of administrative controls include the corporate security policy, password policy, hiring policies, and disciplinary policies.

Administrative controls form the basis for the selection and implementation of logical and physical controls. Logical and physical controls are manifestations of administrative controls, which are of paramount importance.

Logical

Logical controls (also called technical controls) use software and data to monitor and control access to information and computing systems. Passwords, network and host-based firewalls, network intrusion detection systems, access control lists, and data encryption are examples of logical controls.

An important logical control that is frequently overlooked is the principle of least privilege, which requires that an individual, program or system process not be granted any more access privileges than are necessary to perform the task.[49] A blatant example of the failure to adhere to the principle of least privilege is logging into Windows as user Administrator to read email and surf the web. Violations of this principle can also occur when an individual collects additional access privileges over time. This happens when employees' job duties change, employees are promoted to a new position, or employees are transferred to another department. The access privileges required by their new duties are frequently added onto their already existing access privileges, which may no longer be necessary or appropriate.

Physical

Physical controls monitor and control the environment of the work place and computing facilities. They also monitor and control access to and from such facilities and include doors, locks, heating and air conditioning, smoke and fire alarms, fire suppression systems, cameras, barricades, fencing, security guards, cable locks, etc. Separating the network and workplace into functional areas are also physical controls.

An important physical control that is frequently overlooked is separation of duties, which ensures that an individual can not complete a critical task by himself. For example, an employee who submits a request for reimbursement should not also be able to authorize payment or print the check. An applications programmer should not also be the server administrator or the database administrator; these roles and responsibilities must be separated from one another.[50]

Defense in depth

Information security must protect information throughout its lifespan, from the initial creation of the information on through to the final disposal of the information. The information must be protected while in motion and while at rest. During its lifetime, information may pass through many different information processing systems and through many different parts of information processing systems. There are many different ways the information and information systems can be threatened. To fully protect the information during its lifetime, each component of the information processing system must have its own protection mechanisms. The building up, layering on and overlapping of security measures is called "defense in depth." In contrast to a metal chain, which is famously only as strong as its weakest link, the defense in depth strategy aims at a structure where, should one defensive measure fail, other measures will continue to provide protection.[51]

Recall the earlier discussion about administrative controls, logical controls, and physical controls. The three types of controls can be used to form the basis upon which to build a defense in depth strategy. With this approach, defense in depth can be conceptualized as three distinct layers or planes laid one on top of the other. Additional insight into defense in depth can be gained by thinking of it as forming the layers of an onion, with data at the core of the onion, people the next outer layer of the onion, and network security, host-based security and application security forming the outermost layers of the onion. Both perspectives are equally valid, and each provides valuable insight into the implementation of a good defense in depth strategy.

Security classification for information

An important aspect of information security and risk management is recognizing the value of information and defining appropriate procedures and protection requirements for the information. Not all information is equal and so not all information requires the same degree of protection. This requires information to be assigned a security classification. The first step in information classification is to identify a member of senior management as the owner of the particular information to be classified. Next, develop a classification policy. The policy should describe the different classification labels, define the criteria for information to be assigned a particular label, and list the required security controls for each classification. [52]

Some factors that influence which classification information should be assigned include how much value that information has to the organization, how old the information is and whether or not the information has become obsolete. Laws and other regulatory requirements are also important considerations when classifying information. The Information Systems Audit and Control Association (ISACA) and its *Business Model for Information Security* also serves as a tool for security professionals to examine security from a systems perspective, creating an environment where security can be managed holistically, allowing actual risks to be addressed.[53]

The type of information security classification labels selected and used will depend on the nature of the organization, with examples being:[52]

- In the business sector, labels such as: Public, Sensitive, Private, Confidential.
- In the government sector, labels such as: Unclassified, Unofficial, Protected, Confidential, Secret, Top Secret and their non-English equivalents.
- In cross-sectoral formations, the Traffic Light Protocol, which consists of: White, Green, Amber, and Red.

All employees in the organization, as well as business partners, must be trained on the classification schema and understand the required security controls and handling procedures for each classification. The classification of a particular information asset that has been assigned should be reviewed periodically to ensure the classification is still appropriate for the information and to ensure the security controls required by the classification are in place and are followed in their right procedures.

Access control

Access to protected information must be restricted to people who are authorized to access the information. The computer programs, and in many cases the computers that process the information, must also be authorized. This requires that mechanisms be in place to control the access to protected information. The sophistication of the access control mechanisms should be in parity with the value of the information being protected; the more sensitive or valuable the information the stronger the control mechanisms need to be. The foundation on which access control mechanisms are built start with identification and authentication.

Access control is generally considered in three steps: identification, authentication, and authorization.[36]

Identification

Identification is an assertion of who someone is or what something is. If a person makes the statement

"Hello, my name is John Doe" they are making a claim of who they are. However, their claim may or may not be true. Before John Doe can be granted access to protected information it will be necessary to verify that the person claiming to be John Doe really is John Doe. Typically the claim is in the form of a username. By entering that username you are claiming "I am the person the username belongs to".

Authentication

Authentication is the act of verifying a claim of identity. When John Doe goes into a bank to make a withdrawal, he tells the bank teller he is John Doe, a claim of identity. The bank teller asks to see a photo ID, so he hands the teller his driver's license. The bank teller checks the license to make sure it has John Doe printed on it and compares the photograph on the license against the person claiming to be John Doe. If the photo and name match the person, then the teller has authenticated that John Doe is who he claimed to be. Similarly, by entering the correct password, the user is providing evidence that he/she is the person the username belongs to.

There are three different types of information that can be used for authentication:

- Something you know: things such as a PIN, a password, or your mother's maiden name
- Something you have: a driver's license or a magnetic swipe card
- Something you are: biometrics, including palm prints, fingerprints, voice prints and retina (eye) scans

Strong authentication requires providing more than one type of authentication information (two-factor authentication). The username is the most common form of identification on computer systems today and the password is the most common form of authentication. Usernames and passwords have served their purpose, but they are increasingly inadequate.[54] Usernames and passwords are slowly being replaced or supplemented with more sophisticated authentication mechanisms such as Time-based One-time Password algorithms.

Authorization

After a person, program or computer has successfully been identified and authenticated then it must be determined what informational resources they are permitted to access and what actions they will be allowed to perform (run, view, create, delete, or change). This is called authorization. Authorization to access information and other computing services begins with administrative policies and procedures. The policies prescribe what information and computing services can be accessed, by whom, and under what conditions. The access control mechanisms are then configured to enforce these policies. Different computing systems are equipped with different kinds of access control mechanisms. Some may even offer a choice of different access control mechanisms. The access control mechanism a system offers will be based upon one of three approaches to access control, or it may be derived from a combination of the three approaches.[36]

The non-discretionary approach consolidates all access control under a centralized administration. The access to information and other resources is usually based on the individuals function (role) in the organization or the tasks the individual must perform. The discretionary approach gives the creator or owner of the information resource the ability to control access to those resources. In the mandatory access control approach, access is granted or denied basing upon the security classification assigned to the information resource.

Examples of common access control mechanisms in use today include role-based access control, available in many advanced database management systems; simple file permissions provided in the UNIX and Windows operating systems; Group Policy Objects provided in Windows network systems; and Kerberos,

RADIUS, TACACS, and the simple access lists used in many firewalls and routers.

To be effective, policies and other security controls must be enforceable and upheld. Effective policies ensure that people are held accountable for their actions. The U.S. Treasury's guidelines for systems processing sensitive or proprietary information, for example, states that all failed and successful authentication and access attempts must be logged, and all access to information must leave some type of audit trail.[55]

Also, the need-to-know principle needs to be in effect when talking about access control. This principle gives access rights to a person to perform their job functions. This principle is used in the government when dealing with difference clearances. Even though two employees in different departments have a top-secret clearance, they must have a need-to-know in order for information to be exchanged. Within the need-to-know principle, network administrators grant the employee the least amount of privilege to prevent employees from accessing more than what they are supposed to. Need-to-know helps to enforce the confidentiality-integrity-availability triad. Need-to-know directly impacts the confidential area of the triad.

Cryptography

Information security uses cryptography to transform usable information into a form that renders it unusable by anyone other than an authorized user; this process is called encryption. Information that has been encrypted (rendered unusable) can be transformed back into its original usable form by an authorized user who possesses the cryptographic key, through the process of decryption. Cryptography is used in information security to protect information from unauthorized or accidental disclosure while the information is in transit (either electronically or physically) and while information is in storage.[36]

Cryptography provides information security with other useful applications as well, including improved authentication methods, message digests, digital signatures, non-repudiation, and encrypted network communications. Older, less secure applications such as Telnet and File Transfer Protocol (FTP) are slowly being replaced with more secure applications such as Secure Shell (SSH) that use encrypted network communications. Wireless communications can be encrypted using protocols such as WPA/WPA2 or the older (and less secure) WEP. Wired communications (such as ITU-T G.hn) are secured using AES for encryption and X.1035 for authentication and key exchange. Software applications such as GnuPG or PGP can be used to encrypt data files and email.

Cryptography can introduce security problems when it is not implemented correctly. Cryptographic solutions need to be implemented using industry-accepted solutions that have undergone rigorous peer review by independent experts in cryptography. The length and strength of the encryption key is also an important consideration. A key that is weak or too short will produce weak encryption. The keys used for encryption and decryption must be protected with the same degree of rigor as any other confidential information. They must be protected from unauthorized disclosure and destruction and they must be available when needed. Public key infrastructure (PKI) solutions address many of the problems that surround key management.[36]

Process

The terms "reasonable and prudent person," "due care" and "due diligence" have been used in the fields of finance, securities, and law for many years. In recent years these terms have found their way into the fields of computing and information security.[45] U.S. Federal Sentencing Guidelines now make it possible to hold corporate officers liable for failing to exercise due care and due diligence in the management of their information systems.[56]

In the business world, stockholders, customers, business partners and governments have the expectation that corporate officers will run the business in accordance with accepted business practices and in compliance with laws and other regulatory requirements. This is often described as the "reasonable and prudent person" rule. A prudent person takes due care to ensure that everything necessary is done to operate the business by sound business principles and in a legal, ethical manner. A prudent person is also diligent (mindful, attentive, ongoing) in their due care of the business.

In the field of information security, Harris[57] offers the following definitions of due care and due diligence:

> *"Due care are steps that are taken to show that a company has taken responsibility for the activities that take place within the corporation and has taken the necessary steps to help protect the company, its resources, and employees."* And, [Due diligence are the] *"continual activities that make sure the protection mechanisms are continually maintained and operational."*

Attention should be made to two important points in these definitions. First, in due care, steps are taken to show; this means that the steps can be verified, measured, or even produce tangible artifacts. Second, in due diligence, there are continual activities; this means that people are actually doing things to monitor and maintain the protection mechanisms, and these activities are ongoing.

Organizations have a responsibility with practicing duty of care when applying information security. The Duty of Care Risk Analysis Standard (DoCRA)[58] provides principles and practices for evaluating risk. It considers all parties that could be affected by those risks. DoCRA helps evaluate safeguards if they are appropriate in protecting others from harm while presenting a reasonable burden. With increased data breach litigation, companies must balance security controls, compliance, and its mission.

Security governance

The Software Engineering Institute at Carnegie Mellon University, in a publication titled *Governing for Enterprise Security (GES) Implementation Guide*, defines characteristics of effective security governance. These include:[59]

- An enterprise-wide issue
- Leaders are accountable
- Viewed as a business requirement
- Risk-based
- Roles, responsibilities, and segregation of duties defined
- Addressed and enforced in policy
- Adequate resources committed
- Staff aware and trained
- A development life cycle requirement
- Planned, managed, measurable, and measured
- Reviewed and audited

Incident response plans

An incident response plan is a group of policies that dictate an organizations reaction to a cyber attack. Once an security breach has been identified the plan is initiated. It is important to note that there can be legal implications to a data breach. Knowing local and federal laws is critical. Every plan is unique to the needs of the organization, and it can involve skill set that are not part of an IT team. For example, a lawyer may be included in the response plan to help navigate legal implications to a data breach.[60]

As mentioned above every plan is unique but most plans will include the following:[61]

Preparation

Good preparation includes the development of an Incident Response Team (IRT). Skills need to be used by this team would be, penetration testing, computer forensics, network security, etc. This team should also keep track of trends in cybersecurity and modern attack strategies. A training program for end users is important as well as most modern attack strategies target users on the network.[61]

Identification

This part of the incident response plan identifies if there was a security event. When an end user reports information or an admin notices irregularities, an investigation is launched. An incident log is a crucial part of this step. All of the members of the team should be updating this log to ensure that information flows as fast as possible. If it has been identified that a security breach has occurred the next step should be activated.[62]

Containment

In this phase, the IRT works to isolate the areas that the breach took place to limit the scope of the security event. During this phase it is important to preserve information forensically so it can be analyzed later in the process. Containment could be as simple as physically containing a server room or as complex as segmenting a network to not allow the spread of a virus.[63]

Eradication

This is where the threat that was identified is removed from the affected systems. This could include using deleting malicious files, terminating compromised accounts, or deleting other components. Some events do not require this step, however it is important to fully understand the event before moving to this step. This will help to ensure that the threat is completely removed.[63]

Recovery

This stage is where the systems are restored back to original operation. This stage could include the recovery of data, changing user access information, or updating firewall rules or policies to prevent a breach in the future. Without executing this step, the system could still be vulnerable to future security threats.[63]

Lessons Learned

In this step information that has been gathered during this process is used to make future decisions on security. This step is crucial to the ensure that future events are prevented. Using this information to further train admins is critical to the process. This step can also be used to process information that is distributed from other entities who have experienced a security event.[64]

Change management

Change management is a formal process for directing and controlling alterations to the information processing environment. This includes alterations to desktop computers, the network, servers and software. The objectives of change management are to reduce the risks posed by changes to the information processing environment and improve the stability and reliability of the processing environment as changes are made. It is not the objective of change management to prevent or hinder necessary changes from being implemented.[65]

Any change to the information processing environment introduces an element of risk. Even apparently simple changes can have unexpected effects. One of management's many responsibilities is the management of risk. Change management is a tool for managing the risks introduced by changes to the information processing environment. Part of the change management process ensures that changes are not implemented at inopportune times when they may disrupt critical business processes or interfere with other changes being implemented.

Not every change needs to be managed. Some kinds of changes are a part of the everyday routine of information processing and adhere to a predefined procedure, which reduces the overall level of risk to the processing environment. Creating a new user account or deploying a new desktop computer are examples of changes that do not generally require change management. However, relocating user file shares, or upgrading the Email server pose a much higher level of risk to the processing environment and are not a normal everyday activity. The critical first steps in change management are (a) defining change (and communicating that definition) and (b) defining the scope of the change system.

Change management is usually overseen by a change review board composed of representatives from key business areas, security, networking, systems administrators, database administration, application developers, desktop support and the help desk. The tasks of the change review board can be facilitated with the use of automated work flow application. The responsibility of the change review board is to ensure the organization's documented change management procedures are followed. The change management process is as follows[66]

- **Request:** Anyone can request a change. The person making the change request may or may not be the same person that performs the analysis or implements the change. When a request for change is received, it may undergo a preliminary review to determine if the requested change is compatible with the organizations business model and practices, and to determine the amount of resources needed to implement the change.
- **Approve:** Management runs the business and controls the allocation of resources therefore, management must approve requests for changes and assign a priority for every change. Management might choose to reject a change request if the change is not compatible with the business model, industry standards or best practices. Management might also choose to reject a change request if the change requires more resources than can be allocated for the change.
- **Plan:** Planning a change involves discovering the scope and impact of the proposed change; analyzing the complexity of the change; allocation of resources and, developing, testing and documenting both implementation and back-out plans. Need to define the criteria on which a decision to back out will be made.
- **Test:** Every change must be tested in a safe test environment, which closely reflects the actual production environment, before the change is applied to the production environment. The backout plan must also be tested.
- **Schedule:** Part of the change review board's responsibility is to assist in the scheduling of changes by reviewing the proposed implementation date for potential conflicts with other scheduled changes

or critical business activities.

- **Communicate:** Once a change has been scheduled it must be communicated. The communication is to give others the opportunity to remind the change review board about other changes or critical business activities that might have been overlooked when scheduling the change. The communication also serves to make the help desk and users aware that a change is about to occur. Another responsibility of the change review board is to ensure that scheduled changes have been properly communicated to those who will be affected by the change or otherwise have an interest in the change.
- **Implement:** At the appointed date and time, the changes must be implemented. Part of the planning process was to develop an implementation plan, testing plan and, a back out plan. If the implementation of the change should fail or, the post implementation testing fails or, other "drop dead" criteria have been met, the back out plan should be implemented.
- **Document:** All changes must be documented. The documentation includes the initial request for change, its approval, the priority assigned to it, the implementation, testing and back out plans, the results of the change review board critique, the date/time the change was implemented, who implemented it, and whether the change was implemented successfully, failed or postponed.
- **Post-change review:** The change review board should hold a post-implementation review of changes. It is particularly important to review failed and backed out changes. The review board should try to understand the problems that were encountered, and look for areas for improvement.

Change management procedures that are simple to follow and easy to use can greatly reduce the overall risks created when changes are made to the information processing environment. Good change management procedures improve the overall quality and success of changes as they are implemented. This is accomplished through planning, peer review, documentation and communication.

Cloud Computing

Cloud computing is the on-demand availability of computer system resources, especially data storage (cloud storage) and computing power, without direct active management by the user. The term is generally used to describe data centers available to many users over the Internet.[1] Large clouds, predominant today, often have functions distributed over multiple locations from central servers. If the connection to the user is relatively close, it may be designated an edge server.

Clouds may be limited to a single organization (enterprise clouds[2][3]), or be available to many organizations (public cloud).

Cloud computing relies on sharing of resources to achieve coherence and economies of scale.

Advocates of public and hybrid clouds note that cloud computing allows companies to avoid or minimize up-front IT infrastructure costs. Proponents also claim that cloud computing allows enterprises to get their applications up and running faster, with improved manageability and less maintenance, and that it enables IT teams to more rapidly adjust resources to meet fluctuating and unpredictable demand,[3][4][5] providing the **burst computing** capability: high computing power at certain periods of peak demand.[6]

Cloud providers typically use a "pay-as-you-go" model, which can lead to unexpected operating expenses if administrators are not familiarized with cloud-pricing models.[7]

The availability of high-capacity networks, low-cost computers and storage devices as well as the widespread adoption of hardware virtualization, service-oriented architecture and autonomic and utility computing has led to growth in cloud computing.[8][9][10] By 2019, Linux was the most widely used operating system, including in Microsoft's offerings and is thus described as dominant.[11] The Cloud Service Provider (CSP) will screen, keep up and gather data about the firewalls, intrusion identification or/and counteractive action frameworks and information stream inside the network.[12]

History

Cloud computing was popularized with Amazon.com releasing its Elastic Compute Cloud product in 2006. [13]

References to the phrase "cloud computing" appeared as early as 1996, with the first known mention in a Compaq internal document.[14]

The cloud symbol was used to represent networks of computing equipment in the original ARPANET by as early as 1977,[15] and the CSNET by 1981[16]—both predecessors to the Internet itself. The word *cloud* was used as a metaphor for the Internet and a standardized cloud-like shape was used to denote a network on telephony schematics. With this simplification, the implication is that the specifics of how the endpoints of a network are connected are not relevant to understanding the diagram.[17]

The term *cloud* was used to refer to platforms for distributed computing as early as 1993, when Apple spin-off General Magic and AT&T used it in describing their (paired) Telescript and PersonaLink technologies. [18] In *Wired's* April 1994 feature "Bill and Andy's Excellent Adventure II", Andy Hertzfeld commented on Telescript, General Magic's distributed programming language:

> "The beauty of Telescript ... is that now, instead of just having a device to program, we now have the entire Cloud out there, where a single program can go and travel to many different sources of information and create a sort of a virtual service. No one had conceived that before. The example Jim White [the designer of Telescript, X.400 and ASN.1] uses now is a date-arranging service where a software agent goes to the flower store and orders flowers and then goes to the ticket shop and gets the tickets for the show, and everything is communicated to both parties."[19]

Early history

During the 1960s, the initial concepts of time-sharing became popularized via RJE (Remote Job Entry);[20] this terminology was mostly associated with large vendors such as IBM and DEC. Full-time-sharing solutions were available by the early 1970s on such platforms as Multics (on GE hardware), Cambridge CTSS, and the earliest UNIX ports (on DEC hardware). Yet, the "data center" model where users submitted jobs to operators to run on IBM's mainframes was overwhelmingly predominant.

In the 1990s, telecommunications companies, who previously offered primarily dedicated point-to-point data circuits, began offering virtual private network (VPN) services with comparable quality of service, but at a lower cost. By switching traffic as they saw fit to balance server use, they could use overall network bandwidth more effectively.[21] They began to use the cloud symbol to denote the demarcation point between what the provider was responsible for and what users were responsible for. Cloud computing extended this boundary to cover all servers as well as the network infrastructure.[22] As computers became more diffused, scientists and technologists explored ways to make large-scale computing power available to more users through time-sharing.[23] They experimented with algorithms to optimize the infrastructure, platform, and applications to prioritize CPUs and increase efficiency for end users.[24][25]

The use of the cloud metaphor for virtualized services dates at least to General Magic in 1994, where it was used to describe the universe of "places" that mobile agents in the Telescript environment could go. As described by Andy Hertzfeld:

> "The beauty of Telescript," says Andy, "is that now, instead of just having a device to program, we now have the entire Cloud out there, where a single program can go and travel to many different sources of information and create a sort of a virtual service."[26]

The use of the cloud metaphor is credited to General Magic communications employee David Hoffman, based on long-standing use in networking and telecom. In addition, to use by General Magic itself, it was also used in promoting AT&T's associated PersonaLink Services.[27]

2000s

In August 2006, Amazon created subsidiary Amazon Web Services and introduced its Elastic Compute Cloud (EC2).[13]

In April 2008, Google released the beta version of Google App Engine.[28]

In early 2008, NASA's OpenNebula, enhanced in the RESERVOIR European Commission-funded project, became the first open-source software for deploying private and hybrid clouds, and for the federation of clouds.[29]

By mid-2008, Gartner saw an opportunity for cloud computing "to shape the relationship among consumers of IT services, those who use IT services and those who sell them"[30] and observed that "organizations are switching from company-owned hardware and software assets to per-use service-based models" so that the "projected shift to computing ... will result in dramatic growth in IT products in some areas and significant reductions in other areas."[31]

In 2008, the U.S. National Science Foundation began the Cluster Exploratory program to fund academic research using Google-IBM cluster technology to analyze massive amounts of data.[32]

2010s

In February 2010, Microsoft released Microsoft Azure, which was announced in October 2008.[33]

In July 2010, Rackspace Hosting and NASA jointly launched an open-source cloud-software initiative known as OpenStack. The OpenStack project intended to help organizations offering cloud-computing services running on standard hardware. The early code came from NASA's Nebula platform as well as from Rackspace's Cloud Files platform. As an open-source offering and along with other open-source solutions such as CloudStack, Ganeti, and OpenNebula, it has attracted attention by several key communities. Several studies aim at comparing these open source offerings based on a set of criteria.[34][35][36][37][38][39][40]

On March 1, 2011, IBM announced the IBM SmartCloud framework to support Smarter Planet.[41] Among the various components of the Smarter Computing foundation, cloud computing is a critical part. On June 7, 2012, Oracle announced the Oracle Cloud.[42] This cloud offering is poised to be the first to provide users with access to an integrated set of IT solutions, including the Applications (SaaS), Platform (PaaS), and Infrastructure (IaaS) layers.[43][44][45]

In May 2012, Google Compute Engine was released in preview, before being rolled out into General Availability in December 2013.[46]

In 2019, it was revealed that Linux is most used on Microsoft Azure.[11]

Similar concepts

The goal of cloud computing is to allow users to take benefit from all of these technologies, without the need for deep knowledge about or expertise with each one of them. The cloud aims to cut costs and helps the users focus on their core business instead of being impeded by IT obstacles.[47] The main enabling technology for cloud computing is virtualization. Virtualization software separates a physical computing device into one or more "virtual" devices, each of which can be easily used and managed to perform computing tasks. With operating system–level virtualization essentially creating a scalable system of multiple independent computing devices, idle computing resources can be allocated and used more efficiently. Virtualization provides the agility required to speed up IT operations and reduces cost by increasing infrastructure utilization. Autonomic computing automates the process through which the user can provision resources on-demand. By minimizing user involvement, automation speeds up the process, reduces labor costs and reduces the possibility of human errors.[47]

Cloud computing uses concepts from utility computing to provide metrics for the services used. Cloud computing attempts to address QoS (quality of service) and reliability problems of other grid computing models.[47]

Cloud computing shares characteristics with:

- Client–server model—*Client–server computing* refers broadly to any distributed application that distinguishes between service providers (servers) and service requestors (clients).[48]
- Computer bureau—A service bureau providing computer services, particularly from the 1960s to 1980s.
- Grid computing—A form of distributed and parallel computing, whereby a 'super and virtual computer' is composed of a cluster of networked, loosely coupled computers acting in concert to perform very large tasks.
- Fog computing—Distributed computing paradigm that provides data, compute, storage and application services closer to the client or near-user edge devices, such as network routers. Furthermore, fog computing handles data at the network level, on smart devices and on the end-user client-side (e.g. mobile devices), instead of sending data to a remote location for processing.
- Mainframe computer—Powerful computers used mainly by large organizations for critical applications, typically bulk data processing such as census; industry and consumer statistics; police and secret intelligence services; enterprise resource planning; and financial transaction processing.
- Utility computing—The "packaging of computing resources, such as computation and storage, as a metered service similar to a traditional public utility, such as electricity."[49][50]
- Peer-to-peer—A distributed architecture without the need for central coordination. Participants are both suppliers and consumers of resources (in contrast to the traditional client-server model).
- Green computing
- Cloud sandbox—A live, isolated computer environment in which a program, code or file can run without affecting the application in which it runs.

Characteristics

Cloud computing exhibits the following key characteristics:

- Agility for organizations may be improved, as cloud computing may increase users' flexibility with re-provisioning, adding, or expanding technological infrastructure resources.

- Cost reductions are claimed by cloud providers. A public-cloud delivery model converts capital expenditures (e.g., buying servers) to operational expenditure.[51] This purportedly lowers barriers to entry, as infrastructure is typically provided by a third party and need not be purchased for one-time or infrequent intensive computing tasks. Pricing on a utility computing basis is "fine-grained", with usage-based billing options. As well, less in-house IT skills are required for implementation of projects that use cloud computing.[52] The e-FISCAL project's state-of-the-art repository[53] contains several articles looking into cost aspects in more detail, most of them concluding that costs savings depend on the type of activities supported and the type of infrastructure available in-house.

- Device and location independence[54] enable users to access systems using a web browser regardless of their location or what device they use (e.g., PC, mobile phone). As infrastructure is off-site (typically provided by a third-party) and accessed via the Internet, users can connect to it from anywhere.[52]

- Maintenance of cloud computing applications is easier, because they do not need to be installed on each user's computer and can be accessed from different places (e.g., different work locations, while travelling, etc.).

- Multitenancy enables sharing of resources and costs across a large pool of users thus allowing for:
  - centralization of infrastructure in locations with lower costs (such as real estate, electricity, etc.)
  - peak-load capacity increases (users need not engineer and pay for the resources and equipment to meet their highest possible load-levels)
  - utilisation and efficiency improvements for systems that are often only 10–20% utilised.[55][56]

- Performance is monitored by IT experts from the service provider, and consistent and loosely coupled architectures are constructed using web services as the system interface.[52][57]

- Productivity may be increased when multiple users can work on the same data simultaneously, rather than waiting for it to be saved and emailed. Time may be saved as information does not need to be re-entered when fields are matched, nor do users need to install application software upgrades to their computer.[58]

- Availability improves with the use of multiple redundant sites, which makes well-designed cloud computing suitable for business continuity and disaster recovery.[59]

- Scalability and elasticity via dynamic ("on-demand") provisioning of resources on a fine-grained, self-service basis in near real-time[60][61] (Note, the VM startup time varies by VM type, location, OS and cloud providers[60]), without users having to engineer for peak loads.[62][63][64] This gives the ability to scale up when the usage need increases or down if resources are not being used.[65] Emerging approaches for managing elasticity include the use of machine learning techniques to propose efficient elasticity models.[66]

- Security can improve due to centralization of data, increased security-focused resources, etc., but concerns can persist about loss of control over certain sensitive data, and the lack of security for stored kernels. Security is often as good as or better than other traditional systems, in part because service providers are able to devote resources to solving security issues that many customers cannot afford to tackle or which they lack the technical skills to address.[67] However, the complexity of security is greatly increased when data is distributed over a wider area or over a greater number of devices, as well as in multi-tenant systems shared by unrelated users. In addition, user access to security audit logs may be difficult or impossible. Private cloud installations are in part motivated by users' desire to retain control over the infrastructure and avoid losing control of information security.

The National Institute of Standards and Technology's definition of cloud computing identifies "five essential characteristics":

On-demand self-service. A consumer can unilaterally provision computing capabilities, such as server time and network storage, as needed automatically without requiring human interaction with each service provider.

Broad network access. Capabilities are available over the network and accessed through standard mechanisms that promote use by heterogeneous thin or thick client platforms (e.g., mobile phones, tablets, laptops, and workstations).

Resource pooling. The provider's computing resources are pooled to serve multiple consumers using a multi-tenant model, with different physical and virtual resources dynamically assigned and reassigned according to consumer demand.

Rapid elasticity. Capabilities can be elastically provisioned and released, in some cases automatically, to scale rapidly outward and inward commensurate with demand. To the consumer, the capabilities available for provisioning often appear unlimited and can be appropriated in any quantity at any time.

Measured service. Cloud systems automatically control and optimize resource use by leveraging a metering capability at some level of abstraction appropriate to the type of service (e.g., storage, processing, bandwidth, and active user accounts). Resource usage can be monitored, controlled, and reported, providing transparency for both the provider and consumer of the utilized service.

— *National Institute of Standards and Technology[68]*

Service models

Though service-oriented architecture advocates "Everything as a service" (with the acronyms **EaaS** or **XaaS**,[69] or simply **aas**), cloud-computing providers offer their "services" according to different models, of which the three standard models per NIST are Infrastructure as a Service (IaaS), Platform as a Service (PaaS), and Software as a Service (SaaS).[68] These models offer increasing abstraction; they are thus often portrayed as *layers* in a stack: infrastructure-, platform- and software-as-a-service, but these need not be related. For example, one can provide SaaS implemented on physical machines (bare metal), without using underlying PaaS or IaaS layers, and conversely one can run a program on IaaS and access it directly, without wrapping it as SaaS.

Infrastructure as a service (IaaS)

"Infrastructure as a service" (IaaS) refers to online services that provide high-level APIs used to abstract various low-level details of underlying network infrastructure like physical computing resources, location, data partitioning, scaling, security, backup, etc. A hypervisor runs the virtual machines as guests. Pools of hypervisors within the cloud operational system can support large numbers of virtual machines and the ability to scale services up and down according to customers' varying requirements. Linux containers run in isolated partitions of a single Linux kernel running directly on the physical hardware. Linux cgroups and namespaces are the underlying Linux kernel technologies used to isolate, secure and manage the containers. Containerisation offers higher performance than virtualization because there is no hypervisor overhead. Also, container capacity auto-scales dynamically with computing load, which eliminates the problem of over-provisioning and enables usage-based billing.[70] IaaS clouds often offer additional resources such as a virtual-machine disk-image library, raw block storage, file or object storage, firewalls, load balancers, IP addresses, virtual local area networks (VLANs), and software bundles.[71]

The NIST's definition of cloud computing describes IaaS as "where the consumer is able to deploy and run arbitrary software, which can include operating systems and applications. The consumer does not manage or control the underlying cloud infrastructure but has control over operating systems, storage, and deployed applications; and possibly limited control of select networking components (e.g., host firewalls)."[68]

IaaS-cloud providers supply these resources on-demand from their large pools of equipment installed in data centers. For wide-area connectivity, customers can use either the Internet or carrier clouds (dedicated virtual private networks). To deploy their applications, cloud users install operating-system images and their application software on the cloud infrastructure. In this model, the cloud user patches and maintains the operating systems and the application software. Cloud providers typically bill IaaS services on a utility computing basis: cost reflects the amount of resources allocated and consumed.[72]

Platform as a service (PaaS)

The NIST's definition of cloud computing defines Platform as a Service as:[68]

> The capability provided to the consumer is to deploy onto the cloud infrastructure consumer-created or acquired applications created using programming languages, libraries, services, and tools supported by the provider. The consumer does not manage or control the underlying cloud infrastructure including network, servers, operating systems, or storage, but has control over the deployed applications and possibly configuration settings for the application-hosting environment.

PaaS vendors offer a development environment to application developers. The provider typically develops toolkit and standards for development and channels for distribution and payment. In the PaaS models, cloud providers deliver a computing platform, typically including operating system, programming-language execution environment, database, and web server. Application developers develop and run their software on a cloud platform instead of directly buying and managing the underlying hardware and software layers. With some PaaS, the underlying computer and storage resources scale automatically to match application demand so that the cloud user does not have to allocate resources manually.[73][*need quotation to verify*]

Some integration and data management providers also use specialized applications of PaaS as delivery models for data. Examples include **iPaaS (Integration Platform as a Service)** and **dPaaS (Data Platform as a Service)**. iPaaS enables customers to develop, execute and govern integration flows.[74] Under the iPaaS integration model, customers drive the development and deployment of integrations without installing or managing any hardware or middleware.[75] dPaaS delivers integration—and data-management —products as a fully managed service.[76] Under the dPaaS model, the PaaS provider, not the customer, manages the development and execution of programs by building data applications for the customer. dPaaS users access data through data-visualization tools.[77] Platform as a Service (PaaS) consumers do not manage or control the underlying cloud infrastructure including network, servers, operating systems, or storage, but have control over the deployed applications and possibly configuration settings for the application-hosting environment.

Software as a service (SaaS)

The NIST's definition of cloud computing defines Software as a Service as:[68]

> The capability provided to the consumer is to use the provider's applications running on a cloud infrastructure. The applications are accessible from various client devices through either a thin client interface, such as a web browser (e.g., web-based email), or a program interface. The consumer does not manage or control the underlying cloud infrastructure including network, servers, operating systems, storage, or even individual application capabilities, with the possible exception of limited user-specific application configuration settings.

In the software as a service (SaaS) model, users gain access to application software and databases. Cloud providers manage the infrastructure and platforms that run the applications. SaaS is sometimes referred to as "on-demand software" and is usually priced on a pay-per-use basis or using a subscription fee.[78] In the SaaS model, cloud providers install and operate application software in the cloud and cloud users access the software from cloud clients. Cloud users do not manage the cloud infrastructure and platform where the application runs. This eliminates the need to install and run the application on the cloud user's own computers, which simplifies maintenance and support. Cloud applications differ from other applications in their scalability—which can be achieved by cloning tasks onto multiple virtual machines at run-time to meet changing work demand.[79] Load balancers distribute the work over the set of virtual machines. This process is transparent to the cloud user, who sees only a single access-point. To accommodate a large number of cloud users, cloud applications can be *multitenant*, meaning that any machine may serve more than one cloud-user organization.

The pricing model for SaaS applications is typically a monthly or yearly flat fee per user,[80] so prices become scalable and adjustable if users are added or removed at any point. It may also be free.[81] Proponents claim that SaaS gives a business the potential to reduce IT operational costs by outsourcing hardware and software maintenance and support to the cloud provider. This enables the business to reallocate IT operations costs away from hardware/software spending and from personnel expenses, towards meeting other goals. In addition, with applications hosted centrally, updates can be released without the need for users to install new software. One drawback of SaaS comes with storing the users' data on the cloud provider's server. As a result,[*citation needed*] there could be unauthorized access to the data. [*citation needed*] Examples of applications offered as SaaS are games and productivity software like Google Docs and Word Online. SaaS applications may be integrated with cloud storage or File hosting services, which is the case with Google Docs being integrated with Google Drive and Word Online being integrated with Onedrive.[*citation needed*]

Mobile "backend" as a service (MBaaS)

In the mobile "backend" as a service (m) model, also known as **backend as a service (BaaS)**, web app and mobile app developers are provided with a way to link their applications to cloud storage and cloud computing services with application programming interfaces (APIs) exposed to their applications and custom software development kits (SDKs). Services include user management, push notifications, integration with social networking services[82] and more. This is a relatively recent model in cloud computing,[83] with most BaaS startups dating from 2011 or later[84][85][86] but trends indicate that these services are gaining significant mainstream traction with enterprise consumers.[87]

Serverless computing

Serverless computing is a cloud computing code execution model in which the cloud provider fully manages starting and stopping virtual machines as necessary to serve requests, and requests are billed by an abstract measure of the resources required to satisfy the request, rather than per virtual machine, per hour. [88] Despite the name, it does not actually involve running code without servers.[88] Serverless computing is so named because the business or person that owns the system does not have to purchase, rent or provision servers or virtual machines for the back-end code to run on.

Function as a service (FaaS)

Function as a service (FaaS) is a service-hosted remote procedure call that leverages serverless computing to enable the deployment of individual functions in the cloud that run in response to events.[89] FaaS is included under the broader term *serverless computing*, but the terms may also be used interchangeably.[90]

Deployment models

Private cloud

Private cloud is cloud infrastructure operated solely for a single organization, whether managed internally or by a third party, and hosted either internally or externally.[68] Undertaking a private cloud project requires significant engagement to virtualize the business environment, and requires the organization to reevaluate decisions about existing resources. It can improve business, but every step in the project raises security issues that must be addressed to prevent serious vulnerabilities. Self-run data centers[91] are generally capital intensive. They have a significant physical footprint, requiring allocations of space, hardware, and environmental controls. These assets have to be refreshed periodically, resulting in additional capital expenditures. They have attracted criticism because users "still have to buy, build, and manage them" and thus do not benefit from less hands-on management,[92] essentially "[lacking] the economic model that makes cloud computing such an intriguing concept".[93][94]

Public cloud

For a comparison of cloud-computing software and providers, see Cloud-computing comparison

Cloud services are considered "public" when they are delivered over the public Internet, and they may be offered as a paid subscription, or free of charge.[95] Architecturally, there are few differences between public- and private-cloud services, but security concerns increase substantially when services (applications, storage, and other resources) are shared by multiple customers. Most public-cloud providers offer direct-connection services that allow customers to securely link their legacy data centers to their cloud-resident applications.[52][96]

Hybrid cloud

Hybrid cloud is a composition of a public cloud and a private environment, such as a private cloud or on-premises resources,[97][98] that remain distinct entities but are bound together, offering the benefits of multiple deployment models. Hybrid cloud can also mean the ability to connect collocation, managed and/or dedicated services with cloud resources.[68] Gartner defines a hybrid cloud service as a cloud computing service that is composed of some combination of private, public and community cloud services, from different service providers.[99] A hybrid cloud service crosses isolation and provider boundaries so that it can't be simply put in one category of private, public, or community cloud service. It allows one to extend either the capacity or the capability of a cloud service, by aggregation, integration or customization with another cloud service.

Varied use cases for hybrid cloud composition exist. For example, an organization may store sensitive client data in house on a private cloud application, but interconnect that application to a business intelligence application provided on a public cloud as a software service.[100] This example of hybrid cloud extends the capabilities of the enterprise to deliver a specific business service through the addition of externally available public cloud services. Hybrid cloud adoption depends on a number of factors such as data security and compliance requirements, level of control needed over data, and the applications an organization uses.[101]

Another example of hybrid cloud is one where IT organizations use public cloud computing resources to meet temporary capacity needs that can not be met by the private cloud.[102] This capability enables hybrid clouds to employ cloud bursting for scaling across clouds.[68] Cloud bursting is an application deployment model in which an application runs in a private cloud or data center and "bursts" to a public cloud when the demand for computing capacity increases. A primary advantage of cloud bursting and a hybrid cloud model is that an organization pays for extra compute resources only when they are needed. [103] Cloud bursting enables data centers to create an in-house IT infrastructure that supports average workloads, and use cloud resources from public or private clouds, during spikes in processing demands. [104] The specialized model of hybrid cloud, which is built atop heterogeneous hardware, is called "Cross-platform Hybrid Cloud". A cross-platform hybrid cloud is usually powered by different CPU architectures, for example, x86-64 and ARM, underneath. Users can transparently deploy and scale applications without knowledge of the cloud's hardware diversity.[105] This kind of cloud emerges from the rise of ARM-based system-on-chip for server-class computing.

Hybrid cloud infrastructure essentially serves to eliminate limitations inherent to the multi-access relay characteristics of private cloud networking. The advantages include enhanced runtime flexibility and adaptive memory processing unique to virtualized interface models.[106]

Others

Community cloud

Community cloud shares infrastructure between several organizations from a specific community with common concerns (security, compliance, jurisdiction, etc.), whether managed internally or by a third-party, and either hosted internally or externally. The costs are spread over fewer users than a public cloud (but more than a private cloud), so only some of the cost savings potential of cloud computing are realized.[68]

Distributed cloud

A cloud computing platform can be assembled from a distributed set of machines in different locations, connected to a single network or hub service. It is possible to distinguish between two types of distributed clouds: public-resource computing and volunteer cloud.

- **Public-resource computing**—This type of distributed cloud results from an expansive definition of cloud computing, because they are more akin to distributed computing than cloud computing. Nonetheless, it is considered a sub-class of cloud computing.

- **Volunteer cloud**—Volunteer cloud computing is characterized as the intersection of public-resource computing and cloud computing, where a cloud computing infrastructure is built using volunteered resources. Many challenges arise from this type of infrastructure, because of the volatility of the resources used to build it and the dynamic environment it operates in. It can also be called peer-to-peer clouds, or ad-hoc clouds. An interesting effort in such direction is Cloud@Home, it aims to implement a cloud computing infrastructure using volunteered resources providing a business-model to incentivize contributions through financial restitution.[107]

Multicloud

Multicloud is the use of multiple cloud computing services in a single heterogeneous architecture to reduce reliance on single vendors, increase flexibility through choice, mitigate against disasters, etc. It differs from hybrid cloud in that it refers to multiple cloud services, rather than multiple deployment modes (public, private, legacy).[108][109][110]

Poly cloud

Poly cloud refers to the use of multiple public clouds for the purpose of leveraging specific services that each provider offers. It differs from multicloud in that it is not designed to increase flexibility or mitigate against failures but is rather used to allow an organization to achieve more that could be done with a single provider.[111]

Big Data cloud

The issues of transferring large amounts of data to the cloud as well as data security once the data is in the cloud initially hampered adoption of cloud for big data, but now that much data originates in the cloud and with the advent of bare-metal servers, the cloud has become[112] a solution for use cases including business analytics and geospatial analysis.[113]

HPC cloud

HPC cloud refers to the use of cloud computing services and infrastructure to execute high-performance computing (HPC) applications.[114] These applications consume considerable amount of computing power and memory and are traditionally executed on clusters of computers. In 2016 a handful of companies, including R-HPC, Amazon Web Services, Univa, Silicon Graphics International, Sabalcore, Gomput, and Penguin Computing offered a high performance computing cloud. The Penguin On Demand (POD) cloud was one of the first non-virtualized remote HPC services offered on a pay-as-you-go basis.[115][116] Penguin Computing launched its HPC cloud in 2016 as alternative to Amazon's EC2 Elastic Compute Cloud, which uses virtualized computing nodes.[117][118]

Architecture

Cloud architecture,[119] the systems architecture of the software systems involved in the delivery of cloud computing, typically involves multiple *cloud components* communicating with each other over a loose coupling mechanism such as a messaging queue. Elastic provision implies intelligence in the use of tight or loose coupling as applied to mechanisms such as these and others.

Cloud engineering

Cloud engineering is the application of engineering disciplines to cloud computing. It brings a systematic approach to the high-level concerns of commercialization, standardization and governance in conceiving, developing, operating and maintaining cloud computing systems. It is a multidisciplinary method encompassing contributions from diverse areas such as systems, software, web, performance, information technology engineering, security, platform, risk, and quality engineering.

Security and privacy

Cloud computing poses privacy concerns because the service provider can access the data that is in the cloud at any time. It could accidentally or deliberately alter or delete information.[120] Many cloud providers can share information with third parties if necessary for purposes of law and order without a warrant. That is permitted in their privacy policies, which users must agree to before they start using cloud services. Solutions to privacy include policy and legislation as well as end-users' choices for how data is stored.[120] Users can encrypt data that is processed or stored within the cloud to prevent unauthorized access.[121][120] Identity management systems can also provide practical solutions to privacy concerns in cloud computing. These systems distinguish between authorized and unauthorized users and determine the amount of data that is accessible to each entity.[122] The systems work by creating and describing identities, recording activities, and getting rid of unused identities.

According to the Cloud Security Alliance, the top three threats in the cloud are *Insecure Interfaces and APIs*, *Data Loss & Leakage*, and *Hardware Failure*—which accounted for 29%, 25% and 10% of all cloud security outages respectively. Together, these form shared technology vulnerabilities. In a cloud provider platform being shared by different users, there may be a possibility that information belonging to different customers resides on the same data server. Additionally, Eugene Schultz, chief technology officer at Emagined Security, said that hackers are spending substantial time and effort looking for ways to penetrate the cloud. "There are some real Achilles' heels in the cloud infrastructure that are making big holes for the bad guys to get into". Because data from hundreds or thousands of companies can be stored on large cloud servers, hackers can theoretically gain control of huge stores of information through a single attack—a process he called "hyperjacking". Some examples of this include the Dropbox security breach, and iCloud 2014 leak.[123] Dropbox had been breached in October 2014, having over 7 million of its users passwords stolen by hackers in an effort to get monetary value from it by Bitcoins (BTC). By having these passwords, they are able to read private data as well as have this data be indexed by search engines (making the information public).[123]

There is the problem of legal ownership of the data (If a user stores some data in the cloud, can the cloud provider profit from it?). Many Terms of Service agreements are silent on the question of ownership.[124] Physical control of the computer equipment (private cloud) is more secure than having the equipment off-site and under someone else's control (public cloud). This delivers great incentive to public cloud computing service providers to prioritize building and maintaining strong management of secure services. [125] Some small businesses that don't have expertise in IT security could find that it's more secure for them to use a public cloud. There is the risk that end users do not understand the issues involved when signing on to a cloud service (persons sometimes don't read the many pages of the terms of service agreement, and just click "Accept" without reading). This is important now that cloud computing is becoming popular and required for some services to work, for example for an intelligent personal assistant (Apple's Siri or Google Now). Fundamentally, private cloud is seen as more secure with higher levels of control for the owner, however public cloud is seen to be more flexible and requires less time and money investment from the user.[126]

Limitations and disadvantages

According to Bruce Schneier, "The downside is that you will have limited customization options. Cloud computing is cheaper because of economics of scale, and—like any outsourced task—you tend to get what you want. A restaurant with a limited menu is cheaper than a personal chef who can cook anything you want. Fewer options at a much cheaper price: it's a feature, not a bug." He also suggests that "the cloud provider might not meet your legal needs" and that businesses need to weigh the benefits of cloud computing against the risks.[127] In cloud computing, the control of the back end infrastructure is limited to the cloud vendor only. Cloud providers often decide on the management policies, which moderates what the cloud users are able to do with their deployment.[128] Cloud users are also limited to the control and management of their applications, data and services.[129] This includes data caps, which are placed on cloud users by the cloud vendor allocating a certain amount of bandwidth for each customer and are often shared among other cloud users.[129]

Privacy and confidentiality are big concerns in some activities. For instance, sworn translators working under the stipulations of an NDA, might face problems regarding sensitive data that are not encrypted.[130]

Cloud computing is beneficial to many enterprises; it lowers costs and allows them to focus on competence instead of on matters of IT and infrastructure. Nevertheless, cloud computing has proven to have some limitations and disadvantages, especially for smaller business operations, particularly regarding security and downtime. Technical outages are inevitable and occur sometimes when cloud service providers (CSPs) become overwhelmed in the process of serving their clients. This may result in temporary business suspension. Since this technology's systems rely on the Internet, an individual cannot access their applications, server or data from the cloud during an outage.[131] However, many large enterprises maintain at least two internet providers, using different entry points into their workplaces, some even use 4G as a third fallback.

Emerging trends

Cloud computing is still a subject of research.[132] A driving factor in the evolution of cloud computing has been chief technology officers seeking to minimize risk of internal outages and mitigate the complexity of housing network and computing hardware in-house.[133] Major cloud technology companies invest billions of dollars per year in cloud Research and Development. For example, in 2011 Microsoft committed 90 percent of its $9.6 billion R&D budget to its cloud.[134] Research by investment bank Centaur Partners in late 2015 forecasted that SaaS revenue would grow from $13.5 billion in 2011 to $32.8 billion in 2016.[135]

Digital forensics in the cloud

The issue of carrying out investigations where the cloud storage devices cannot be physically accessed has generated a number of changes to the way that digital evidence is located and collected.[136] New process models have been developed to formalize collection.[137]

In some scenarios existing digital forensics tools can be employed to access cloud storage as networked drives (although this is a slow process generating a large amount of internet traffic).[*citation needed*]

An alternative approach is to deploy a tool that processes in the cloud itself.[138]

For organizations using Office 365 with an 'E5' subscription, there is the option to use Microsoft's built-in ediscovery resources, although these do not provide all the functionality that is typically required for a forensic process.[139]

Electronic Authentication

Electronic authentication is the process of establishing confidence in user identities electronically presented to an information system.[1] **Digital authentication** or **e-authentication** may be used synonymously when referring to the authentication process that confirms or certifies a person's identity and works. When used in conjunction with an electronic signature, it can provide evidence of whether data received has been tampered with after being signed by its original sender. Electronic authentication can reduce the risk of fraud and identity theft by verifying that a person is who they say they are when performing transactions online.[2]

There are various e-authentication methods that can be used to authenticate a user's identify ranging from a password to higher levels of security that utilize multifactor authentication (MFA).[3] Depending on the level of security used, the user might need to prove his or her identity through the use of security tokens, challenge questions or being in possession of a certificate from a third-party certificate authority that attests to their identity.[4]

Overview

The American National Institute of Standards and Technology (NIST) has developed a generic electronic authentication model[5] that provides a basic framework on how the authentication process is accomplished regardless of jurisdiction or geographic region. According to this model, the enrollment process begins with an individual applying to a Credential Service Provider (CSP). The CSP will need to prove the applicant's identity before proceeding with the transaction. Once the applicant's identity has been confirmed by the CSP, he or she receives the status of "subscriber", is given an authenticator, such as a token and a credential, which may be in the form of a username.

The CSP is responsible for managing the credential along with the subscriber's enrollment data for the life of the credential. The subscriber will be tasked with maintaining the authenticators. An example of this is when a user normally uses a specific computer to do their online banking. If he or she attempts to access their bank account from another computer, the authenticator will not be present. In order to gain access, the subscriber would need to verify their identity to the CSP, which might be in the form of answering a challenge question successfully before being given access.[4]

History

The need for authentication has been prevalent throughout history. In ancient times, people would identify each other through eye contact and physical appearance. The Sumerians in ancient Mesopotamia attested to the authenticity of their writings by using seals embellished with identifying symbols. As time moved on, the most common way to provide authentication would be the handwritten signature.[2]

Authentication factors

There are three generally accepted factors that are used to establish a digital identity for electronic authentication, including:

- Knowledge factor, which is something that the user knows, such as a password, answers to challenge questions, ID numbers or a PIN.
- Possession factor, which is something that the user has, such as mobile phone, PC or token
- Biometric factor, which is something that the user is, such as his or her fingerprints, eye scan or voice pattern

Out of the three factors, the biometric factor is the most convenient and convincing to prove an individual's identity; but it is the most expensive to implement. Each factor has its weaknesses, so reliable and strong authentication depends on combining two or more factors. This is known as multi-factor authentication,[2] of which two-factor authentication and two-step verification are subtypes.

Multi-factor authentication can still be vulnerable to attacks, including man-in-the-middle attacks and Trojan attacks.[6]

Methods

Token

Tokens generically are something the claimant possesses and controls that may be used to authenticate the claimant's identity. In e-authentication, the claimant authenticates to a system or application over a network. Therefore, a token used for e-authentication is a secret and the token must be protected. The token may, for example, be a cryptographic key, that is protected by encrypting it under a password. An impostor must steal the encrypted key and learn the password to use the token.

Passwords and PIN-based authentication

Passwords and PINs are categorized as "something you know" method. A combination of numbers, symbols, and mixed cases are considered to be stronger than all-letter password. Also, the adoption of Transport Layer Security (TLS) or Secure Socket Layer (SSL) features during the information transmission process will as well create an encrypted channel for data exchange and to further protect information delivered. Currently, most security attacks target on password-based authentication systems.[7]

Public-key authentication

This type of authentication has two parts. One is a public key, the other is a private key. A public key is issued by a Certification Authority and is available to any user or server. A private key is known by the user only.[8]

Symmetric-key authentication

The user shares a unique key with an authentication server. When the user sends a randomly generated message (the challenge) encrypted by the secret key to the authentication server, if the message can be matched by the server using its shared secret key, the user is authenticated. When implemented together with the password authentication, this method also provides a possible solution for two-factor authentication systems.[9]

SMS-based authentication

The user receives password by reading the message in the cell phone, and types back the password to complete the authentication. Short Message Service (SMS) is very effective when cell phones are commonly adopted. SMS is also suitable against man-in-the-middle (MITM) attacks, since the use of SMS does not involve the Internet.[10]

Biometric authentication

Biometric authentication is the use of unique physical attributes and body measurements as the intermediate for better identification and access control. Physical characteristics that are often used for authentication include fingerprints, voice recognition, face, recognition, and iris scans because all of these are unique to every individual separately. Traditionally, Biometric Authentication based on token-based identification systems, such as passport, and nowadays becomes one of the most secure identification systems to user protections. A new technological innovation which provides a wide variety of either behavioral or physical characteristics which are defining the proper concept of Biometric Authentication. [11]

Digital identity authentication

Digital identity authentication refers to the combined use of device, behavior, location and other data, including email address, account and credit card information, to authenticate online users in real time.

Electronic credentials

Paper credentials are documents that attest to the identity or other attributes of an individual or entity called the subject of the credentials. Some common paper credentials include passports, birth certificates, driver's licenses, and employee identity cards. The credentials themselves are authenticated in a variety of ways: traditionally perhaps by a signature or a seal, special papers and inks, high quality engraving, and today by more complex mechanisms, such as holograms, that make the credentials recognizable and difficult to copy or forge. In some cases, simple possession of the credentials is sufficient to establish that the physical holder of the credentials is indeed the subject of the credentials. More commonly, the credentials contain biometric information such as the subject's description, a picture of the subject or the handwritten signature of the subject that can be used to authenticate that the holder of the credentials is indeed the subject of the credentials. When these paper credentials are presented in-person, authentication biometrics contained in those credentials can be checked to confirm that the physical holder of the credential is the subject.

Electronic identity credentials bind a name and perhaps other attributes to a token. There are a variety of electronic credential types in use today, and new types of credentials are constantly being created (eID, electronic voter ID card, biometric passports, bank cards, etc.) At a minimum, credentials include identifying information that permits recovery of the records of the registration associated with the credentials and a name that is associated with the subscriber.[*citation needed*]

Verifiers

In any authenticated on-line transaction, the verifier is the party that verifies that the claimant has possession and control of the token that verifies his or her identity. A claimant authenticates his or her identity to a verifier by the use of a token and an authentication protocol. This is called Proof of Possession (PoP). Many PoP protocols are designed so that a verifier, with no knowledge of the token before the authentication protocol run, learns nothing about the token from the run. The verifier and CSP may be the same entity, the verifier and relying party may be the same entity or they may all three be separate entities. It is undesirable for verifiers to learn shared secrets unless they are a part of the same entity as the CSP that registered the tokens. Where the verifier and the relying party are separate entities, the verifier must convey the result of the authentication protocol to the relying party. The object created by the verifier to convey this result is called an assertion.[12]

Authentication schemes

There are four types of authentication schemes: local authentication, centralized authentication, global centralized authentication, global authentication and web application (portal).

When using a local authentication scheme, the application retains the data that pertains to the user's credentials. This information is not usually shared with other applications. The onus is on the user to maintain and remember the types and number of credentials that are associated with the service in which they need to access. This is a high risk scheme because of the possibility that the storage area for passwords might become compromised.

Using the central authentication scheme allows for each user to use the same credentials to access various services. Each application is different and must be designed with interfaces and the ability to interact with a central system to successfully provide authentication for the user. This allows the user to access important information and be able to access private keys that will allow him or her to electronically sign documents.

Using a third party through a global centralized authentication scheme allows the user direct access to authentication services. This then allows the user to access the particular services they need.

The most secure scheme is the global centralized authentication and web application (portal). It is ideal for E-Government use because it allows a wide range of services. It uses a single authentication mechanism involving a minimum of two factors to allow access to required services and the ability to sign documents. [2]

Authentication and digital signing working together

Often, authentication and digital signing are applied in conjunction. In advanced electronic signatures, the signatory has authenticated and uniquely linked to a signature. In the case of a qualified electronic signature as defined in the eIDAS-regulation, the signer's identity is even certified by a qualified trust service provider. This linking of signature and authentication firstly supports the probative value of the signature – commonly referred to as non-repudiation of origin. The protection of the message on the network-level is called non-repudiation of emission. The authenticated sender and the message content are linked to each other. If a 3rd party tries to change the message content, the signature loses validity.[13]

Characteristics biometric authentication

Homogenization and decoupling

Biometric authentication can be defined by many different procedures and sensors which are being used to produce security. Biometric can be separated into physical or behavioral security. Physical protection is based on identification through fingerprint, face, hand, iris, etc. On the other hand, behavioral safety is succeeded by keystroke, signature, and voice.[14] The main point is that all of these different procedures and mechanism that exist, produce the same homogeneous result, namely the security of the system and users. When thinking of the decoupling of hardware, the hardware is not coded in the same form by digitization which directly makes decoupling more difficult. Because of unlinkability and irreversibility of biometric templates, this technology can secure user authentication.

Digital traces

Biometric authentication has a substantial impact on digital traces. For example, when the user decides to use his fingerprint to protect his data on his smartphone, then the system memorizes the input so it will be able to be re-used again. During this procedure and many other similar applications proves that the digital trace is vital and exist on biometric authentication.

Connectivity

Another characteristic of biometric authentication is that it combines different components such as security tokens with computer systems to protect the user. Another example is the connection between devices, such as camera and computer systems to scan the user's retina and produce new ways of security. So biometric authentication could be defined by connectivity as long it connects different applications or components and through these users are getting connected and can work under the same roof and especially on a safe environment on the cyber world.

Reprogrammable & smart

As new kinds of cybercrime are appearing, the ways of authentication must be able to adapt. This adaptation means that it is always ready for evolution and updating, and so it will be able to protect the users at any time. At first biometric authentication started in the sampler form of user's access and defining user profiles and policies. Over time the need of biometric authentication became more complex, so cybersecurity organizations started reprogramming their products/technology from simple personal user's access to allow interoperability of identities across multiple solutions. Through this evolution, business value also rises.[15]

Risk assessment

When developing electronic systems, there are some industry standards requiring United States agencies to ensure the transactions provide an appropriate level of assurance. Generally, servers adopt the US' Office of Management and Budget's (OMB's) E-Authentication Guidance for Federal Agencies (M-04-04) as a guideline, which is published to help federal agencies provide secure electronic services that protect individual privacy. It asks agencies to check whether their transactions require e-authentication, and determine a proper level of assurance.[16]

It established four levels of assurance:[17]

Assurance Level 1: Little or no confidence in the asserted identity's validity.
Assurance Level 2: Some confidence in the asserted identity's validity.
Assurance Level 3: High confidence in the asserted identity's validity.
Assurance Level 4: Very high confidence in the asserted identity's validity.

Determining assurance levels

The OMB proposes a five-step process to determine the appropriate assurance level for their applications:

- Conduct a risk assessment, which measures possible negative impacts.
- Compare with the five assurance levels and decide which one suits this case.
- Select technology according to the technical guidance issued by NIST.
- Confirm the selected authentication process satisfies requirements.
- Reassess the system regularly and adjust it with changes.[18]

The required level of authentication assurance are assessed through the factors below:

- Inconvenience, distress, or damage to standing or reputation;
- Financial loss or agency liability;
- Harm to agency programs or public interests;
- Unauthorized release of sensitive information;
- Personal safety; and/or civil or criminal violations.[18]

Determining technical requirements

National Institute of Standards and Technology (NIST) guidance defines technical requirements for each of the four levels of assurance in the following areas:[19]

- Tokens are used for proving identity. Passwords and symmetric cryptographic keys are private information that the verifier needs to protect. Asymmetric cryptographic keys have a private key (which only the subscriber knows) and a related public key.
- Identity proofing, registration, and the delivery of credentials that bind an identity to a token. This process can involve a far distance operation.
- Credentials, tokens, and authentication protocols can also be combined together to identify that a claimant is in fact the claimed subscriber.
- An assertion mechanism that involves either a digital signature of the claimant or is acquired directly by a trusted third party through a secure authentication protocol.

Physical Security

Physical security describes security measures that are designed to deny unauthorized access to facilities, equipment and resources and to protect personnel and property from damage or harm (such as espionage, theft, or terrorist attacks).[1] Physical security involves the use of multiple layers of interdependent systems that can include CCTV surveillance, security guards, protective barriers, locks, access control, perimeter intrusion detection, deterrent systems, fire protection, and other systems designed to protect persons and property.

Overview

Physical security systems for protected facilities are generally intended to:[2][3][4]

- deter potential intruders (e.g. warning signs, security lighting and perimeter markings);
- detect intrusions and monitor/record intruders (e.g. intruder alarms and CCTV systems); and
- trigger appropriate incident responses (e.g. by security guards and police).

It is up to security designers, architects and analysts to balance security controls against risks, taking into account the costs of specifying, developing, testing, implementing, using, managing, monitoring and maintaining the controls, along with broader issues such as aesthetics, human rights, health and safety, and societal norms or conventions. Physical access security measures that are appropriate for a high security prison or a military site may be inappropriate in an office, a home or a vehicle, although the principles are similar.

Elements and design

Deterrence methods

The goal of *deterrence* methods is to convince potential attackers that a successful attack is unlikely due to strong defenses.

The initial layer of security for a campus, building, office, or other physical space uses crime prevention through environmental design to deter threats. Some of the most common examples are also the most basic: warning signs or window stickers, fences, vehicle barriers, vehicle height-restrictors, restricted access points, security lighting and trenches.[5][6][7][8]

Physical barriers

Physical barriers such as fences, walls, and vehicle barriers act as the outermost layer of security. They serve to prevent, or at least delay, attacks, and also act as a psychological deterrent by defining the perimeter of the facility and making intrusions seem more difficult. Tall fencing, topped with barbed wire, razor wire or metal spikes are often emplaced on the perimeter of a property, generally with some type of signage that warns people not to attempt entry. However, in some facilities imposing perimeter walls/fencing will not be possible (e.g. an urban office building that is directly adjacent to public sidewalks) or it may be aesthetically unacceptable (e.g. surrounding a shopping center with tall fences topped with razor wire); in this case, the outer security perimeter will be defined as the walls/windows/doors of the structure itself.[9]

Combination barriers

Barriers are typically designed to defeat defined threats. This is part of building codes as well as fire codes. Apart from external threats, there are internal threats of fire, smoke migration as well as sabotage. The National Building Code of Canada, as an example, indicates the need to defeat external explosions with the building envelope, where they are possible, such as where large electrical transformers are located close to a building. High-voltage transformer fire barriers can be examples of walls designed to simultaneously defeat fire, ballistics and fragmentation as a result of transformer ruptures, as well as incoming small weapons fire. Similarly, buildings may have internal barriers to defeat weapons as well as fire and heat. An example would be a counter at a police station or embassy, where the public may access a room but talk through security glass to employees in behind. If such a barrier aligns with a fire compartment as part of building code compliance, then multiple threats must be defeated simultaneously, which must be considered in the design.

Natural surveillance

Another major form of deterrence that can be incorporated into the design of facilities is natural surveillance, whereby architects seek to build spaces that are more open and visible to security personnel and authorized users, so that intruders/attackers are unable to perform unauthorized activity without being seen. An example would be decreasing the amount of dense, tall vegetation in the landscaping so that attackers cannot conceal themselves within it, or placing critical resources in areas where intruders would have to cross over a wide, open space to reach them (making it likely that someone would notice them).

Security lighting

Security lighting is another effective form of deterrence. Intruders are less likely to enter well-lit areas for fear of being seen. Doors, gates, and other entrances, in particular, should be well lit to allow close observation of people entering and exiting. When lighting the grounds of a facility, widely distributed low-intensity lighting is generally superior to small patches of high-intensity lighting, because the latter can have a tendency to create blind spots for security personnel and CCTV cameras. It is important to place lighting in a manner that makes it difficult to tamper with (e.g. suspending lights from tall poles), and to ensure that there is a backup power supply so that security lights will not go out if the electricity is cut off. [10] The introduction of low-voltage LED-based lighting products has enabled new security capabilities, such as instant-on or strobing, while substantially reducing electrical consumption[11].

Intrusion detection and electronic surveillance

Alarm systems and sensors

Alarm systems can be installed to alert security personnel when unauthorized access is attempted. Alarm systems work in tandem with physical barriers, mechanical systems, and security guards, serving to trigger a response when these other forms of security have been breached. They consist of sensors including perimeter sensors, motion sensors, contact sensors, and glass break detectors.[12]

However, alarms are only useful if there is a prompt response when they are triggered. In the reconnaissance phase prior to an actual attack, some intruders will test the response time of security personnel to a deliberately tripped alarm system. By measuring the length of time it takes for a security team to arrive (if they arrive at all), the attacker can determine if an attack could succeed before authorities arrive to neutralize the threat. Loud audible alarms can also act as a psychological deterrent, by notifying intruders that their presence has been detected.[13] In some jurisdictions, law enforcement will not respond to alarms from intrusion detection systems unless the activation has been verified by an eyewitness or video.[14] Policies like this one have been created to combat the 94–99 percent rate of false alarm activation in the United States.[15]

Video surveillance

Surveillance cameras can be a deterrent[16] when placed in highly visible locations and are useful for incident assessment and historical analysis. For example, if alarms are being generated and there is a camera in place, security personnel assess the situation via the camera feed. In instances when an attack has already occurred and a camera is in place at the point of attack, the recorded video can be reviewed. Although the term closed-circuit television (CCTV) is common, it is quickly becoming outdated as more video systems lose the closed circuit for signal transmission and are instead transmitting on IP camera networks.

Video monitoring does not necessarily guarantee a human response. A human must be monitoring the situation in real time in order to respond in a timely manner; otherwise, video monitoring is simply a means to gather evidence for later analysis. However, technological advances like video analytics are reducing the amount of work required for video monitoring as security personnel can be automatically notified of potential security events.[17][18][19]

Access control

Access control methods are used to monitor and control traffic through specific access points and areas of the secure facility. This is done using a variety of systems including CCTV surveillance, identification cards, security guards, biometric readers, and electronic/mechanical control systems such as locks, doors, turnstiles and gates.[20][21][22]

Mechanical access control systems

Mechanical access control systems include turnstiles, gates, doors, and locks. Key control of the locks becomes a problem with large user populations and any user turnover. Keys quickly become unmanageable, often forcing the adoption of electronic access control.

Electronic access control systems

Electronic access control manages large user populations, controlling for user life cycles times, dates, and individual access points. For example, a user's access rights could allow access from 0700h to 1900h Monday through Friday and expire in 90 days.[*citation needed*] These access control systems are often interfaced with turnstiles for entry control in buildings to prevent unauthorized access. The use of turnstiles also reduces the need for additional security personnel to monitor each individual entering the building allowing faster throughput.

An additional sub-layer of mechanical/electronic access control protection is reached by integrating a key management system to manage the possession and usage of mechanical keys to locks or property within a building or campus.[*citation needed*]

Identification systems and access policies

Another form of access control (*procedural*) includes the use of policies, processes and procedures to manage the ingress into the restricted area. An example of this is the deployment of security personnel conducting checks for authorized entry at predetermined points of entry. This form of access control is usually supplemented by the earlier forms of access control (i.e. mechanical and electronic access control), or simple devices such as physical passes.

Security personnel

Security personnel play a central role in all layers of security. All of the technological systems that are employed to enhance physical security are useless without a security force that is trained in their use and maintenance, and which knows how to properly respond to breaches in security. Security personnel perform many functions: patrolling facilities, administering electronic access control, responding to alarms, and monitoring and analyzing video footage.[23]

Cryptography

Cryptography, or **cryptology** (from Ancient Greek: κρυπτός, romanized: *kryptós* "hidden, secret"; and γράφειν *graphein*, "to write", or -λογία *-logia*, "study", respectively[1]), is the practice and study of techniques for secure communication in the presence of third parties called adversaries.[2] More generally, cryptography is about constructing and analyzing protocols that prevent third parties or the public from reading private messages;[3] various aspects in information security such as data confidentiality, data integrity, authentication, and non-repudiation[4] are central to modern cryptography. Modern cryptography exists at the intersection of the disciplines of mathematics, computer science, electrical engineering, communication science, and physics. Applications of cryptography include electronic commerce, chip-based payment cards, digital currencies, computer passwords, and military communications. Cryptography prior to the modern age was effectively synonymous with *encryption*, the conversion of information from a readable state to apparent nonsense. The originator of an encrypted message shares the decoding technique only with intended recipients to preclude access from adversaries. The cryptography literature often uses the names Alice ("A") for the sender, Bob ("B") for the intended recipient, and Eve ("eavesdropper") for the adversary.[5] Since the development of rotor cipher machines in World War I and the advent of computers in World War II, the methods used to carry out cryptology have become increasingly complex and its application more widespread.

Modern cryptography is heavily based on mathematical theory and computer science practice; cryptographic algorithms are designed around computational hardness assumptions, making such algorithms hard to break in practice by any adversary. It is theoretically possible to break such a system, but it is infeasible to do so by any known practical means. These schemes are therefore termed computationally secure; theoretical advances, e.g., improvements in integer factorization algorithms, and faster computing technology require these solutions to be continually adapted. There exist information-theoretically secure schemes that provably cannot be broken even with unlimited computing power—an example is the one-time pad—but these schemes are more difficult to use in practice than the best theoretically breakable but computationally secure mechanisms.

The growth of cryptographic technology has raised a number of legal issues in the information age. Cryptography's potential for use as a tool for espionage and sedition has led many governments to classify it as a weapon and to limit or even prohibit its use and export.[6] In some jurisdictions where the use of cryptography is legal, laws permit investigators to compel the disclosure of encryption keys for documents relevant to an investigation.[7][8] Cryptography also plays a major role in digital rights management and copyright infringement of digital media.[9]

Terminology

The first use of the term *cryptograph* (as opposed to *cryptogram*) dates back to the 19th century— originating from *The Gold-Bug*, a novel by Edgar Allan Poe.[10][11][*broken footnote*]

Until modern times, cryptography referred almost exclusively to *encryption*, which is the process of converting ordinary information (called plaintext) into unintelligible form (called ciphertext).[12] Decryption is the reverse, in other words, moving from the unintelligible ciphertext back to plaintext. A *cipher* (or *cypher*) is a pair of algorithms that create the encryption and the reversing decryption. The detailed operation of a cipher is controlled both by the algorithm and in each instance by a "key". The key is a secret (ideally known only to the communicants), usually a short string of characters, which is needed to decrypt the ciphertext. Formally, a "cryptosystem" is the ordered list of elements of finite possible plaintexts, finite possible cyphertexts, finite possible keys, and the encryption and decryption algorithms which correspond to each key. Keys are important both formally and in actual practice, as ciphers without variable keys can be trivially broken with only the knowledge of the cipher used and are therefore useless (or even counter-productive) for most purposes.

Historically, ciphers were often used directly for encryption or decryption without additional procedures such as authentication or integrity checks. There are two kinds of cryptosystems: symmetric and asymmetric. In symmetric systems the same key (the secret key) is used to encrypt and decrypt a message. Data manipulation in symmetric systems is faster than asymmetric systems as they generally use shorter key lengths. Asymmetric systems use a public key to encrypt a message and a private key to decrypt it. Use of asymmetric systems enhances the security of communication.[13] Examples of asymmetric systems include RSA (Rivest–Shamir–Adleman), and ECC (Elliptic Curve Cryptography). Symmetric models include the commonly used AES (Advanced Encryption Standard) which replaced the older DES (Data Encryption Standard).[14]

In colloquial use, the term "code" is often used to mean any method of encryption or concealment of meaning. However, in cryptography, *code* has a more specific meaning: the replacement of a unit of plaintext (i.e., a meaningful word or phrase) with a code word (for example, "wallaby" replaces "attack at dawn").

Cryptanalysis is the term used for the study of methods for obtaining the meaning of encrypted information without access to the key normally required to do so; i.e., it is the study of how to crack encryption algorithms or their implementations.

Some use the terms *cryptography* and *cryptology* interchangeably in English, while others (including US military practice generally) use *cryptography* to refer specifically to the use and practice of cryptographic techniques and *cryptology* to refer to the combined study of cryptography and cryptanalysis.[15][16] English is more flexible than several other languages in which *cryptology* (done by cryptologists) is always used in the second sense above. RFC 2828 advises that steganography is sometimes included in cryptology. [17]

The study of characteristics of languages that have some application in cryptography or cryptology (e.g. frequency data, letter combinations, universal patterns, etc.) is called cryptolinguistics.

History of cryptography and cryptanalysis

Before the modern era, cryptography focused on message confidentiality (i.e., encryption)—conversion of messages from a comprehensible form into an incomprehensible one and back again at the other end, rendering it unreadable by interceptors or eavesdroppers without secret knowledge (namely the key needed for decryption of that message). Encryption attempted to ensure secrecy in communications, such as those of spies, military leaders, and diplomats. In recent decades, the field has expanded beyond confidentiality concerns to include techniques for message integrity checking, sender/receiver identity authentication, digital signatures, interactive proofs and secure computation, among others.

Classic cryptography

The main classical cipher types are transposition ciphers, which rearrange the order of letters in a message (e.g., 'hello world' becomes 'ehlol owrdl' in a trivially simple rearrangement scheme), and substitution ciphers, which systematically replace letters or groups of letters with other letters or groups of letters (e.g., 'fly at once' becomes 'gmz bu podf' by replacing each letter with the one following it in the Latin alphabet). Simple versions of either have never offered much confidentiality from enterprising opponents. An early substitution cipher was the Caesar cipher, in which each letter in the plaintext was replaced by a letter some fixed number of positions further down the alphabet. Suetonius reports that Julius Caesar used it with a shift of three to communicate with his generals. Atbash is an example of an early Hebrew cipher. The earliest known use of cryptography is some carved ciphertext on stone in Egypt (ca 1900 BCE), but this may have been done for the amusement of literate observers rather than as a way of concealing information.

The Greeks of Classical times are said to have known of ciphers (e.g., the scytale transposition cipher claimed to have been used by the Spartan military).[18] Steganography (i.e., hiding even the existence of a message so as to keep it confidential) was also first developed in ancient times. An early example, from Herodotus, was a message tattooed on a slave's shaved head and concealed under the regrown hair.[12] More modern examples of steganography include the use of invisible ink, microdots, and digital watermarks to conceal information.

In India, the 2000-year-old Kamasutra of Vātsyāyana speaks of two different kinds of ciphers called Kautiliyam and Mulavediya. In the Kautiliyam, the cipher letter substitutions are based on phonetic relations, such as vowels becoming consonants. In the Mulavediya, the cipher alphabet consists of pairing letters and using the reciprocal ones.[12]

In Sassanid Persia, there were two secret scripts, according to the Muslim author Ibn al-Nadim: the šāh-dabīrīya (literally "King's script") which was used for official correspondence, and the rāz-saharīya which was used to communicate secret messages with other countries.[19]

David Kahn notes in *The Codebreakers* that modern cryptology originated among the Arabs, the first people to systematically document cryptanalytic methods.[20] Al-Khalil (717–786) wrote the *Book of Cryptographic Messages*, which contains the first use of permutations and combinations to list all possible Arabic words with and without vowels.[21]

Ciphertexts produced by a classical cipher (and some modern ciphers) will reveal statistical information about the plaintext, and that information can often be used to break the cipher. After the discovery of frequency analysis, by the Arab mathematician and polymath Al-Kindi (also known as *Alkindus*) in the 9th century,[22][23][24] nearly all such ciphers could be broken by an informed attacker. Such classical ciphers still enjoy popularity today, though mostly as puzzles. Al-Kindi wrote a book on cryptography entitled *Risalah fi Istikhraj al-Mu'amma* (*Manuscript for the Deciphering Cryptographic Messages*), which described the first known use of frequency analysis and cryptanalysis techniques.[22][25] An important contribution of Ibn Adlan (1187–1268) was on sample size for use of frequency analysis.[21]

Language letter frequencies may offer little help for some extended historical encryption techniques such as homophonic cipher that tend to flatten the frequency distribution. For those ciphers, language letter group (or n-gram) frequencies may provide an attack.

Essentially all ciphers remained vulnerable to cryptanalysis using the frequency analysis technique until the development of the polyalphabetic cipher. While it was known to Al-Kindi to some extent,[25][26] it was first clearly described in the work of Al-Qalqashandi (1355–1418), based on the earlier work of Ibn al-Durayhim (1312–1359), describing a polyalphabetic cipher in which each plaintext letter is assigned more than one substitute.[27] It was later also described by Leon Battista Alberti around the year 1467, though there is some indication that Alberti's method was to use different ciphers (i.e., substitution alphabets) for various parts of a message (perhaps for each successive plaintext letter at the limit). He also invented what was probably the first automatic cipher device, a wheel which implemented a partial realization of his invention. In the Vigenère cipher, a polyalphabetic cipher, encryption uses a *key word*, which controls letter substitution depending on which letter of the key word is used. In the mid-19th century Charles Babbage showed that the Vigenère cipher was vulnerable to Kasiski examination, but this was first published about ten years later by Friedrich Kasiski.[28]

Although frequency analysis can be a powerful and general technique against many ciphers, encryption has still often been effective in practice, as many a would-be cryptanalyst was unaware of the technique. Breaking a message without using frequency analysis essentially required knowledge of the cipher used and perhaps of the key involved, thus making espionage, bribery, burglary, defection, etc., more attractive approaches to the cryptanalytically uninformed. It was finally explicitly recognized in the 19th century that secrecy of a cipher's algorithm is not a sensible nor practical safeguard of message security; in fact, it was further realized that any adequate cryptographic scheme (including ciphers) should remain secure even if the adversary fully understands the cipher algorithm itself. Security of the key used should alone be sufficient for a good cipher to maintain confidentiality under an attack. This fundamental principle was first explicitly stated in 1883 by Auguste Kerckhoffs and is generally called Kerckhoffs's Principle; alternatively and more bluntly, it was restated by Claude Shannon, the inventor of information theory and the fundamentals of theoretical cryptography, as *Shannon's Maxim*—'the enemy knows the system'.

Different physical devices and aids have been used to assist with ciphers. One of the earliest may have been the scytale of ancient Greece, a rod supposedly used by the Spartans as an aid for a transposition cipher. In medieval times, other aids were invented such as the cipher grille, which was also used for a kind of steganography. With the invention of polyalphabetic ciphers came more sophisticated aids such as Alberti's own cipher disk, Johannes Trithemius' tabula recta scheme, and Thomas Jefferson's wheel cypher (not publicly known, and reinvented independently by Bazeries around 1900). Many mechanical encryption/decryption devices were invented early in the 20th century, and several patented, among them rotor machines—famously including the Enigma machine used by the German government and military from the late 1920s and during World War II.[29] The ciphers implemented by better quality examples of these machine designs brought about a substantial increase in cryptanalytic difficulty after WWI.[30]

Computer era

Prior to the early 20th century, cryptography was mainly concerned with linguistic and lexicographic patterns. Since then the emphasis has shifted, and cryptography now makes extensive use of mathematics, including aspects of information theory, computational complexity, statistics, combinatorics, abstract algebra, number theory, and finite mathematics generally. Cryptography is also a branch of engineering, but an unusual one since it deals with active, intelligent, and malevolent opposition; other kinds of engineering (e.g., civil or chemical engineering) need deal only with neutral natural forces. There is also active research examining the relationship between cryptographic problems and quantum physics.

Just as the development of digital computers and electronics helped in cryptanalysis, it made possible much more complex ciphers. Furthermore, computers allowed for the encryption of any kind of data representable in any binary format, unlike classical ciphers which only encrypted written language texts; this was new and significant. Computer use has thus supplanted linguistic cryptography, both for cipher design and cryptanalysis. Many computer ciphers can be characterized by their operation on binary bit sequences (sometimes in groups or blocks), unlike classical and mechanical schemes, which generally manipulate traditional characters (i.e., letters and digits) directly. However, computers have also assisted cryptanalysis, which has compensated to some extent for increased cipher complexity. Nonetheless, good modern ciphers have stayed ahead of cryptanalysis; it is typically the case that use of a quality cipher is very efficient (i.e., fast and requiring few resources, such as memory or CPU capability), while breaking it requires an effort many orders of magnitude larger, and vastly larger than that required for any classical cipher, making cryptanalysis so inefficient and impractical as to be effectively impossible.

Advent of modern cryptography

Cryptanalysis of the new mechanical devices proved to be both difficult and laborious. In the United Kingdom, cryptanalytic efforts at Bletchley Park during WWII spurred the development of more efficient means for carrying out repetitious tasks. This culminated in the development of the Colossus, the world's first fully electronic, digital, programmable computer, which assisted in the decryption of ciphers generated by the German Army's Lorenz SZ40/42 machine.

Extensive open academic research into cryptography is relatively recent; it began only in the mid-1970s. In recent times, IBM personnel designed the algorithm that became the Federal (i.e., US) Data Encryption Standard; Whitfield Diffie and Martin Hellman published their key agreement algorithm;[31] and the RSA algorithm was published in Martin Gardner's *Scientific American* column. Following their work in 1976, it became popular to consider cryptography systems based on mathematical problems that are easy to state but have been found difficult to solve.[32] Since then, cryptography has become a widely used tool in communications, computer networks, and computer security generally. Some modern cryptographic techniques can only keep their keys secret if certain mathematical problems are intractable, such as the integer factorization or the discrete logarithm problems, so there are deep connections with abstract mathematics. There are very few cryptosystems that are proven to be unconditionally secure. The one-time pad is one, and was proven to be so by Claude Shannon. There are a few important algorithms that have been proven secure under certain assumptions. For example, the infeasibility of factoring extremely large integers is the basis for believing that RSA is secure, and some other systems, but even so proof of unbreakability is unavailable since the underlying mathematical problem remains open. In practice, these are widely used, and are believed unbreakable in practice by most competent observers. There are systems similar to RSA, such as one by Michael O. Rabin that are provably secure provided factoring $n = pq$ is impossible; it is quite unusable in practice. The discrete logarithm problem is the basis for believing some other cryptosystems are secure, and again, there are related, less practical systems that are provably secure relative to the solvability or insolvability discrete log problem.[33]

As well as being aware of cryptographic history, cryptographic algorithm and system designers must also sensibly consider probable future developments while working on their designs. For instance, continuous improvements in computer processing power have increased the scope of brute-force attacks, so when specifying key lengths, the required key lengths are similarly advancing.[34] The potential effects of quantum computing are already being considered by some cryptographic system designers developing post-quantum cryptography; the announced imminence of small implementations of these machines may be making the need for preemptive caution rather more than merely speculative.[4]

Modern cryptography

Symmetric-key cryptography

Symmetric-key cryptography refers to encryption methods in which both the sender and receiver share the same key (or, less commonly, in which their keys are different, but related in an easily computable way). This was the only kind of encryption publicly known until June 1976.[31]

Symmetric key ciphers are implemented as either block ciphers or stream ciphers. A block cipher enciphers input in blocks of plaintext as opposed to individual characters, the input form used by a stream cipher.

The Data Encryption Standard (DES) and the Advanced Encryption Standard (AES) are block cipher designs that have been designated cryptography standards by the US government (though DES's designation was finally withdrawn after the AES was adopted).[35] Despite its deprecation as an official standard, DES (especially its still-approved and much more secure triple-DES variant) remains quite popular; it is used across a wide range of applications, from ATM encryption[36] to e-mail privacy[37] and secure remote access.[38] Many other block ciphers have been designed and released, with considerable variation in quality. Many, even some designed by capable practitioners, have been thoroughly broken, such as FEAL.[4][39]

Stream ciphers, in contrast to the 'block' type, create an arbitrarily long stream of key material, which is combined with the plaintext bit-by-bit or character-by-character, somewhat like the one-time pad. In a stream cipher, the output stream is created based on a hidden internal state that changes as the cipher operates. That internal state is initially set up using the secret key material. RC4 is a widely used stream cipher.[4] Block ciphers can be used as stream ciphers.

Cryptographic hash functions are a third type of cryptographic algorithm. They take a message of any length as input, and output a short, fixed length hash, which can be used in (for example) a digital signature. For good hash functions, an attacker cannot find two messages that produce the same hash. MD4 is a long-used hash function that is now broken; MD5, a strengthened variant of MD4, is also widely used but broken in practice. The US National Security Agency developed the Secure Hash Algorithm series of MD5-like hash functions: SHA-0 was a flawed algorithm that the agency withdrew; SHA-1 is widely deployed and more secure than MD5, but cryptanalysts have identified attacks against it; the SHA-2 family improves on SHA-1, but is vulnerable to clashes as of 2011; and the US standards authority thought it "prudent" from a security perspective to develop a new standard to "significantly improve the robustness of NIST's overall hash algorithm toolkit."[40] Thus, a hash function design competition was meant to select a new U.S. national standard, to be called SHA-3, by 2012. The competition ended on October 2, 2012 when the NIST announced that Keccak would be the new SHA-3 hash algorithm.[41] Unlike block and stream ciphers that are invertible, cryptographic hash functions produce a hashed output that cannot be used to retrieve the original input data. Cryptographic hash functions are used to verify the authenticity of data retrieved from an untrusted source or to add a layer of security.

Message authentication codes (MACs) are much like cryptographic hash functions, except that a secret key can be used to authenticate the hash value upon receipt;[4] this additional complication blocks an attack scheme against bare digest algorithms, and so has been thought worth the effort.

Public-key cryptography

Symmetric-key cryptosystems use the same key for encryption and decryption of a message, although a message or group of messages can have a different key than others. A significant disadvantage of symmetric ciphers is the key management necessary to use them securely. Each distinct pair of communicating parties must, ideally, share a different key, and perhaps for each ciphertext exchanged as well. The number of keys required increases as the square of the number of network members, which very quickly requires complex key management schemes to keep them all consistent and secret.

In a groundbreaking 1976 paper, Whitfield Diffie and Martin Hellman proposed the notion of *public-key* (also, more generally, called *asymmetric key*) cryptography in which two different but mathematically related keys are used—a *public* key and a *private* key.[42] A public key system is so constructed that calculation of one key (the 'private key') is computationally infeasible from the other (the 'public key'), even though they are necessarily related. Instead, both keys are generated secretly, as an interrelated pair.[43] The historian David Kahn described public-key cryptography as "the most revolutionary new concept in the field since polyalphabetic substitution emerged in the Renaissance".[44]

In public-key cryptosystems, the public key may be freely distributed, while its paired private key must remain secret. In a public-key encryption system, the *public key* is used for encryption, while the *private* or *secret key* is used for decryption. While Diffie and Hellman could not find such a system, they showed that public-key cryptography was indeed possible by presenting the Diffie–Hellman key exchange protocol, a solution that is now widely used in secure communications to allow two parties to secretly agree on a shared encryption key.[31] The X.509 standard defines the most commonly used format for public key certificates.[45]

Diffie and Hellman's publication sparked widespread academic efforts in finding a practical public-key encryption system. This race was finally won in 1978 by Ronald Rivest, Adi Shamir, and Len Adleman, whose solution has since become known as the RSA algorithm.[46]

The Diffie–Hellman and RSA algorithms, in addition to being the first publicly known examples of high quality public-key algorithms, have been among the most widely used. Other asymmetric-key algorithms include the Cramer–Shoup cryptosystem, ElGamal encryption, and various elliptic curve techniques. [*citation needed*]

A document published in 1997 by the Government Communications Headquarters (GCHQ), a British intelligence organization, revealed that cryptographers at GCHQ had anticipated several academic developments.[47] Reportedly, around 1970, James H. Ellis had conceived the principles of asymmetric key cryptography. In 1973, Clifford Cocks invented a solution that very similar in design rationale to RSA. [47][48] And in 1974, Malcolm J. Williamson is claimed to have developed the Diffie–Hellman key exchange.[49]

Public-key cryptography is also used for implementing digital signature schemes. A digital signature is reminiscent of an ordinary signature; they both have the characteristic of being easy for a user to produce, but difficult for anyone else to forge. Digital signatures can also be permanently tied to the content of the message being signed; they cannot then be 'moved' from one document to another, for any attempt will be detectable. In digital signature schemes, there are two algorithms: one for *signing*, in which a secret key is used to process the message (or a hash of the message, or both), and one for *verification*, in which the matching public key is used with the message to check the validity of the signature. RSA and DSA are two of the most popular digital signature schemes. Digital signatures are central to the operation of public key infrastructures and many network security schemes (e.g., SSL/TLS, many VPNs, etc.).[39]

Public-key algorithms are most often based on the computational complexity of "hard" problems, often from number theory. For example, the hardness of RSA is related to the integer factorization problem, while Diffie–Hellman and DSA are related to the discrete logarithm problem. The security of elliptic curve cryptography is based on number theoretic problems involving elliptic curves. Because of the difficulty of the underlying problems, most public-key algorithms involve operations such as modular multiplication and exponentiation, which are much more computationally expensive than the techniques used in most block ciphers, especially with typical key sizes. As a result, public-key cryptosystems are commonly hybrid cryptosystems, in which a fast high-quality symmetric-key encryption algorithm is used for the message itself, while the relevant symmetric key is sent with the message, but encrypted using a public-key algorithm. Similarly, hybrid signature schemes are often used, in which a cryptographic hash function is computed, and only the resulting hash is digitally signed.[4]

Computer Network

A **computer network** is a group of computers that use a set of common communication protocols over digital interconnections for the purpose of sharing resources located on or provided by the network nodes. The interconnections between nodes are formed from a broad spectrum of telecommunication network technologies, based on physically wired, optical, and wireless radio-frequency methods that may be arranged in a variety of network topologies.

The nodes of a computer network may be classified by many means as personal computers, servers, networking hardware, or general purpose hosts. They are identified by hostnames and network addresses. Hostnames serve as memorable labels for the nodes, rarely changed after initial assignment. Network addresses serve for locating and identifying the nodes by communication protocols such as the Internet Protocol.

Computer networks may be classified by many criteria, for example, the transmission medium used to carry signals, bandwidth, communications protocols to organize network traffic, the network size, the topology, traffic control mechanism, and organizational intent.

Computer networks support many applications and services, such as access to the World Wide Web, digital video, digital audio, shared use of application and storage servers, printers, and fax machines, and use of email and instant messaging applications.

History

Computer networking may be considered a branch of computer science, computer engineering, and telecommunications, since it relies on the theoretical and practical application of the related disciplines. Computer networking was influenced by a wide array of technology developments and historical milestones.

- In the late 1950s, early networks of computers included the U.S. military radar system Semi-Automatic Ground Environment (SAGE).
- In 1959, Christopher Strachey filed a patent application for time-sharing and John McCarthy initiated the first project to implement time-sharing of user programs at MIT.[1][2][3][4] Stratchey passed the concept on to J. C. R. Licklider at the inaugural UNESCO Information Processing Conference in Paris that year.[5] McCarthy was instrumental in the creation of three of the earliest time-sharing systems (Compatible Time-Sharing System in 1961, BBN Time-Sharing System in 1962, and Dartmouth Time Sharing System in 1963).
- In 1959, Anatolii Ivanovich Kitov proposed to the Central Committee of the Communist Party of the Soviet Union a detailed plan for the re-organisation of the control of the Soviet armed forces and of the Soviet economy on the basis of a network of computing centres, the OGAS.[6]
- In 1959, the MOS transistor was invented by Mohamed Atalla and Dawon Kahng at Bell Labs.[7] It

later became one of the basic building blocks and "work horses" of virtually any element of communications infrastructure.[8]

- In 1960, the commercial airline reservation system semi-automatic business research environment (SABRE) went online with two connected mainframes.
- In 1963, J. C. R. Licklider sent a memorandum to office colleagues discussing the concept of the "Intergalactic Computer Network", a computer network intended to allow general communications among computer users.
- Throughout the 1960s, Paul Baran and Donald Davies independently developed the concept of packet switching to transfer information between computers over a network. Davies pioneered the implementation of the concept with the NPL network, a local area network at the National Physical Laboratory (United Kingdom) using a line speed of 768 kbit/s.[9][10][11]
- In 1965, Western Electric introduced the first widely used telephone switch that implemented computer control in the switching fabric.
- In 1969, the first four nodes of the ARPANET were connected using 50 kbit/s circuits between the University of California at Los Angeles, the Stanford Research Institute, the University of California at Santa Barbara, and the University of Utah.[12] In the 1970s, Leonard Kleinrock carried out mathematical work to model the performance of packet-switched networks, which underpinned the development of the ARPANET.[13][14] His theoretical work on hierarchical routing in the late 1970s with student Farouk Kamoun remains critical to the operation of the Internet today.
- In 1972, commercial services using X.25 were deployed, and later used as an underlying infrastructure for expanding TCP/IP networks.
- In 1973, the French CYCLADES network was the first to make the hosts responsible for the reliable delivery of data, rather than this being a centralized service of the network itself.[15]
- In 1973, Robert Metcalfe wrote a formal memo at Xerox PARC describing Ethernet, a networking system that was based on the Aloha network, developed in the 1960s by Norman Abramson and colleagues at the University of Hawaii. In July 1976, Robert Metcalfe and David Boggs published their paper "Ethernet: Distributed Packet Switching for Local Computer Networks"[16] and collaborated on several patents received in 1977 and 1978.
- In 1974, Vint Cerf, Yogen Dalal, and Carl Sunshine published the Transmission Control Protocol (TCP) specification, RFC 675, coining the term Internet as a shorthand for internetworking.[17]
- In 1976, John Murphy of Datapoint Corporation created ARCNET, a token-passing network first used to share storage devices.
- In 1977, the first long-distance fiber network was deployed by GTE in Long Beach, California.
- In 1977, Xerox Network Systems (XNS) was developed by Robert Metcalfe and Yogen Dalal at Xerox.[18]
- In 1979, Robert Metcalfe pursued making Ethernet an open standard.[19]
- In 1980, Ethernet was upgraded from the original 2.94 Mbit/s protocol to the 10 Mbit/s protocol, which was developed by Ron Crane, Bob Garner, Roy Ogus,[20] and Yogen Dalal.[21]
- In 1995, the transmission speed capacity for Ethernet increased from 10 Mbit/s to 100 Mbit/s. By 1998, Ethernet supported transmission speeds of a Gigabit. Subsequently, higher speeds of up to 400 Gbit/s were added (as of 2018). The scaling of Ethernet has been a contributing factor to its continued use.[19]

Use

A computer network extends interpersonal communications by electronic means with various technologies, such as email, instant messaging, online chat, voice and video telephone calls, and video conferencing. A network allows sharing of network and computing resources. Users may access and use resources provided by devices on the network, such as printing a document on a shared network printer or use of a shared storage device. A network allows sharing of files, data, and other types of information giving authorized users the ability to access information stored on other computers on the network. Distributed computing uses computing resources across a network to accomplish tasks.

Network packet

Most modern computer networks use protocols based on packet-mode transmission. A network packet is a formatted unit of data carried by a packet-switched network. The physical link technologies of packet network typically limit the size of packets to a certain maximum transmission unit (MTU). A longer message is fragmented before it is transferred and once the packets arrive, they are reassembled to construct the original message.

Packets consist of two types of data: control information and user data (payload). The control information provides data the network needs to deliver the user data, for example, source and destination network addresses, error detection codes, and sequencing information. Typically, control information is found in packet headers and trailers, with payload data in between.

With packets, the bandwidth of the transmission medium can be better shared among users than if the network were circuit switched. When one user is not sending packets, the link can be filled with packets from other users, and so the cost can be shared, with relatively little interference, provided the link isn't overused. Often the route a packet needs to take through a network is not immediately available. In that case, the packet is queued and waits until a link is free.

Network topology

Network topology is the layout, pattern, or organizational hierarchy of the interconnection of network hosts, in contrast to their physical or geographic location. Typically, most diagrams describing networks are arranged by their topology. The network topology can affect throughput, but reliability is often more critical.[*citation needed*] With many technologies, such as bus networks, a single failure can cause the network to fail entirely. In general, the more interconnections there are, the more robust the network is; but the more expensive it is to install.

Common layouts are:

- Bus network: all nodes are connected to a common medium along this medium. This was the layout used in the original Ethernet, called 10BASE5 and 10BASE2. This is still a common topology on the data link layer, although modern physical layer variants use point-to-point links instead.
- Star network: all nodes are connected to a special central node. This is the typical layout found in a Wireless LAN, where each wireless client connects to the central Wireless access point.
- Ring network: each node is connected to its left and right neighbour node, such that all nodes are connected and that each node can reach each other node by traversing nodes left- or rightwards. The Fiber Distributed Data Interface (FDDI) made use of such a topology.
- Mesh network: each node is connected to an arbitrary number of neighbours in such a way that there is at least one traversal from any node to any other.
- Fully connected network: each node is connected to every other node in the network.
- Tree network: nodes are arranged hierarchically.

The physical layout of the nodes in a network may not necessarily reflect the network topology. As an example, with FDDI, the network topology is a ring, but the physical topology is often a star, because all neighboring connections can be routed via a central physical location. Physical layout is not completely irrelevant, however, as common ducting and equipment locations can represent single points of failure due to issues like fires, power failures and flooding.

Overlay network

An overlay network is a virtual network that is built on top of another network. Nodes in the overlay network are connected by virtual or logical links. Each link corresponds to a path, perhaps through many physical links, in the underlying network. The topology of the overlay network may (and often does) differ from that of the underlying one. For example, many peer-to-peer networks are overlay networks. They are organized as nodes of a virtual system of links that run on top of the Internet.[22]

Overlay networks have been around since the invention of networking when computer systems were connected over telephone lines using modems, before any data network existed.

The most striking example of an overlay network is the Internet itself. The Internet itself was initially built as an overlay on the telephone network.[22] Even today, each Internet node can communicate with virtually any other through an underlying mesh of sub-networks of wildly different topologies and technologies. Address resolution and routing are the means that allow mapping of a fully connected IP overlay network to its underlying network.

Another example of an overlay network is a distributed hash table, which maps keys to nodes in the network. In this case, the underlying network is an IP network, and the overlay network is a table (actually a map) indexed by keys.

Overlay networks have also been proposed as a way to improve Internet routing, such as through quality of service guarantees to achieve higher-quality streaming media. Previous proposals such as IntServ, DiffServ, and IP Multicast have not seen wide acceptance largely because they require modification of all routers in the network.[*citation needed*] On the other hand, an overlay network can be incrementally deployed on end-hosts running the overlay protocol software, without cooperation from Internet service providers. The overlay network has no control over how packets are routed in the underlying network between two overlay nodes, but it can control, for example, the sequence of overlay nodes that a message traverses before it reaches its destination.

For example, Akamai Technologies manages an overlay network that provides reliable, efficient content delivery (a kind of multicast). Academic research includes end system multicast,[23] resilient routing and quality of service studies, among others.

Network links

The transmission media (often referred to in the literature as the *physical medium*) used to link devices to form a computer network include electrical cable, optical fiber, and free space. In the OSI model, the software to handle the media are defined at layers 1 and 2 — the physical layer and the data link layer.

A widely adopted *family* that uses copper and fiber media in local area network (LAN) technology is collectively known as Ethernet. The media and protocol standards that enable communication between networked devices over Ethernet are defined by IEEE 802.3. Wireless LAN standards use radio waves, others use infrared signals as a transmission medium. Power line communication uses a building's power cabling to transmit data.

Wired technologies

The following classes of wired technologies are used in computer networking.

- *Coaxial cable* is widely used for cable television systems, office buildings, and other work-sites for local area networks. Transmission speed ranges from 200 million bits per second to more than 500 million bits per second.[*citation needed*]
- ITU-T G.hn technology uses existing home wiring (coaxial cable, phone lines and power lines) to create a high-speed local area network.
- *Twisted pair* cabling is used for wired Ethernet and other standards. It typically consists of 4 pairs of copper cabling that can be utilized for both voice and data transmission. The use of two wires twisted together helps to reduce crosstalk and electromagnetic induction. The transmission speed ranges from 2 Mbit/s to 10 Gbit/s. Twisted pair cabling comes in two forms: unshielded twisted pair (UTP) and shielded twisted-pair (STP). Each form comes in several category ratings, designed for use in various scenarios.
- An *optical fiber* is a glass fiber. It carries pulses of light that represent data via lasers and optical amplifiers. Some advantages of optical fibers over metal wires are very low transmission loss and immunity to electrical interference. Using dense wave division multiplexing, optical fibers can simultaneously carry multiple streams of data on different wavelengths of light, which greatly increases the rate that data can be sent to up to trillions of bits per second. Optic fibers can be used for long runs of cable carrying very high data rates, and are used for undersea cables to interconnect continents. There are two basic types of fiber optics, single-mode optical fiber (SMF) and multi-mode optical fiber (MMF). Single-mode fiber has the advantage of being able to sustain a coherent signal for dozens or even a hundred kilometers. Multimode fiber is cheaper to terminate but is limited to a few hundred or even only a few dozens of meters, depending on the data rate and cable grade.[24]

Wireless technologies

Network connections can be established wirelessly using radio or other electromagnetic means of communication.

- *Terrestrial microwave* – Terrestrial microwave communication uses Earth-based transmitters and receivers resembling satellite dishes. Terrestrial microwaves are in the low gigahertz range, which limits all communications to line-of-sight. Relay stations are spaced approximately 40 miles (64 km) apart.
- *Communications satellites* – Satellites also communicate via microwave. The satellites are stationed in space, typically in geosynchronous orbit 35,400 km (22,000 mi) above the equator. These Earth-orbiting systems are capable of receiving and relaying voice, data, and TV signals.
- *Cellular networks* use several radio communications technologies. The systems divide the region covered into multiple geographic areas. Each area is served by a low-power transceiver.
- *Radio and spread spectrum technologies* – Wireless LANs use a high-frequency radio technology similar to digital cellular. Wireless LANs use spread spectrum technology to enable communication between multiple devices in a limited area. IEEE 802.11 defines a common flavor of open-standards wireless radio-wave technology known as Wi-Fi.
- *Free-space optical communication* uses visible or invisible light for communications. In most cases, line-of-sight propagation is used, which limits the physical positioning of communicating devices.

Exotic technologies

There have been various attempts at transporting data over exotic media.

- IP over Avian Carriers was a humorous April fool's Request for Comments, issued as RFC 1149. It was implemented in real life in 2001.[25]
- Extending the Internet to interplanetary dimensions via radio waves, the Interplanetary Internet.[26]

Both cases have a large round-trip delay time, which gives slow two-way communication but doesn't prevent sending large amounts of information.

Network nodes

Apart from any physical transmission media, networks are built from additional basic system building blocks, such as network interface controllers (NICs), repeaters, hubs, bridges, switches, routers, modems, and firewalls. Any particular piece of equipment will frequently contain multiple building blocks and so may perform multiple functions.

Network interfaces

A network interface controller (NIC) is computer hardware that connects the computer to the network media and has the ability to process low-level network information. For example, the NIC may have a connector for accepting a cable, or an aerial for wireless transmission and reception, and the associated circuitry.

In Ethernet networks, each network interface controller has a unique Media Access Control (MAC) address —usually stored in the controller's permanent memory. To avoid address conflicts between network devices, the Institute of Electrical and Electronics Engineers (IEEE) maintains and administers MAC address uniqueness. The size of an Ethernet MAC address is six octets. The three most significant octets are reserved to identify NIC manufacturers. These manufacturers, using only their assigned prefixes, uniquely assign the three least-significant octets of every Ethernet interface they produce.

Repeaters and hubs

A repeater is an electronic device that receives a network signal, cleans it of unnecessary noise and regenerates it. The signal is retransmitted at a higher power level, or to the other side of an obstruction so that the signal can cover longer distances without degradation. In most twisted pair Ethernet configurations, repeaters are required for cable that runs longer than 100 meters. With fiber optics, repeaters can be tens or even hundreds of kilometers apart.

Repeaters work on the physical layer of the OSI model but still require a small amount of time to regenerate the signal. This can cause a propagation delay that affects network performance and may affect proper function. As a result, many network architectures limit the number of repeaters used in a network, e.g., the Ethernet 5-4-3 rule.

An Ethernet repeater with multiple ports is known as an Ethernet hub. In addition to reconditioning and distributing network signals, a repeater hub assists with collision detection and fault isolation for the network. Hubs and repeaters in LANs have been largely obsoleted by modern network switches.

Bridges

A network bridge opeates at the data link layer (layer 2) of the OSI model and connects and filters traffic between two network segments to form a single network. This divides the network's collision domain but maintains a single broadcast domain. Network segmentation through bridging breaks down a large, congested network into an aggregation of smaller, more efficient networks.

Switches

A network switch is a device that forwards and frames of data between ports based on the destination MAC address in each frame.[27] A switch is distinct from a hub in that it only forwards the frames to the ports involved in the communication whereas a hub forwards to all ports. A switch can be thought of as a multi-port bridge.[28] A switch learns the association of physical ports to MAC addresses by examining the source addresses of received frames. If an unknown destination MAC is targeted, the switch broadcasts to all ports but the source. Switches normally have numerous ports, facilitating a star topology for devices, and for cascading additional switches.

Routers

A router is an internetworking device that forwards packets between networks by processing the addressing or routing information included in the packet. The routing information is often processed in conjunction with the routing table. A router uses its routing table to determine where to forward packets.

Modems

Modems (MOdulator-DEModulator) are used to connect network nodes via wire not originally designed for digital network traffic, or for wireless. To do this one or more carrier signals are modulated by the digital signal to produce an analog signal that can be tailored to give the required properties for transmission. Modems are commonly used for telephone lines, using a digital subscriber line technology.

Firewalls

A firewall is a network device for controlling network security and access rules. Firewalls are typically configured to reject access requests from unrecognized sources while allowing actions from recognized ones. The vital role firewalls play in network security grows in parallel with the constant increase in cyber attacks.

Communication protocols

A communication protocol is a set of rules for exchanging information over a network. In a protocol stack (also see the OSI model), each protocol leverages the services of the protocol layer below it, until the lowest layer controls the hardware that sends information across the media. The use of protocol layering is today ubiquitous across the field of computer networking. An important example of a protocol stack is HTTP (the World Wide Web protocol) running over TCP over IP (the Internet protocols) over IEEE 802.11 (the Wi-Fi protocol). This stack is used between the wireless router and the home user's personal computer when the user is surfing the web.

Communication protocols have various characteristics. They may be connection-oriented or connectionless, they may use circuit mode or packet switching, and they may use hierarchical addressing or flat addressing.

There are many communication protocols, a few of which are described below.

IEEE 802

IEEE 802 is a family of IEEE standards dealing with local area networks and metropolitan area networks. The complete IEEE 802 protocol suite provides a diverse set of networking capabilities. The protocols have a flat addressing scheme. They operate mostly at levels 1 and 2 of the OSI model.

For example, MAC bridging (IEEE 802.1D) deals with the routing of Ethernet packets using a Spanning Tree Protocol. IEEE 802.1Q describes VLANs, and IEEE 802.1X defines a port-based Network Access Control protocol, which forms the basis for the authentication mechanisms used in VLANs (but it is also found in WLANs) – it is what the home user sees when the user has to enter a "wireless access key".

Ethernet

Ethernet, sometimes simply called *LAN*, is a family of protocols used in wired LANs, described by a set of standards together called IEEE 802.3 published by the Institute of Electrical and Electronics Engineers.

Wireless LAN

Wireless LAN, also widely known as WLAN or WiFi, is probably the most well-known member of the IEEE 802 protocol family for home users today. It is standardized by IEEE 802.11 and shares many properties with wired Ethernet.

Internet Protocol Suite

The Internet Protocol Suite, also called TCP/IP, is the foundation of all modern networking. It offers connection-less as well as connection-oriented services over an inherently unreliable network traversed by datagram transmission at the Internet protocol (IP) level. At its core, the protocol suite defines the addressing, identification, and routing specifications for Internet Protocol Version 4 (IPv4) and for IPv6, the next generation of the protocol with a much enlarged addressing capability.

The Internet Protocol Suite is the defining set of protocols for the Internet. Although many computers communicate via the Internet, it is actually a network of networks, as elaborated by Andrew Tannenbaum. [29]

SONET/SDH

Synchronous optical networking (SONET) and Synchronous Digital Hierarchy (SDH) are standardized multiplexing protocols that transfer multiple digital bit streams over optical fiber using lasers. They were originally designed to transport circuit mode communications from a variety of different sources, primarily to support real-time, uncompressed, circuit-switched voice encoded in PCM (Pulse-Code Modulation) format. However, due to its protocol neutrality and transport-oriented features, SONET/SDH also was the obvious choice for transporting Asynchronous Transfer Mode (ATM) frames.

Asynchronous Transfer Mode

Asynchronous Transfer Mode (ATM) is a switching technique for telecommunication networks. It uses asynchronous time-division multiplexing and encodes data into small, fixed-sized cells. This differs from other protocols such as the Internet Protocol Suite or Ethernet that use variable sized packets or frames.

ATM has similarity with both circuit and packet switched networking. This makes it a good choice for a network that must handle both traditional high-throughput data traffic, and real-time, low-latency content such as voice and video. ATM uses a connection-oriented model in which a virtual circuit must be established between two endpoints before the actual data exchange begins.

While the role of ATM is diminishing in favor of next-generation networks, it still plays a role in the last mile, which is the connection between an Internet service provider and the home user.[30]

Cellular standards

There are a number of different digital cellular standards, including: Global System for Mobile Communications (GSM), General Packet Radio Service (GPRS), cdmaOne, CDMA2000, Evolution-Data Optimized (EV-DO), Enhanced Data Rates for GSM Evolution (EDGE), Universal Mobile Telecommunications System (UMTS), Digital Enhanced Cordless Telecommunications (DECT), Digital AMPS (IS-136/TDMA), and Integrated Digital Enhanced Network (iDEN).[31]

Geographic scale

Networks may be characterized by many properties or features, such as physical capacity, organizational purpose, user authorization, access rights, and others. Another distinct classification method is that of physical extent, or geographic scale.

Nanoscale network

A nanoscale communication network has key components implemented at the nanoscale including message carriers and leverages physical principles that differ from macroscale communication mechanisms. Nanoscale communication extends communication to very small sensors and actuators such as those found in biological systems and also tends to operate in environments that would be too harsh for classical communication.[32]

Personal area network

A personal area network (PAN) is a computer network used for communication among computer and different information technological devices close to one person. Some examples of devices that are used in a PAN are personal computers, printers, fax machines, telephones, PDAs, scanners, and even video game consoles. A PAN may include wired and wireless devices. The reach of a PAN typically extends to 10 meters.[33] A wired PAN is usually constructed with USB and FireWire connections while technologies such as Bluetooth and infrared communication typically form a wireless PAN.

Local area network

A local area network (LAN) is a network that connects computers and devices in a limited geographical area such as a home, school, office building, or closely positioned group of buildings. Each computer or device on the network is a node. Wired LANs are most likely based on Ethernet technology. Newer standards such as ITU-T G.hn also provide a way to create a wired LAN using existing wiring, such as coaxial cables, telephone lines, and power lines.[34]

The defining characteristics of a LAN, in contrast to a wide area network (WAN), include higher data transfer rates, limited geographic range, and lack of reliance on leased lines to provide connectivity. Current Ethernet or other IEEE 802.3 LAN technologies operate at data transfer rates up to 100 Gbit/s, standardized by IEEE in 2010.[35] Currently, 400 Gbit/s Ethernet is being developed.

A LAN can be connected to a WAN using a router.

Home area network

A home area network (HAN) is a residential LAN used for communication between digital devices typically deployed in the home, usually a small number of personal computers and accessories, such as printers and mobile computing devices. An important function is the sharing of Internet access, often a broadband service through a cable TV or digital subscriber line (DSL) provider.

Storage area network

A storage area network (SAN) is a dedicated network that provides access to consolidated, block level data storage. SANs are primarily used to make storage devices, such as disk arrays, tape libraries, and optical jukeboxes, accessible to servers so that the devices appear like locally attached devices to the operating system. A SAN typically has its own network of storage devices that are generally not accessible through the local area network by other devices. The cost and complexity of SANs dropped in the early 2000s to levels allowing wider adoption across both enterprise and small to medium-sized business environments.

Campus area network

A campus area network (CAN) is made up of an interconnection of LANs within a limited geographical area. The networking equipment (switches, routers) and transmission media (optical fiber, copper plant, Cat5 cabling, etc.) are almost entirely owned by the campus tenant / owner (an enterprise, university, government, etc.).

For example, a university campus network is likely to link a variety of campus buildings to connect academic colleges or departments, the library, and student residence halls.

Backbone network

A backbone network is part of a computer network infrastructure that provides a path for the exchange of information between different LANs or subnetworks. A backbone can tie together diverse networks within the same building, across different buildings, or over a wide area.

For example, a large company might implement a backbone network to connect departments that are located around the world. The equipment that ties together the departmental networks constitutes the network backbone. When designing a network backbone, network performance and network congestion are critical factors to take into account. Normally, the backbone network's capacity is greater than that of the individual networks connected to it.

Another example of a backbone network is the Internet backbone, which is a massive, global system of fiber-optic cable and optical networking that carry the bulk of data between wide area networks (WANs), metro, regional, national and transoceanic networks.

Metropolitan area network

A Metropolitan area network (MAN) is a large computer network that usually spans a city or a large campus.

Wide area network

A wide area network (WAN) is a computer network that covers a large geographic area such as a city, country, or spans even intercontinental distances. A WAN uses a communications channel that combines many types of media such as telephone lines, cables, and air waves. A WAN often makes use of transmission facilities provided by common carriers, such as telephone companies. WAN technologies generally function at the lower three layers of the OSI reference model: the physical layer, the data link layer, and the network layer.

Enterprise private network

An enterprise private network is a network that a single organization builds to interconnect its office locations (e.g., production sites, head offices, remote offices, shops) so they can share computer resources.

Virtual private network

A virtual private network (VPN) is an overlay network in which some of the links between nodes are carried by open connections or virtual circuits in some larger network (e.g., the Internet) instead of by physical wires. The data link layer protocols of the virtual network are said to be tunneled through the larger network when this is the case. One common application is secure communications through the public Internet, but a VPN need not have explicit security features, such as authentication or content encryption. VPNs, for example, can be used to separate the traffic of different user communities over an underlying network with strong security features.

VPN may have best-effort performance, or may have a defined service level agreement (SLA) between the VPN customer and the VPN service provider. Generally, a VPN has a topology more complex than point-to-point.

Global area network

A global area network (GAN) is a network used for supporting mobile across an arbitrary number of wireless LANs, satellite coverage areas, etc. The key challenge in mobile communications is handing off user communications from one local coverage area to the next. In IEEE Project 802, this involves a succession of terrestrial wireless LANs.[36]

Organizational scope

Networks are typically managed by the organizations that own them. Private enterprise networks may use a combination of intranets and extranets. They may also provide network access to the Internet, which has no single owner and permits virtually unlimited global connectivity.

Intranet

An intranet is a set of networks that are under the control of a single administrative entity. The intranet uses the IP protocol and IP-based tools such as web browsers and file transfer applications. The administrative entity limits use of the intranet to its authorized users. Most commonly, an intranet is the internal LAN of an organization. A large intranet typically has at least one web server to provide users with organizational information. An intranet is also anything behind the router on a local area network.

Extranet

An extranet is a network that is also under the administrative control of a single organization, but supports a limited connection to a specific external network. For example, an organization may provide access to some aspects of its intranet to share data with its business partners or customers. These other entities are not necessarily trusted from a security standpoint. Network connection to an extranet is often, but not always, implemented via WAN technology.

Internetwork

An internetwork is the connection of multiple different types of computer networks to form a single computer network by layering on top of the different networking software and connecting them together using routers.

Internet

The Internet is the largest example of an internetwork. It is a global system of interconnected governmental, academic, corporate, public, and private computer networks. It is based on the networking technologies of the Internet Protocol Suite. It is the successor of the Advanced Research Projects Agency Network (ARPANET) developed by DARPA of the United States Department of Defense. The Internet utilizes copper communications and the optical networking backbone to enable the World Wide Web (WWW), the Internet of Things, video transfer and a broad range of information services.

Participants in the Internet use a diverse array of methods of several hundred documented, and often standardized, protocols compatible with the Internet Protocol Suite and an addressing system (IP addresses) administered by the Internet Assigned Numbers Authority and address registries. Service providers and large enterprises exchange information about the reachability of their address spaces through the Border Gateway Protocol (BGP), forming a redundant worldwide mesh of transmission paths.

Darknet

A darknet is an overlay network, typically running on the Internet, that is only accessible through specialized software. A darknet is an anonymizing network where connections are made only between trusted peers — sometimes called "friends" (F2F)[37] — using non-standard protocols and ports.

Darknets are distinct from other distributed peer-to-peer networks as sharing is anonymous (that is, IP addresses are not publicly shared), and therefore users can communicate with little fear of governmental or corporate interference.[38]

Routing

Routing is the process of selecting network paths to carry network traffic. Routing is performed for many kinds of networks, including circuit switching networks and packet switched networks.

In packet-switched networks, routing directs packet forwarding (the transit of logically addressed network packets from their source toward their ultimate destination) through intermediate nodes. Intermediate nodes are typically network hardware devices such as routers, bridges, gateways, firewalls, or switches. General-purpose computers can also forward packets and perform routing, though they are not specialized hardware and may suffer from limited performance. The routing process usually directs forwarding on the basis of routing tables, which maintain a record of the routes to various network destinations. Thus, constructing routing tables, which are held in the router's memory, is very important for efficient routing.

There are usually multiple routes that can be taken, and to choose between them, different elements can be considered to decide which routes get installed into the routing table, such as (sorted by priority):

1. *Prefix-Length*: where longer subnet masks are preferred (independent if it is within a routing protocol or over different routing protocol)
2. *Metric*: where a lower metric/cost is preferred (only valid within one and the same routing protocol)
3. *Administrative distance*: where a lower distance is preferred (only valid between different routing protocols)

Most routing algorithms use only one network path at a time. Multipath routing techniques enable the use of multiple alternative paths.

Routing, in a more narrow sense of the term, is often contrasted with bridging in its assumption that network addresses are structured and that similar addresses imply proximity within the network. Structured addresses allow a single routing table entry to represent the route to a group of devices. In large networks, structured addressing (routing, in the narrow sense) outperforms unstructured addressing (bridging). Routing has become the dominant form of addressing on the Internet. Bridging is still widely used within localized environments.

Network service

Network services are applications hosted by servers on a computer network, to provide some functionality for members or users of the network, or to help the network itself to operate.

The World Wide Web, E-mail,[39] printing and network file sharing are examples of well-known network services. Network services such as DNS (Domain Name System) give names for IP and MAC addresses (people remember names like "nm.lan" better than numbers like "210.121.67.18"),[40] and DHCP to ensure that the equipment on the network has a valid IP address.[41]

Services are usually based on a service protocol that defines the format and sequencing of messages between clients and servers of that network service.

Network performance

Bandwidth

Bandwidth in bit/s may refer to consumed bandwidth, corresponding to achieved throughput or goodput, i.e., the average rate of successful data transfer through a communication path. The throughput is affected by technologies such as bandwidth shaping, bandwidth management, bandwidth throttling, bandwidth cap, bandwidth allocation (for example bandwidth allocation protocol and dynamic bandwidth allocation), etc. A bit stream's bandwidth is proportional to the average consumed signal bandwidth in hertz (the average spectral bandwidth of the analog signal representing the bit stream) during a studied time interval.

Network delay

Any data sent across a network requires time to travel from source to destination. Depending on the application, the one-way delay or the round-trip time can have a significant impact on performance.

Quality of service

Depending on the installation requirements, network performance is usually measured by the quality of service of a telecommunications product. The parameters that affect this typically can include throughput, jitter, bit error rate and latency.

The following list gives examples of network performance measures for a circuit-switched network and one type of packet-switched network, viz. ATM:

- Circuit-switched networks: In circuit switched networks, network performance is synonymous with the grade of service. The number of rejected calls is a measure of how well the network is performing under heavy traffic loads.[42] Other types of performance measures can include the level of noise and echo.
- ATM: In an Asynchronous Transfer Mode (ATM) network, performance can be measured by line rate, quality of service (QoS), data throughput, connect time, stability, technology, modulation technique and modem enhancements.[43][*verification needed*][*full citation needed*]

There are many ways to measure the performance of a network, as each network is different in nature and design. Performance can also be modelled instead of measured. For example, state transition diagrams are often used to model queuing performance in a circuit-switched network. The network planner uses these diagrams to analyze how the network performs in each state, ensuring that the network is optimally designed.[44]

Network congestion

Network congestion occurs when a link or node is subjected to a greater data load than it is rated for, resulting in a deterioration of its quality of service. Typical effects include queueing delay, packet loss or the blocking of new connections. A consequence of these latter two is that incremental increases in offered load lead either to only a small increase in network throughput, or to a reduction in network throughput.

Network protocols that use aggressive retransmissions to compensate for packet loss tend to keep systems in a state of network congestion—even after the initial load is reduced to a level that would not normally induce network congestion. Thus, networks using these protocols can exhibit two stable states under the same level of load. The stable state with low throughput is known as *congestive collapse*.

Modern networks use congestion control, congestion avoidance and traffic control techniques to try to avoid congestion collapse. These include: exponential backoff in protocols such as 802.11's CSMA/CA and the original Ethernet, window reduction in TCP, and fair queueing in devices such as routers. Another method to avoid the negative effects of network congestion is implementing priority schemes, so that some packets are transmitted with higher priority than others. Priority schemes do not solve network congestion by themselves, but they help to alleviate the effects of congestion for some services. An example of this is 802.1p. A third method to avoid network congestion is the explicit allocation of network resources to specific flows. One example of this is the use of Contention-Free Transmission Opportunities (CFTXOPs) in the ITU-T G.hn standard, which provides high-speed (up to 1 Gbit/s) Local area networking over existing home wires (power lines, phone lines and coaxial cables).

For the Internet, RFC 2914 addresses the subject of congestion control in detail.

Network resilience

Network resilience is "the ability to provide and maintain an acceptable level of service in the face of faults and challenges to normal operation."[45]

Security

Computer networks are also used by security hackers to deploy computer viruses or computer worms on devices connected to the network, or to prevent these devices from accessing the network via a denial-of-service attack.

Network security

Network security consists of provisions and policies adopted by the network administrator to prevent and monitor unauthorized access, misuse, modification, or denial of the computer network and its network-accessible resources.[46] Network security is the authorization of access to data in a network, which is controlled by the network administrator. Users are assigned an ID and password that allows them access to information and programs within their authority. Network security is used on a variety of computer networks, both public and private, to secure daily transactions and communications among businesses, government agencies and individuals.

Network surveillance

Network surveillance is the monitoring of data being transferred over computer networks such as the Internet. The monitoring is often done surreptitiously and may be done by or at the behest of governments, by corporations, criminal organizations, or individuals. It may or may not be legal and may or may not require authorization from a court or other independent agency.

Computer and network surveillance programs are widespread today, and almost all Internet traffic is or could potentially be monitored for clues to illegal activity.

Surveillance is very useful to governments and law enforcement to maintain social control, recognize and monitor threats, and prevent/investigate criminal activity. With the advent of programs such as the Total Information Awareness program, technologies such as high-speed surveillance computers and biometrics software, and laws such as the Communications Assistance For Law Enforcement Act, governments now possess an unprecedented ability to monitor the activities of citizens.[47]

However, many civil rights and privacy groups—such as Reporters Without Borders, the Electronic Frontier Foundation, and the American Civil Liberties Union—have expressed concern that increasing surveillance of citizens may lead to a mass surveillance society, with limited political and personal freedoms. Fears such as this have led to numerous lawsuits such as *Hepting v. AT&T*.[47][48] The hacktivist group Anonymous has hacked into government websites in protest of what it considers "draconian surveillance".[49][50]

End to end encryption

End-to-end encryption (E2EE) is a digital communications paradigm of uninterrupted protection of data traveling between two communicating parties. It involves the originating party encrypting data so only the intended recipient can decrypt it, with no dependency on third parties. End-to-end encryption prevents intermediaries, such as Internet providers or application service providers, from discovering or tampering with communications. End-to-end encryption generally protects both confidentiality and integrity.

Examples of end-to-end encryption include HTTPS for web traffic, PGP for email, OTR for instant messaging, ZRTP for telephony, and TETRA for radio.

Typical server-based communications systems do not include end-to-end encryption. These systems can only guarantee protection of communications between clients and servers, not between the communicating parties themselves. Examples of non-E2EE systems are Google Talk, Yahoo Messenger, Facebook, and Dropbox. Some such systems, for example LavaBit and SecretInk, have even described themselves as offering "end-to-end" encryption when they do not. Some systems that normally offer end-to-end encryption have turned out to contain a back door that subverts negotiation of the encryption key between the communicating parties, for example Skype or Hushmail.

The end-to-end encryption paradigm does not directly address risks at the communications endpoints themselves, such as the technical exploitation of clients, poor quality random number generators, or key escrow. E2EE also does not address traffic analysis, which relates to things such as the identities of the endpoints and the times and quantities of messages that are sent.

SSL/TLS

The introduction and rapid growth of e-commerce on the World Wide Web in the mid-1990s made it obvious that some form of authentication and encryption was needed. Netscape took the first shot at a new standard. At the time, the dominant web browser was Netscape Navigator. Netscape created a standard called secure socket layer (SSL). SSL requires a server with a certificate. When a client requests access to an SSL-secured server, the server sends a copy of the certificate to the client. The SSL client checks this certificate (all web browsers come with an exhaustive list of CA root certificates preloaded), and if the certificate checks out, the server is authenticated and the client negotiates a symmetric-key cipher for use in the session. The session is now in a very secure encrypted tunnel between the SSL server and the SSL client.[24]

Wireless Security

Wireless security is the prevention of unauthorized access or damage to computers or data using wireless networks, which include Wi-Fi networks. The most common type is **Wi-Fi security**, which includes Wired Equivalent Privacy (WEP) and Wi-Fi Protected Access (WPA). WEP is a notoriously weak security standard[*citation needed*]: the password it uses can often be cracked in a few minutes with a basic laptop computer and widely available software tools. WEP is an old IEEE 802.11 standard from 1997,[1] which was superseded in 2003 by WPA, or Wi-Fi Protected Access. WPA was a quick alternative to improve security over WEP. The current standard is WPA2; some hardware cannot support WPA2 without firmware upgrade or replacement. WPA2 uses an encryption device that encrypts the network with a 256-bit key; the longer key length improves security over WEP. Enterprises often enforce security using a certificate-based system to authenticate the connecting device, following the standard 802.1X.

Many laptop computers have wireless cards pre-installed. The ability to enter a network while mobile has great benefits. However, wireless networking is prone to some security issues. Hackers have found wireless networks relatively easy to break into, and even use wireless technology to hack into wired networks. As a result, it is very important that enterprises define effective wireless security policies that guard against unauthorized access to important resources.[2] Wireless Intrusion Prevention Systems (WIPS) or Wireless Intrusion Detection Systems (WIDS) are commonly used to enforce wireless security policies.

The risks to users of wireless technology have increased as the service has become more popular. There were relatively few dangers when wireless technology was first introduced. Hackers had not yet had time to latch on to the new technology, and wireless networks were not commonly found in the work place. However, there are many security risks associated with the current wireless protocols and encryption methods, and in the carelessness and ignorance that exists at the user and corporate IT level.[3] Hacking methods have become much more sophisticated and innovative with wireless access. Hacking has also become much easier and more accessible with easy-to-use Windows- or Linux-based tools being made available on the web at no charge.

Some organizations that have no wireless access points installed do not feel that they need to address wireless security concerns. In-Stat MDR and META Group have estimated that 95% of all corporate laptop computers that were planned to be purchased in 2005 were equipped with wireless cards. Issues can arise in a supposedly non-wireless organization when a wireless laptop is plugged into the corporate network. A hacker could sit out in the parking lot and gather information from it through laptops and/or other devices, or even break in through this wireless card–equipped laptop and gain access to the wired network.

Background

Anyone within the geographical network range of an open, unencrypted wireless network can "sniff", or capture and record, the traffic, gain unauthorized access to internal network resources as well as to the internet, and then use the information and resources to perform disruptive or illegal acts. Such security breaches have become important concerns for both enterprise and home networks.

If router security is not activated or if the owner deactivates it for convenience, it creates a free hotspot. Since most 21st-century laptop PCs have wireless networking built in (see Intel "Centrino" technology), they don't need a third-party adapter such as a PCMCIA Card or USB dongle. Built-in wireless networking might be enabled by default, without the owner realizing it, thus broadcasting the laptop's accessibility to any computer nearby.

Modern operating systems such as Linux, macOS, or Microsoft Windows make it fairly easy to set up a PC as a wireless LAN "base station" using Internet Connection Sharing, thus allowing all the PCs in the home to access the Internet through the "base" PC. However, lack of knowledge among users about the security issues inherent in setting up such systems often may allow others nearby access to the connection. Such "piggybacking" is usually achieved without the wireless network operator's knowledge; it may even be without the knowledge of the intruding user if their computer automatically selects a nearby unsecured wireless network to use as an access point.

The threat situation

Wireless security is just an aspect of computer security; however, organizations may be particularly vulnerable to security breaches[4] caused by rogue access points.

If an employee (trusted entity) brings in a wireless router and plugs it into an unsecured switchport, the entire network can be exposed to anyone within range of the signals. Similarly, if an employee adds a wireless interface to a networked computer using an open USB port, they may create a breach in network security that would allow access to confidential materials. However, there are effective countermeasures (like disabling open switchports during switch configuration and VLAN configuration to limit network access) that are available to protect both the network and the information it contains, but such countermeasures must be applied uniformly to all network devices.

Threats and Vulnerabilites in an industrial (M2M) context

Due to its availability and low cost, the use of wireless communication technologies increases in domains beyond the originally intended usage areas, e.g. M2M communication in industrial applications. Such industrial applications often have specific security requirements. Hence, it is important to understand the characteristics of such applications and evaluate the vulnerabilities bearing the highest risk in this context. Evaluation of these vulnerabilities and the resulting vulnerability catalogs in an industrial context when considering WLAN, NFC and ZigBee are available.[5]

The mobility advantage

Wireless networks are very common, both for organizations and individuals. Many laptop computers have wireless cards pre-installed. The ability to enter a network while mobile has great benefits. However, wireless networking is prone to some security issues.[6] Hackers have found wireless networks relatively easy to break into, and even use wireless technology to hack into wired networks.[7] As a result, it is very important that enterprises define effective wireless security policies that guard against unauthorized access to important resources.[2] Wireless Intrusion Prevention Systems (WIPS) or Wireless Intrusion Detection Systems (WIDS) are commonly used to enforce wireless security policies.

The air interface and link corruption risk

There were relatively few dangers when wireless technology was first introduced, as the effort to maintain the communication was high and the effort to intrude is always higher. The variety of risks to users of wireless technology have increased as the service has become more popular and the technology more commonly available. Today there are a great number of security risks associated with the current wireless protocols and encryption methods, as carelessness and ignorance exists at the user and corporate IT level. [3] Hacking methods have become much more sophisticated and innovative with wireless.

Modes of unauthorized access

The modes of unauthorised access to links, to functions and to data is as variable as the respective entities make use of program code. There does not exist a full scope model of such threat. To some extent the prevention relies on known modes and methods of attack and relevant methods for suppression of the applied methods. However, each new mode of operation will create new options of threatening. Hence prevention requires a steady drive for improvement. The described modes of attack are just a snapshot of typical methods and scenarios where to apply.

Accidental association

Violation of the security perimeter of a corporate network can come from a number of different methods and intents. One of these methods is referred to as "accidental association". When a user turns on a computer and it latches on to a wireless access point from a neighboring company's overlapping network, the user may not even know that this has occurred. However, it is a security breach in that proprietary company information is exposed and now there could exist a link from one company to the other. This is especially true if the laptop is also hooked to a wired network.

Accidental association is a case of wireless vulnerability called as "mis-association".[8] Mis-association can be accidental, deliberate (for example, done to bypass corporate firewall) or it can result from deliberate attempts on wireless clients to lure them into connecting to attacker's APs.

Malicious association

"Malicious associations" are when wireless devices can be actively made by attackers to connect to a company network through their laptop instead of a company access point (AP). These types of laptops are known as "soft APs" and are created when a cyber criminal runs some software that makes his/her wireless network card look like a legitimate access point. Once the thief has gained access, he/she can steal passwords, launch attacks on the wired network, or plant trojans. Since wireless networks operate at the Layer 2 level, Layer 3 protections such as network authentication and virtual private networks (VPNs) offer no barrier. Wireless 802.1X authentications do help with some protection but are still vulnerable to hacking. The idea behind this type of attack may not be to break into a VPN or other security measures. Most likely the criminal is just trying to take over the client at the Layer 2 level.

Ad hoc networks

Ad hoc networks can pose a security threat. Ad hoc networks are defined as [peer to peer] networks between wireless computers that do not have an access point in between them. While these types of networks usually have little protection, encryption methods can be used to provide security.[9]

The security hole provided by Ad hoc networking is not the Ad hoc network itself but the bridge it provides into other networks, usually in the corporate environment, and the unfortunate default settings in most versions of Microsoft Windows to have this feature turned on unless explicitly disabled. Thus the user may not even know they have an unsecured Ad hoc network in operation on their computer. If they are also using a wired or wireless infrastructure network at the same time, they are providing a bridge to the secured organizational network through the unsecured Ad hoc connection. Bridging is in two forms. A direct bridge, which requires the user actually configure a bridge between the two connections and is thus unlikely to be initiated unless explicitly desired, and an indirect bridge which is the shared resources on the user computer. The indirect bridge may expose private data that is shared from the user's computer to LAN connections, such as shared folders or private Network Attached Storage, making no distinction between authenticated or private connections and unauthenticated Ad-Hoc networks. This presents no threats not already familiar to open/public or unsecured wifi access points, but firewall rules may be circumvented in the case of poorly configured operating systems or local settings.[10]

Non-traditional networks

Non-traditional networks such as personal network Bluetooth devices are not safe from hacking and should be regarded as a security risk. Even barcode readers, handheld PDAs, and wireless printers and copiers should be secured. These non-traditional networks can be easily overlooked by IT personnel who have narrowly focused on laptops and access points.

Identity theft (MAC spoofing)

Identity theft (or MAC spoofing) occurs when a hacker is able to listen in on network traffic and identify the MAC address of a computer with network privileges. Most wireless systems allow some kind of MAC filtering to allow only authorized computers with specific MAC IDs to gain access and utilize the network. However, programs exist that have network "sniffing" capabilities. Combine these programs with other software that allow a computer to pretend it has any MAC address that the hacker desires,[11] and the hacker can easily get around that hurdle.

MAC filtering is effective only for small residential (SOHO) networks, since it provides protection only when the wireless device is "off the air". Any 802.11 device "on the air" freely transmits its unencrypted MAC address in its 802.11 headers, and it requires no special equipment or software to detect it. Anyone with an 802.11 receiver (laptop and wireless adapter) and a freeware wireless packet analyzer can obtain the MAC address of any transmitting 802.11 within range. In an organizational environment, where most wireless devices are "on the air" throughout the active working shift, MAC filtering provides only a false sense of security since it prevents only "casual" or unintended connections to the organizational infrastructure and does nothing to prevent a directed attack.

Man-in-the-middle attacks

A man-in-the-middle attacker entices computers to log into a computer which is set up as a soft AP (Access Point). Once this is done, the hacker connects to a real access point through another wireless card offering a steady flow of traffic through the transparent hacking computer to the real network. The hacker can then sniff the traffic. One type of man-in-the-middle attack relies on security faults in challenge and handshake protocols to execute a "de-authentication attack". This attack forces AP-connected computers to drop their connections and reconnect with the hacker's soft AP (disconnects the user from the modem so they have to connect again using their password which one can extract from the recording of the event). Man-in-the-middle attacks are enhanced by software such as LANjack and AirJack which automate multiple steps of the process, meaning what once required some skill can now be done by script kiddies. Hotspots are particularly vulnerable to any attack since there is little to no security on these networks.

Denial of service

A Denial-of-Service attack (DoS) occurs when an attacker continually bombards a targeted AP (Access Point) or network with bogus requests, premature successful connection messages, failure messages, and/or other commands. These cause legitimate users to not be able to get on the network and may even cause the network to crash. These attacks rely on the abuse of protocols such as the Extensible Authentication Protocol (EAP).

The DoS attack in itself does little to expose organizational data to a malicious attacker, since the interruption of the network prevents the flow of data and actually indirectly protects data by preventing it from being transmitted. The usual reason for performing a DoS attack is to observe the recovery of the wireless network, during which all of the initial handshake codes are re-transmitted by all devices, providing an opportunity for the malicious attacker to record these codes and use various cracking tools to analyze security weaknesses and exploit them to gain unauthorized access to the system. This works best on weakly encrypted systems such as WEP, where there are a number of tools available which can launch a dictionary style attack of "possibly accepted" security keys based on the "model" security key captured during the network recovery.

Network injection

In a network injection attack, a hacker can make use of access points that are exposed to non-filtered network traffic, specifically broadcasting network traffic such as "Spanning Tree" (802.1D), OSPF, RIP, and HSRP. The hacker injects bogus networking re-configuration commands that affect routers, switches, and intelligent hubs. A whole network can be brought down in this manner and require rebooting or even reprogramming of all intelligent networking devices.

Caffe Latte attack

The Caffe Latte attack is another way to defeat WEP. It is not necessary for the attacker to be in the area of the network using this exploit. By using a process that targets the Windows wireless stack, it is possible to obtain the WEP key from a remote client.[12] By sending a flood of encrypted ARP requests, the assailant takes advantage of the shared key authentication and the message modification flaws in 802.11 WEP. The attacker uses the ARP responses to obtain the WEP key in less than 6 minutes.[13]

Wireless intrusion prevention concepts

There are three principal ways to secure a wireless network.

- For closed networks (like home users and organizations) the most common way is to configure access restrictions in the access points. Those restrictions may include encryption and checks on MAC address. Wireless Intrusion Prevention Systems can be used to provide wireless LAN security in this network model.
- For commercial providers, hotspots, and large organizations, the preferred solution is often to have an open and unencrypted, but completely isolated wireless network. The users will at first have no access to the Internet nor to any local network resources. Commercial providers usually forward all web traffic to a captive portal which provides for payment and/or authorization. Another solution is to require the users to connect securely to a privileged network using VPN.
- Wireless networks are less secure than wired ones; in many offices intruders can easily visit and hook up their own computer to the wired network without problems, gaining access to the network, and it is also often possible for remote intruders to gain access to the network through backdoors like Back Orifice. One general solution may be end-to-end encryption, with independent authentication on all resources that shouldn't be available to the public.

There is no ready designed system to prevent from fraudulent usage of wireless communication or to protect data and functions with wirelessly communicating computers and other entities. However, there is a system of qualifying the taken measures as a whole according to a common understanding what shall be seen as state of the art. The system of qualifying is an international consensus as specified in ISO/IEC 15408.

A wireless intrusion prevention system

A Wireless Intrusion Prevention System (WIPS) is a concept for the most robust way to counteract wireless security risks.[14] However such WIPS does not exist as a ready designed solution to implement as a software package. A WIPS is typically implemented as an overlay to an existing Wireless LAN infrastructure, although it may be deployed standalone to enforce no-wireless policies within an organization. WIPS is considered so important to wireless security that in July 2009, the Payment Card Industry Security Standards Council published wireless guidelines[15] for PCI DSS recommending the use of WIPS to automate wireless scanning and protection for large organizations.

Security measures

There are a range of wireless security measures, of varying effectiveness and practicality.

SSID hiding

Further information: SSID § Security of SSID hiding, and Network cloaking

A simple but ineffective method to attempt to secure a wireless network is to hide the SSID (Service Set Identifier).[16] This provides very little protection against anything but the most casual intrusion efforts.

MAC ID filtering

One of the simplest techniques is to only allow access from known, pre-approved MAC addresses. Most wireless access points contain some type of MAC ID filtering. However, an attacker can simply sniff the MAC address of an authorized client and spoof this address.

Static IP addressing

Typical wireless access points provide IP addresses to clients via DHCP. Requiring clients to set their own addresses makes it more difficult for a casual or unsophisticated intruder to log onto the network, but provides little protection against a sophisticated attacker.[16]

802.11 security

IEEE 802.1X is the IEEE Standard authentication mechanisms to devices wishing to attach to a Wireless LAN.

Regular WEP

The Wired Equivalent Privacy (WEP) encryption standard was the original encryption standard for wireless, but since 2004 with the ratification WPA2 the IEEE has declared it "deprecated",[17] and while often supported, it is seldom or never the default on modern equipment.

Concerns were raised about its security as early as 2001,[18] dramatically demonstrated in 2005 by the FBI,[19] yet in 2007 T.J. Maxx admitted a massive security breach due in part to a reliance on WEP[20] and the Payment Card Industry took until 2008 to prohibit its use – and even then allowed existing use to continue until June 2010.[21]

WPAv1

The Wi-Fi Protected Access (WPA and WPA2) security protocols were later created to address the problems with WEP. If a weak password, such as a dictionary word or short character string is used, WPA and WPA2 can be cracked. Using a long enough random password (e.g. 14 random letters) or passphrase (e.g. 5 randomly chosen words) makes pre-shared key WPA virtually uncrackable. The second generation of the WPA security protocol (WPA2) is based on the final IEEE 802.11i amendment to the 802.11 standard and is eligible for FIPS 140-2 compliance. With all those encryption schemes, any client in the network that knows the keys can read all the traffic.

Wi-Fi Protected Access (WPA) is a software/firmware improvement over WEP. All regular WLAN-equipment that worked with WEP are able to be simply upgraded and no new equipment needs to be bought. WPA is a trimmed-down version of the 802.11i security standard that was developed by the IEEE 802.11 to replace WEP. The TKIP encryption algorithm was developed for WPA to provide improvements to WEP that could be fielded as firmware upgrades to existing 802.11 devices. The WPA profile also provides optional support for the AES-CCMP algorithm that is the preferred algorithm in 802.11i and WPA2.

WPA Enterprise provides RADIUS based authentication using 802.1X. WPA Personal uses a pre-shared Shared Key (PSK) to establish the security using an 8 to 63 character passphrase. The PSK may also be entered as a 64 character hexadecimal string. Weak PSK passphrases can be broken using off-line dictionary attacks by capturing the messages in the four-way exchange when the client reconnects after being deauthenticated. Wireless suites such as aircrack-ng can crack a weak passphrase in less than a minute. Other WEP/WPA crackers are AirSnort and Auditor Security Collection.[22] Still, WPA Personal is secure when used with 'good' passphrases or a full 64-character hexadecimal key.

There was information, however, that Erik Tews (the man who created the fragmentation attack against WEP) was going to reveal a way of breaking the WPA TKIP implementation at Tokyo's PacSec security conference in November 2008, cracking the encryption on a packet in between 12–15 minutes.[23] Still, the announcement of this 'crack' was somewhat overblown by the media, because as of August, 2009, the best attack on WPA (the Beck-Tews attack) is only partially successful in that it only works on short data packets, it cannot decipher the WPA key, and it requires very specific WPA implementations in order to work.[24]

Additions to WPAv1

In addition to WPAv1, TKIP, WIDS and EAP may be added alongside. Also, VPN-networks (non-continuous secure network connections) may be set up under the 802.11-standard. VPN implementations include PPTP, L2TP, IPsec and SSH. However, this extra layer of security may also be cracked with tools such as Anger, Deceit and Ettercap for PPTP;[25] and ike-scan, IKEProbe, ipsectrace, and IKEcrack for IPsec-connections.

TKIP

This stands for Temporal Key Integrity Protocol and the acronym is pronounced as tee-kip. This is part of the IEEE 802.11i standard. TKIP implements per-packet key mixing with a re-keying system and also provides a message integrity check. These avoid the problems of WEP.

EAP

The WPA-improvement over the IEEE 802.1X standard already improved the authentication and authorization for access of wireless and wired LANs. In addition to this, extra measures such as the Extensible Authentication Protocol (EAP) have initiated an even greater amount of security. This, as EAP uses a central authentication server. Unfortunately, during 2002 a Maryland professor discovered some shortcomings[*citation needed*]. Over the next few years these shortcomings were addressed with the use of TLS and other enhancements.[26] This new version of EAP is now called Extended EAP and is available in several versions; these include: EAP-MD5, PEAPv0, PEAPv1, EAP-MSCHAPv2, LEAP, EAP-FAST, EAP-TLS, EAP-TTLS, MSCHAPv2, and EAP-SIM.

EAP-versions

EAP-versions include LEAP, PEAP and other EAP's.

LEAP

This stands for the Lightweight Extensible Authentication Protocol. This protocol is based on 802.1X and helps minimize the original security flaws by using WEP and a sophisticated key management system. This

EAP-version is safer than EAP-MD5. This also uses MAC address authentication. LEAP is not secure; THC-LeapCracker can be used to break Cisco's version of LEAP and be used against computers connected to an access point in the form of a dictionary attack. Anwrap and asleap finally are other crackers capable of breaking LEAP.[22]

PEAP

This stands for Protected Extensible Authentication Protocol. This protocol allows for a secure transport of data, passwords, and encryption keys without the need of a certificate server. This was developed by Cisco, Microsoft, and RSA Security.

Other EAPs There are other types of Extensible Authentication Protocol implementations that are based on the EAP framework. The framework that was established supports existing EAP types as well as future authentication methods.[27] EAP-TLS offers very good protection because of its mutual authentication. Both the client and the network are authenticated using certificates and per-session WEP keys.[28] EAP-FAST also offers good protection. EAP-TTLS is another alternative made by Certicom and Funk Software. It is more convenient as one does not need to distribute certificates to users, yet offers slightly less protection than EAP-TLS.[29]

Restricted access networks

Solutions include a newer system for authentication, IEEE 802.1X, that promises to enhance security on both wired and wireless networks. Wireless access points that incorporate technologies like these often also have routers built in, thus becoming wireless gateways.

End-to-end encryption

One can argue that both layer 2 and layer 3 encryption methods are not good enough for protecting valuable data like passwords and personal emails. Those technologies add encryption only to parts of the communication path, still allowing people to spy on the traffic if they have gained access to the wired network somehow. The solution may be encryption and authorization in the application layer, using technologies like SSL, SSH, GnuPG, PGP and similar.

The disadvantage with the end-to-end method is, it may fail to cover all traffic. With encryption on the router level or VPN, a single switch encrypts all traffic, even UDP and DNS lookups. With end-to-end encryption on the other hand, each service to be secured must have its encryption "turned on", and often every connection must also be "turned on" separately. For sending emails, every recipient must support the encryption method, and must exchange keys correctly. For Web, not all web sites offer https, and even if they do, the browser sends out IP addresses in clear text.

The most prized resource is often access to the Internet. An office LAN owner seeking to restrict such access will face the nontrivial enforcement task of having each user authenticate themselves for the router.

802.11i security

The newest and most rigorous security to implement into WLAN's today is the 802.11i RSN-standard. This full-fledged 802.11i standard (which uses WPAv2) however does require the newest hardware (unlike WPAv1), thus potentially requiring the purchase of new equipment. This new hardware required may be either AES-WRAP (an early version of 802.11i) or the newer and better AES-CCMP-equipment. One should make sure one needs WRAP or CCMP-equipment, as the 2 hardware standards are not compatible.

WPAv2

WPA2 is a WiFi Alliance branded version of the final 802.11i standard.[30] The primary enhancement over WPA is the inclusion of the AES-CCMP algorithm as a mandatory feature. Both WPA and WPA2 support EAP authentication methods using RADIUS servers and preshared key (PSK).

The number of WPA and WPA2 networks are increasing, while the number of WEP networks are decreasing,[31] because of the security vulnerabilities in WEP.

WPA2 has been found to have at least one security vulnerability, nicknamed Hole196. The vulnerability uses the WPA2 Group Temporal Key (GTK), which is a shared key among all users of the same BSSID, to launch attacks on other users of the same BSSID. It is named after page 196 of the IEEE 802.11i specification, where the vulnerability is discussed. In order for this exploit to be performed, the GTK must be known by the attacker.[32]

Additions to WPAv2

Unlike 802.1X, 802.11i already has most other additional security-services such as TKIP. Just as with WPAv1, WPAv2 may work in cooperation with EAP and a WIDS.

WAPI

This stands for WLAN Authentication and Privacy Infrastructure. This is a wireless security standard defined by the Chinese government.

Smart cards, USB tokens, and software tokens

This is a very strong form of security. When combined with some server software, the hardware or software card or token will use its internal identity code combined with a user entered PIN to create a powerful algorithm that will very frequently generate a new encryption code. The server will be time synced to the card or token. This is a very secure way to conduct wireless transmissions. Companies in this area make USB tokens, software tokens, and smart cards. They even make hardware versions that double as an employee picture badge. Currently the safest security measures are the smart cards / USB tokens. However, these are expensive. The next safest methods are WPA2 or WPA with a RADIUS server. Any one of the three will provide a good base foundation for security. The third item on the list is to educate both employees and contractors on security risks and personal preventive measures. It is also IT's task to keep the company workers' knowledge base up-to-date on any new dangers that they should be cautious about. If the employees are educated, there will be a much lower chance that anyone will accidentally cause a breach in security by not locking down their laptop or bring in a wide open home access point to extend their mobile range. Employees need to be made aware that company laptop security extends to outside of their site walls as well. This includes places such as coffee houses where workers can be at their most vulnerable. The last item on the list deals with 24/7 active defense measures to ensure that the company network is secure and compliant. This can take the form of regularly looking at access point, server, and firewall logs to try to detect any unusual activity. For instance, if any large files went through an access point in the early hours of the morning, a serious investigation into the incident would be called for. There are a number of software and hardware devices that can be used to supplement the usual logs and usual other safety measures.

RF shielding

It's practical in some cases to apply specialized wall paint and window film to a room or building to significantly attenuate wireless signals, which keeps the signals from propagating outside a facility. This can significantly improve wireless security because it's difficult for hackers to receive the signals beyond the controlled area of a facility, such as from a parking lot.[33]

Denial of service defense

Most DoS attacks are easy to detect. However, a lot of them are difficult to stop even after detection. Here are three of the most common ways to stop a DoS attack.

Black holing

Black holing is one possible way of stopping a DoS attack. This is a situation where we drop all IP packets from an attacker. This is not a very good long-term strategy because attackers can change their source address very quickly.

This may have negative effects if done automatically. An attacker could knowingly spoof attack packets with the IP address of a corporate partner. Automated defenses could block legitimate traffic from that partner and cause additional problems.

Validating the handshake

Validating the handshake involves creating false opens, and not setting aside resources until the sender acknowledges. Some firewalls address SYN floods by pre-validating the TCP handshake. This is done by creating false opens. Whenever a SYN segment arrives, the firewall sends back a SYN/ACK segment, without passing the SYN segment on to the target server.

Only when the firewall gets back an ACK, which would happen only in a legitimate connection, would the firewall send the original SYN segment on to the server for which it was originally intended. The firewall doesn't set aside resources for a connection when a SYN segment arrives, so handling a large number of false SYN segments is only a small burden.

Rate limiting

Rate limiting can be used to reduce a certain type of traffic down to an amount the can be reasonably dealt with. Broadcasting to the internal network could still be used, but only at a limited rate for example. This is for more subtle DoS attacks. This is good if an attack is aimed at a single server because it keeps transmission lines at least partially open for other communication.

Rate limiting frustrates both the attacker, and the legitimate users. This helps but does not fully solve the problem. Once DoS traffic clogs the access line going to the internet, there is nothing a border firewall can do to help the situation. Most DoS attacks are problems of the community which can only be stopped with the help of ISP's and organizations whose computers are taken over as bots and used to attack other firms.

Mobile devices

With increasing number of mobile devices with 802.1X interfaces, security of such mobile devices becomes a concern. While open standards such as Kismet are targeted towards securing laptops,[34] access points solutions should extend towards covering mobile devices also. Host based solutions for mobile handsets and PDA's with 802.1X interface.

Security within mobile devices fall under three categories:

1. Protecting against ad hoc networks
2. Connecting to rogue access points
3. Mutual authentication schemes such as WPA2 as described above

Wireless IPS solutions now offer wireless security for mobile devices.[35]

Mobile patient monitoring devices are becoming an integral part of healthcare industry and these devices will eventually become the method of choice for accessing and implementing health checks for patients located in remote areas. For these types of patient monitoring systems, security and reliability are critical, because they can influence the condition of patients, and could leave medical professionals in the dark about the condition of the patient if compromised.[36]

Implementing network encryption

In order to implement 802.11i, one must first make sure both that the router/access point(s), as well as all client devices are indeed equipped to support the network encryption. If this is done, a server such as RADIUS, ADS, NDS, or LDAP needs to be integrated. This server can be a computer on the local network, an access point / router with integrated authentication server, or a remote server. AP's/routers with integrated authentication servers are often very expensive and specifically an option for commercial usage like hot spots. Hosted 802.1X servers via the Internet require a monthly fee; running a private server is free yet has the disadvantage that one must set it up and that the server needs to be on continuously.[37]

To set up a server, server and client software must be installed. Server software required is an enterprise authentication server such as RADIUS, ADS, NDS, or LDAP. The required software can be picked from various suppliers as Microsoft, Cisco, Funk Software, Meetinghouse Data, and from some open-source projects. Software includes:

- Aradial RADIUS Server
- Cisco Secure Access Control Software
- freeRADIUS (open-source)
- Funk Software Steel Belted RADIUS (Odyssey)
- Microsoft Internet Authentication Service
- Meetinghouse Data EAGIS
- SkyFriendz (free cloud solution based on freeRADIUS)

Client software comes built-in with Windows XP and may be integrated into other OS's using any of following software:

- AEGIS-client
- Cisco ACU-client
- Intel PROSet/Wireless Software
- Odyssey client
- Xsupplicant (open1X)-project

RADIUS

Remote Authentication Dial In User Service (RADIUS) is an AAA (authentication, authorization and accounting) protocol used for remote network access. RADIUS was originally proprietary but was later published under ISOC documents RFC 2138 and RFC 2139. The idea is to have an inside server act as a gatekeeper by verifying identities through a username and password that is already pre-determined by the user. A RADIUS server can also be configured to enforce user policies and restrictions as well as record accounting information such as connection time for purposes such as billing.

Open access points

Today, there is almost full wireless network coverage in many urban areas – the infrastructure for the wireless community network (which some consider to be the future of the internet[*who?*]) is already in place. One could roam around and always be connected to Internet if the nodes were open to the public, but due to security concerns, most nodes are encrypted and the users don't know how to disable encryption. Many people[*who?*] consider it proper etiquette to leave access points open to the public, allowing free access to Internet. Others[*who?*] think the default encryption provides substantial protection at small inconvenience, against dangers of open access that they fear may be substantial even on a home DSL router.

The density of access points can even be a problem – there are a limited number of channels available, and they partly overlap. Each channel can handle multiple networks, but places with many private wireless networks (for example, apartment complexes), the limited number of Wi-Fi radio channels might cause slowness and other problems.

According to the advocates of Open Access Points, it shouldn't involve any significant risks to open up wireless networks for the public:

- The wireless network is after all confined to a small geographical area. A computer connected to the Internet and having improper configurations or other security problems can be exploited by anyone from anywhere in the world, while only clients in a small geographical range can exploit an open wireless access point. Thus the exposure is low with an open wireless access point, and the risks with having an open wireless network are small. However, one should be aware that an open wireless router will give access to the local network, often including access to file shares and printers.
- The only way to keep communication truly secure is to use end-to-end encryption. For example, when accessing an internet bank, one would almost always use strong encryption from the web browser and all the way to the bank – thus it shouldn't be risky to do banking over an unencrypted wireless network. The argument is that anyone can sniff the traffic applies to wired networks too, where system administrators and possible hackers have access to the links and can read the traffic. Also, anyone knowing the keys for an encrypted wireless network can gain access to the data being transferred over the network.
- If services like file shares, access to printers etc. are available on the local net, it is advisable to have authentication (i.e. by password) for accessing it (one should never assume that the private network is not accessible from the outside). Correctly set up, it should be safe to allow access to the local network to outsiders.
- With the most popular encryption algorithms today, a sniffer will usually be able to compute the network key in a few minutes.
- It is very common to pay a fixed monthly fee for the Internet connection, and not for the traffic –

thus extra traffic will not be detrimental.

- Where Internet connections are plentiful and cheap, freeloaders will seldom be a prominent nuisance.

On the other hand, in some countries including Germany,[38] persons providing an open access point may be made (partially) liable for any illegal activity conducted via this access point. Also, many contracts with ISPs specify that the connection may not be shared with other persons.

Computer Access Control

In computer security, general access control includes identification, authorization, authentication, access approval, and audit. A more narrow definition of access control would cover only access approval, whereby the system makes a decision to grant or reject an access request from an already authenticated subject, based on what the subject is authorized to access. Authentication and access control are often combined into a single operation, so that access is approved based on successful authentication, or based on an anonymous access token. Authentication methods and tokens include passwords, biometric scans, physical keys, electronic keys and devices, hidden paths, social barriers, and monitoring by humans and automated systems.[*citation needed*]

Software entities

In any access-control model, the entities that can perform actions on the system are called *subjects*, and the entities representing resources to which access may need to be controlled are called *objects* (see also Access Control Matrix). Subjects and objects should both be considered as software entities, rather than as human users: any human users can only have an effect on the system via the software entities that they control.[*citation needed*]

Although some systems equate subjects with *user IDs*, so that all processes started by a user by default have the same authority, this level of control is not fine-grained enough to satisfy the principle of least privilege, and arguably is responsible for the prevalence of malware in such systems (see computer insecurity).[*citation needed*]

In some models, for example the object-capability model, any software entity can potentially act as both subject and object.[*citation needed*]

As of 2014, access-control models tend to fall into one of two classes: those based on capabilities and those based on access control lists (ACLs).

- In a capability-based model, holding an unforge-able reference or *capability* to an object provides access to the object (roughly analogous to how possession of one's house key grants one access to one's house); access is conveyed to another party by transmitting such a capability over a secure channel
- In an ACL-based model, a subject's access to an object depends on whether its identity appears on a list associated with the object (roughly analogous to how a bouncer at a private party would check

an ID to see if a name appears on the guest list); access is conveyed by editing the list. (Different ACL systems have a variety of different conventions regarding who or what is responsible for editing the list and how it is edited.)[*citation needed*]

Both capability-based and ACL-based models have mechanisms to allow access rights to be granted to all members of a *group* of subjects (often the group is itself modeled as a subject).[*citation needed*]

Services

Access control systems provide the essential services of *authorization, identification and authentication (I&A)*, *access approval*, and *accountability* where:[*citation needed*]

- authorization specifies what a subject can do
- identification and authentication ensure that only legitimate subjects can log on to a system
- access approval grants access during operations, by association of users with the resources that they are allowed to access, based on the authorization policy
- accountability identifies what a subject (or all subjects associated with a user) did

Authorization

Authorization involves the act of defining access-rights for subjects. An authorization policy specifies the operations that subjects are allowed to execute within a system.[*citation needed*]

Most modern operating systems implement authorization policies as formal sets of permissions that are variations or extensions of three basic types of access:[*citation needed*]

- Read (R): The subject can
  - Read file contents
  - List directory contents
- Write (W): The subject can change the contents of a file or directory with the following tasks:
  - Add
  - Update
  - Delete
  - Rename
- Execute (X): If the file is a program, the subject can cause the program to be run. (In Unix-style systems, the "execute" permission doubles as a "traverse directory" permission when granted for a directory.)

These rights and permissions are implemented differently in systems based on *discretionary access control (DAC)* and *mandatory access control (MAC)*.

Identification and authentication

Identification and authentication (I&A) is the process of verifying that an identity is bound to the entity that makes an assertion or claim of identity. The I&A process assumes that there was an initial validation of the identity, commonly called identity proofing. Various methods of identity proofing are available, ranging from in-person validation using government issued identification, to anonymous methods that allow the claimant to remain anonymous, but known to the system if they return. The method used for identity proofing and validation should provide an assurance level commensurate with the intended use of the identity within the system. Subsequently, the entity asserts an identity together with an authenticator as a means for validation. The only requirements for the identifier is that it must be unique within its security domain.[*citation needed*]

Authenticators are commonly based on at least one of the following four factors:[*citation needed*]

- *Something you know*, such as a password or a personal identification number (PIN). This assumes that only the owner of the account knows the password or PIN needed to access the account.
- *Something you have*, such as a smart card or security token. This assumes that only the owner of the account has the necessary smart card or token needed to unlock the account.
- *Something you are*, such as fingerprint, voice, retina, or iris characteristics.
- *Where you are*, for example inside or outside a company firewall, or proximity of login location to a personal GPS device.

Access approval

Access approval is the function that actually grants or rejects access during operations.[1]

During access approval, the system compares the formal representation of the authorization policy with the access request, to determine whether the request shall be granted or rejected. Moreover, the access evaluation can be done online/ongoing.[2]

Accountability

Accountability uses such system components as *audit trails* (records) and *logs,* to associate a subject with its actions. The information recorded should be sufficient to map the subject to a controlling user. Audit trails and logs are important for[*citation needed*]

- Detecting security violations
- Re-creating security incidents

If no one is regularly reviewing your logs and they are not maintained in a secure and consistent manner, they may not be admissible as evidence.[*citation needed*]

Many systems can generate automated reports, based on certain predefined criteria or thresholds, known as clipping levels. *For example, a clipping level may be set to generate a report for the following:[citation needed]*

- More than three failed logon attempts in a given period
- Any attempt to use a disabled user account

These reports help a system administrator or security administrator to more easily identify possible break-in attempts.

Definition of clipping level:[3] a disk's ability to maintain its magnetic properties and hold its content. A high-quality level range is 65–70%; low quality is below 55%.

Access controls

Access control models are sometimes categorized as either discretionary or non-discretionary. The three most widely recognized models are Discretionary Access Control (DAC), Mandatory Access Control (MAC), and Role Based Access Control (RBAC). MAC is non-discretionary.[*citation needed*]

Discretionary access control

Discretionary access control (DAC) is a policy determined by the owner of an object. The owner decides who is allowed to access the object, and what privileges they have.

Two important concepts in DAC are[*citation needed*]

- File and data ownership: Every object in the system has an *owner*. In most DAC systems, each object's initial owner is the subject that caused it to be created. The access policy for an object is determined by its owner.
- Access rights and permissions: These are the controls that an owner can assign to other subjects for specific resources.

Access controls may be discretionary in ACL-based or capability-based access control systems. (In capability-based systems, there is usually no explicit concept of 'owner', but the creator of an object has a similar degree of control over its access policy.)

Mandatory access control

Mandatory access control refers to allowing access to a resource if and only if rules exist that allow a given user to access the resource. It is difficult to manage, but its use is usually justified when used to protect highly sensitive information. Examples include certain government and military information. Management is often simplified (over what can be required) if the information can be protected using hierarchical access control, or by implementing sensitivity labels. What makes the method "mandatory" is the use of either rules or sensitivity labels.[*citation needed*]

- Sensitivity labels: In such a system subjects and objects must have labels assigned to them. A subject's sensitivity label specifies its level of trust. An object's sensitivity label specifies the level of trust required for access. In order to access a given object, the subject must have a sensitivity level equal to or higher than the requested object.
- Data import and export: Controlling the import of information from other systems and export to other systems (including printers) is a critical function of these systems, which must ensure that sensitivity labels are properly maintained and implemented so that sensitive information is appropriately protected at all times.

Two methods are commonly used for applying mandatory access control:[*citation needed*]

- Rule-based (or label-based) access control: This type of control further defines specific conditions for access to a requested object. A Mandatory Access Control system implements a simple form of rule-based access control to determine whether access should be granted or denied by matching:
  - An object's sensitivity label
  - A subject's sensitivity label
- Lattice-based access control: These can be used for complex access control decisions involving multiple objects and/or subjects. A lattice model is a mathematical structure that defines greatest

lower-bound and least upper-bound values for a pair of elements, such as a subject and an object.

Few systems implement MAC; XTS-400 and SELinux are examples of systems that do.

Role-based access control

Role-based access control (RBAC) is an access policy determined by the system, not by the owner. RBAC is used in commercial applications and also in military systems, where multi-level security requirements may also exist. RBAC differs from DAC in that DAC allows users to control access to their resources, while in RBAC, access is controlled at the system level, outside of the user's control. Although RBAC is non-discretionary, it can be distinguished from MAC primarily in the way permissions are handled. MAC controls read and write permissions based on a user's clearance level and additional labels. RBAC controls collections of permissions that may include complex operations such as an e-commerce transaction, or may be as simple as read or write. A role in RBAC can be viewed as a set of permissions.

Three primary rules are defined for RBAC:

1. Role assignment: A subject can execute a transaction only if the subject has selected or been assigned a suitable role.
2. Role authorization: A subject's active role must be authorized for the subject. With rule 1 above, this rule ensures that users can take on only roles for which they are authorized.
3. Transaction authorization: A subject can execute a transaction only if the transaction is authorized for the subject's active role. With rules 1 and 2, this rule ensures that users can execute only transactions for which they are authorized.

Additional constraints may be applied as well, and roles can be combined in a hierarchy where higher-level roles subsume permissions owned by lower-level sub-roles.

Most IT vendors offer RBAC in one or more products.

Attribute-based access control

In attribute-based access control (ABAC),[4][5] access is granted not based on the rights of the subject associated with a user after authentication, but based on attributes of the user. The user has to prove so-called claims about his attributes to the access control engine. An attribute-based access control policy specifies which claims need to be satisfied in order to grant access to an object. For instance the claim could be "older than 18". Any user that can prove this claim is granted access. Users can be anonymous when authentication and identification are not strictly required. One does, however, require means for proving claims anonymously. This can for instance be achieved using anonymous credentials.[*citation needed*] XACML (extensible access control markup language) is a standard for attribute-based access control. XACML 3.0 was standardized in January 2013.[6]

Break-Glass Access Control Models

Traditionally, access has the purpose of restricting access, thus most access control models follow the "default deny principle", i.e. if a specific access request is not explicitly allowed, it will be denied. This behavior might conflict with the regular operations of a system. In certain situations, humans are willing to take the risk that might be involved in violating an access control policy, if the potential benefit that can be achieved outweighs this risk. This need is especially visible in the health-care domain, where a denied access to patient records can cause the death of a patient. Break-Glass (also called break-the-glass) try to mitigate this by allowing users to override access control decision. Break-Glass can either be implemented in an access control specific manner (e.g. into RBAC),[7] or generic (i.e., independent from the underlying access control model).[8]

Access control based on the responsibility

In **Aligning Access Rights to Governance Needs with the Responsibility MetaModel (ReMMo) in the Frame of Enterprise Architecture**[9] an expressive responsibility metamodel has been defined and allows representing the existing responsibilities at the business layer and, thereby, allows engineering the access rights required to perform these responsibilities, at the application layer. A method has been proposed to define the access rights more accurately, considering the alignment of the responsibility and RBAC.

Host-based access control (HBAC)

The initialism HBAC stands for "host-based access control".[10]

Access control models

Access to accounts can be enforced through many types of controls.[17]

1. Attribute-based Access Control (ABAC)
   An access control paradigm whereby access rights are granted to users through the use of policies which evaluate attributes (user attributes, resource attributes and environment conditions)[18]
2. Discretionary Access Control (DAC)
   In DAC, the data owner determines who can access specific resources. For example, a system administrator may create a hierarchy of files to be accessed based on certain permissions.
3. Graph-based Access Control (GBAC)
   Compared to other approaches like RBAC or ABAC, the main difference is that in GBAC access rights are defined using an organizational query language instead of total enumeration.
4. History-Based Access Control (HBAC)
   Access is granted or declined based on the real-time evaluation of a history of activities of the inquiring party, e.g. behavior, time between requests, content of requests.[19] For example, the access to a certain service or data source can be granted or declined on the personal behavior, e.g. the request interval exceeds one query per second.
5. History-of-Presence Based Access Control (HPBAC)
   Access control to resources is defined in terms of presence policies that need to be satisfied by presence records stored by the requestor. Policies are usually written in terms of frequency, spread and regularity. An example policy would be "The requestor has made k separate visitations, all within last week, and no two consecutive visitations are apart by more than T hours."[20]
6. Identity-Based Access Control (IBAC)
   Using this network administrators can more effectively manage activity and access based on individual needs.[21]
7. Lattice-Based Access Control (LBAC)
   A lattice is used to define the levels of security that an object may have and that a subject may have access to. The subject is only allowed to access an object if the security level of the subject is greater than or equal to that of the object.
8. Mandatory Access Control (MAC)
   In MAC, users do not have much freedom to determine who has access to their files. For example, security clearance of users and classification of data (as confidential, secret or top secret) are used as

security labels to define the level of trust.

9. Organization-Based Access control (OrBAC)
   OrBAC model allows the policy designer to define a security policy independently of the implementation[22]
10. Role-Based Access Control (RBAC)
    RBAC allows access based on the job title. RBAC largely eliminates discretion when providing access to objects. For example, a human resources specialist should not have permissions to create network accounts; this should be a role reserved for network administrators.
11. Rule-Based Access Control (RAC)
    RAC method, also referred to as Rule-Based Role-Based Access Control (RB-RBAC), is largely context based. Example of this would be allowing students to use labs only during a certain time of day; it is the combination of students' RBAC-based information system access control with the time-based lab access rules.
12. Responsibility Based Access control
    Information is accessed based on the responsibilities assigned to an actor or a business role[23]

Public Key Infrastructure

A **public key infrastructure** (**PKI**) is a set of roles, policies, hardware, software and procedures needed to create, manage, distribute, use, store and revoke digital certificates and manage public-key encryption. The purpose of a PKI is to facilitate the secure electronic transfer of information for a range of network activities such as e-commerce, internet banking and confidential email. It is required for activities where simple passwords are an inadequate authentication method and more rigorous proof is required to confirm the identity of the parties involved in the communication and to validate the information being transferred.

In cryptography, a PKI is an arrangement that *binds* public keys with respective identities of entities (like people and organizations). The binding is established through a process of registration and issuance of certificates at and by a certificate authority (CA). Depending on the assurance level of the binding, this may be carried out by an automated process or under human supervision.

The PKI role that may be delegated by a CA to assure valid and correct registration is called a *registration authority* (RA). Basically, an RA is responsible for accepting requests for digital certificates and authenticating the entity making the request.[1] The Internet Engineering Task Force's RFC 3647 defines an RA as "An entity that is responsible for one or more of the following functions: the identification and authentication of certificate applicants, the approval or rejection of certificate applications, initiating certificate revocations or suspensions under certain circumstances, processing subscriber requests to revoke or suspend their certificates, and approving or rejecting requests by subscribers to renew or re-key their certificates. RAs, however, do not sign or issue certificates (i.e., an RA is delegated certain tasks on behalf of a CA)."[2] While Microsoft may have referred to a subordinate CA as an RA,[3] this is incorrect according to the X.509 PKI standards. RAs do not have the signing authority of a CA and only manage the vetting and provisioning of certificates. So in the Microsoft PKI case, the RA functionality is provided either by the Microsoft Certificate Services web site or through Active Directory Certificate Services which enforces Microsoft Enterprise CA and certificate policy through certificate templates and manages certificate enrollment (manual or auto-enrollment). In the case of Microsoft Standalone CAs, the function of RA does not exist since all of the procedures controlling the CA are based on the administration and access procedure associate with the system hosting the CA and the CA itself rather than Active Directory. Most non-Microsoft commercial PKI solutions offer a stand-alone RA component.

An entity must be uniquely identifiable within each CA domain on the basis of information about that entity. A third-party validation authority (VA) can provide this entity information on behalf of the CA.

The X.509 standard defines the most commonly used format for public key certificates.[4]

Design

Public key cryptography is a cryptographic technique that enables entities to securely communicate on an insecure public network, and reliably verify the identity of an entity via digital signatures.[5]

A public key infrastructure (PKI) is a system for the creation, storage, and distribution of digital certificates which are used to verify that a particular public key belongs to a certain entity. The PKI creates digital certificates which map public keys to entities, securely stores these certificates in a central repository and revokes them if needed.[6][7][8]

A PKI consists of:[7][9][10]

- A *certificate authority* (CA) that stores, issues and signs the digital certificates;
- A *registration authority* (RA) which verifies the identity of entities requesting their digital certificates to be stored at the CA;
- A *central directory*—i.e., a secure location in which keys are stored and indexed;
- A *certificate management system* managing things like the access to stored certificates or the delivery of the certificates to be issued;
- A *certificate policy* stating the PKI's requirements concerning its procedures. Its purpose is to allow outsiders to analyze the PKI's trustworthiness.

Methods of certification

Broadly speaking, there have traditionally been three approaches to getting this trust: certificate authorities (CAs), web of trust (WoT), and simple public key infrastructure (SPKI).[*citation needed*]

Certificate authorities

The primary role of the CA is to digitally sign and publish the public key bound to a given user. This is done using the CA's own private key, so that trust in the user key relies on one's trust in the validity of the CA's key. When the CA is a third party separate from the user and the system, then it is called the Registration Authority (RA), which may or may not be separate from the CA.[11] The key-to-user binding is established, depending on the level of assurance the binding has, by software or under human supervision.

The term trusted third party (TTP) may also be used for certificate authority (CA). Moreover, PKI is itself often used as a synonym for a CA implementation.[12]

Issuer market share

In this model of trust relationships, a CA is a trusted third party – trusted both by the subject (owner) of the certificate and by the party relying upon the certificate.

According to NetCraft report from 2015,[13] the industry standard for monitoring active Transport Layer Security (TLS) certificates, states that "Although the global [TLS] ecosystem is competitive, it is dominated by a handful of major CAs — three certificate authorities (Symantec, Sectigo, GoDaddy) account for three-quarters of all issued [TLS] certificates on public-facing web servers. The top spot has been held by Symantec (or VeriSign before it was purchased by Symantec) ever since [our] survey began, with it currently accounting for just under a third of all certificates. To illustrate the effect of differing methodologies, amongst the million busiest sites Symantec issued 44% of the valid, trusted certificates in use — significantly more than its overall market share."

Following to major issues in how certificate issuing were managed, all major players gradually distrusted Symantec issued certificates starting from 2017.[14][15][16]

Temporary certificates and single sign-on

This approach involves a server that acts as an offline certificate authority within a single sign-on system. A single sign-on server will issue digital certificates into the client system, but never stores them. Users can execute programs, etc. with the temporary certificate. It is common to find this solution variety with X.509-based certificates.[17]

Starting Sep 2020, TLS Certificate Validity reduced to 13 Months.

Web of trust

An alternative approach to the problem of public authentication of public key information is the web-of-trust scheme, which uses self-signed certificates and third-party attestations of those certificates. The singular term "web of trust" does not imply the existence of a single web of trust, or common point of trust, but rather one of any number of potentially disjoint "webs of trust". Examples of implementations of this approach are PGP (Pretty Good Privacy) and GnuPG (an implementation of OpenPGP, the standardized specification of PGP). Because PGP and implementations allow the use of e-mail digital signatures for self-publication of public key information, it is relatively easy to implement one's own web of trust.

One of the benefits of the web of trust, such as in PGP, is that it can interoperate with a PKI CA fully trusted by all parties in a domain (such as an internal CA in a company) that is willing to guarantee certificates, as a trusted introducer. If the "web of trust" is completely trusted then, because of the nature of a web of trust, trusting one certificate is granting trust to all the certificates in that web. A PKI is only as valuable as the standards and practices that control the issuance of certificates and including PGP or a personally instituted web of trust could significantly degrade the trustworthiness of that enterprise's or domain's implementation of PKI.[18]

The web of trust concept was first put forth by PGP creator Phil Zimmermann in 1992 in the manual for PGP version 2.0:

> As time goes on, you will accumulate keys from other people that you may want to designate as trusted introducers. Everyone else will each choose their own trusted introducers. And everyone will gradually accumulate and distribute with their key a collection of certifying signatures from other people, with the expectation that anyone receiving it will trust at least one or two of the signatures. This will cause the emergence of a decentralized fault-tolerant web of

confidence for all public keys.

Simple public key infrastructure

Another alternative, which does not deal with public authentication of public key information, is the simple public key infrastructure (SPKI) that grew out of three independent efforts to overcome the complexities of X.509 and PGP's web of trust. SPKI does not associate users with persons, since the *key* is what is trusted, rather than the person. SPKI does not use any notion of trust, as the verifier is also the issuer. This is called an "authorization loop" in SPKI terminology, where authorization is integral to its design.[*citation needed*] This type of PKI is specially useful for making integrations of PKI that do not rely on third parties for certificate authorization, certificate information, etc.; A good example of this is an Air-gapped network in an office.

Decentralized PKI

Decentralized identifiers (DIDs) eliminates dependence on centralized registries for identifiers as well as centralized certificate authorities for key management, which is the standard in hierarchical PKI. In cases where the DID registry is a distributed ledger, each entity can serve as its own root authority. This architecture is referred to as decentralized PKI (DPKI).[19][20]

Blockchain-based PKI

An emerging approach for PKI is to use the blockchain technology commonly associated with modern cryptocurrency.[21][22] Since blockchain technology aims to provide a distributed and unalterable ledger of information, it has qualities considered highly suitable for the storage and management of public keys. Some cryptocurrencies support the storage of different public key types (SSH, GPG, RFC 2230, etc.) and provides open source software that directly supports PKI for OpenSSH servers.[*citation needed*] While blockchain technology can approximate the proof of work often underpinning the confidence in trust that relying parties have in a PKI, issues remain such as administrative conformance to policy, operational security and software implementation quality. A certificate authority paradigm has these issues regardless of the underlying cryptographic methods and algorithms employed, and PKI that seeks to endow certificates with trustworthy properties must also address these issues.[*citation needed*]

Here is a list of known blockchain-based PKI:

- CertCoin[23]
- FlyClient[24]
- BlockQuick[25]

History

Developments in PKI occurred in the early 1970s at the British intelligence agency GCHQ, where James Ellis, Clifford Cocks and others made important discoveries related to encryption algorithms and key distribution.[26] Because developments at GCHQ are highly classified, the results of this work were kept secret and not publicly acknowledged until the mid-1990s.

The public disclosure of both secure key exchange and asymmetric key algorithms in 1976 by Diffie, Hellman, Rivest, Shamir, and Adleman changed secure communications entirely. With the further development of high-speed digital electronic communications (the Internet and its predecessors), a need became evident for ways in which users could securely communicate with each other, and as a further consequence of that, for ways in which users could be sure with whom they were actually interacting.

Assorted cryptographic protocols were invented and analyzed within which the new cryptographic primitives could be effectively used. With the invention of the World Wide Web and its rapid spread, the need for authentication and secure communication became still more acute. Commercial reasons alone (e.g., e-commerce, online access to proprietary databases from web browsers) were sufficient. Taher Elgamal and others at Netscape developed the SSL protocol ('https' in Web URLs); it included key establishment, server authentication (prior to v3, one-way only), and so on. A PKI structure was thus created for Web users/sites wishing secure communications.

Vendors and entrepreneurs saw the possibility of a large market, started companies (or new projects at existing companies), and began to agitate for legal recognition and protection from liability. An American Bar Association technology project published an extensive analysis of some of the foreseeable legal aspects of PKI operations (see ABA digital signature guidelines), and shortly thereafter, several U.S. states (Utah being the first in 1995) and other jurisdictions throughout the world began to enact laws and adopt regulations. Consumer groups raised questions about privacy, access, and liability considerations, which were more taken into consideration in some jurisdictions than in others.

The enacted laws and regulations differed, there were technical and operational problems in converting PKI schemes into successful commercial operation, and progress has been much slower than pioneers had imagined it would be.

By the first few years of the 21st century, the underlying cryptographic engineering was clearly not easy to deploy correctly. Operating procedures (manual or automatic) were not easy to correctly design (nor even if so designed, to execute perfectly, which the engineering required). The standards that existed were insufficient.

PKI vendors have found a market, but it is not quite the market envisioned in the mid-1990s, and it has grown both more slowly and in somewhat different ways than were anticipated.[27] PKIs have not solved some of the problems they were expected to, and several major vendors have gone out of business or been acquired by others. PKI has had the most success in government implementations; the largest PKI implementation to date is the Defense Information Systems Agency (DISA) PKI infrastructure for the Common Access Cards program.

Uses

PKIs of one type or another, and from any of several vendors, have many uses, including providing public keys and bindings to user identities which are used for:

- Encryption and/or sender authentication of e-mail messages (e.g., using OpenPGP or S/MIME);
- Encryption and/or authentication of documents (e.g., the XML Signature or XML Encryption standards if documents are encoded as XML);
- Authentication of users to applications (e.g., smart card logon, client authentication with SSL). There's experimental usage for digitally signed HTTP authentication in the Enigform and mod_openpgp projects;
- Bootstrapping secure communication protocols, such as Internet key exchange (IKE) and SSL. In both of these, initial set-up of a secure channel (a "security association") uses asymmetric key—i.e., public key—methods, whereas actual communication uses faster symmetric key—i.e., secret key—

methods;

- Mobile signatures are electronic signatures that are created using a mobile device and rely on signature or certification services in a location independent telecommunication environment;[28]
- Internet of things requires secure communication between mutually trusted devices. A public key infrastructure enables devices to obtain and renew X509 certificates which are used to establish trust between devices and encrypt communications using TLS.

Open source implementations

- OpenSSL is the simplest form of CA and tool for PKI. It is a toolkit, developed in C, that is included in all major Linux distributions, and can be used both to build your own (simple) CA and to PKI-enable applications. (Apache licensed)
- EJBCA is a full-featured, enterprise-grade, CA implementation developed in Java. It can be used to set up a CA both for internal use and as a service. (LGPL licensed)
- XiPKI,[29] CA and OCSP responder. With SHA3 support, implemented in Java. (Apache licensed)
- OpenCA is a full-featured CA implementation using a number of different tools. OpenCA uses OpenSSL for the underlying PKI operations.
- XCA is a graphical interface, and database. XCA uses OpenSSL for the underlying PKI operations.
- (Discontinued) TinyCA was a graphical interface for OpenSSL.
- IoT_pki is a simple PKI built using the python cryptography library
- DogTag is a full featured CA developed and maintained as part of the Fedora Project.
- CFSSL[30][31] open source toolkit developed by CloudFlare for signing, verifying, and bundling TLS certificates. (BSD 2-clause licensed)
- Vault[32] tool for securely managing secrets (TLS certificates included) developed by HashiCorp. (Mozilla Public License 2.0 licensed)
- Libhermetik is a self-contained public-key infrastructure system embedded in a C-language library. Hermetik utilizes LibSodium for all cryptographic operations, and SQLite for all data persistence operations. The software is open-source and released under the ISC license.

Public Key Certificate

In cryptography, a **public key certificate,** also known as a **digital certificate** or **identity certificate,** is an electronic document used to prove the ownership of a public key.[1] The certificate includes information about the key, information about the identity of its owner (called the subject), and the digital signature of an entity that has verified the certificate's contents (called the issuer). If the signature is valid, and the software examining the certificate trusts the issuer, then it can use that key to communicate securely with the certificate's subject. In email encryption, code signing, and e-signature systems, a certificate's subject is typically a person or organization. However, in Transport Layer Security (TLS) a certificate's subject is typically a computer or other device, though TLS certificates may identify organizations or individuals in addition to their core role in identifying devices. TLS, sometimes called by its older name Secure Sockets Layer (SSL), is notable for being a part of HTTPS, a protocol for securely browsing the web.

In a typical public-key infrastructure (PKI) scheme, the certificate issuer is a certificate authority (CA), usually a company that charges customers to issue certificates for them. By contrast, in a web of trust scheme, individuals sign each other's keys directly, in a format that performs a similar function to a public key certificate.

The most common format for public key certificates is defined by X.509.[2] Because X.509 is very general, the format is further constrained by profiles defined for certain use cases, such as Public Key Infrastructure (X.509) as defined in RFC 5280.

Types of certificate

TLS/SSL server certificate

In TLS (an updated replacement for SSL), a server is required to present a certificate as part of the initial connection setup. A client connecting to that server will perform the certification path validation algorithm:

1. The subject of the certificate matches the hostname (i.e. domain name) to which the client is trying to connect;
2. The certificate is signed by a trusted certificate authority.

The primary hostname (domain name of the website) is listed as the **Common Name** in the **Subject** field of the certificate. A certificate may be valid for multiple hostnames (multiple websites). Such certificates are commonly called **Subject Alternative Name (SAN) certificates** or **Unified Communications Certificates (UCC)**. These certificates contain the field Subject Alternative Name, though many CAs will also put them into the **Subject Common Name** field for backward compatibility. If some of the hostnames contain an asterisk (*), a certificate may also be called a wildcard certificate.

A TLS server may be configured with a self-signed certificate. When that is the case, clients will generally be unable to verify the certificate, and will terminate the connection unless certificate checking is disabled.

As per the applications, SSL certificates can be classified into three types:[3]

- Domain Validation SSL;
- Organization Validation SSL;
- Extended Validation SSL.

TLS/SSL client certificate

Client certificates are less common than server certificates, and are used to authenticate the client connecting to a TLS service, for instance to provide access control. Because most services provide access to individuals, rather than devices, most client certificates contain an email address or personal name rather than a hostname. Also, because authentication is usually managed by the service provider, client certificates are not usually issued by a public CA that provides server certificates. Instead, the operator of a service that requires client certificates will usually operate their own internal CA to issue them. Client certificates are supported by many web browsers, but most services use passwords and cookies to authenticate users, instead of client certificates.

Client certificates are more common in RPC systems, where they are used to authenticate devices to ensure that only authorized devices can make certain RPC calls.

Email certificate

In the S/MIME protocol for secure email, senders need to discover which public key to use for any given recipient. They get this information from an email certificate. Some publicly trusted certificate authorities provide email certificates, but more commonly S/MIME is used when communicating within a given organization, and that organization runs its own CA, which is trusted by participants in that email system.

EMV certificate

EMV payment cards are preloaded with a card issuer certificate, signed by the EMV certificate authority[4] to validate authenticity of the payment card during the payment transaction. The EMV CA certificate is loaded on ATM or POS card terminals and is used for validating the card issuer certificate.

Code signing certificate

Certificates can also be used to validate signatures on programs to ensure they were not tampered with during delivery.

Qualified certificate

A certificate identifying an individual, typically for electronic signature purposes. These are most commonly used in Europe, where the eIDAS regulation standardizes them and requires their recognition.

Root certificate

A self-signed certificate used to sign other certificates. Also sometimes called a **trust anchor**.

Intermediate certificate

A certificate used to sign other certificates. An intermediate certificate must be signed by another intermediate certificate or a root certificate.

End-entity or leaf certificate

Any certificate that cannot be used to sign other certificates. For instance, TLS/SSL server and client certificates, email certificates, code signing certificates, and qualified certificates are all end-entity certificates.

Self-signed certificate

A certificate with a subject that matches its issuer, and a signature that can be verified by its own public key. Most types of certificate can be self-signed. Self-signed certificates are also often called **snake oil certificates** to emphasize their untrustworthiness.

Common fields

These are some of the most common fields in certificates. Most certificates contain a number of fields not listed here. Note that in terms of a certificate's X.509 representation, a certificate is not "flat" but contains these fields nested in various structures within the certificate.

- **Serial Number**: Used to uniquely identify the certificate within a CA's systems. In particular this is used to track revocation information.
- **Subject**: The entity a certificate belongs to: a machine, an individual, or an organization.
- **Issuer**: The entity that verified the information and signed the certificate.
- **Not Before**: The earliest time and date on which the certificate is valid. Usually set to a few hours or days prior to the moment the certificate was issued, to avoid clock skew problems.
- **Not After**: The time and date past which the certificate is no longer valid.
- **Key Usage**: The valid cryptographic uses of the certificate's public key. Common values include digital signature validation, key encipherment, and certificate signing.
- **Extended Key Usage**: The applications in which the certificate may be used. Common values include TLS server authentication, email protection, and code signing.
- **Public Key**: A public key belonging to the certificate subject.
- **Signature Algorithm**: The algorithm used to sign the public key certificate.
- **Signature**: A signature of the certificate body by the issuer's private key.

Usage in the European Union

In the European Union, (advanced) electronic signatures on legal documents are commonly performed using digital signatures with accompanying identity certificates. However, only qualified electronic signatures (which require using a qualified trust service provider and signature creation device) are given the same power as a physical signature.

Certificate authorities

In the X.509 trust model, a certificate authority (CA) is responsible for signing certificates. These certificates act as an introduction between two parties, which means that a CA acts as a trusted third party. A CA processes requests from people or organizations requesting certificates (called subscribers), verifies the information, and potentially signs an end-entity certificate based on that information. To perform this role effectively, a CA needs to have one or more broadly trusted root certificates or intermediate certificates and the corresponding private keys. CAs may achieve this broad trust by having their root certificates included in popular software, or by obtaining a cross-signature from another CA delegating trust. Other CAs are trusted within a relatively small community, like a business, and are distributed by other mechanisms like Windows Group Policy.

Certificate authorities are also responsible for maintaining up-to-date revocation information about certificates they have issued, indicating whether certificates are still valid. They provide this information through Online Certificate Status Protocol (OCSP) and/or Certificate Revocation Lists (CRLs). Some of the larger certificate authorities in the market include IdenTrust, DigiCert, and Sectigo.[5]

Root programs

Some major software contain a list of certificate authorities that are trusted by default. This makes it easier for end-users to validate certificates, and easier for people or organizations that request certificates to know which certificate authorities can issue a certificate that will be broadly trusted. This is particularly important in HTTPS, where a web site operator generally wants to get a certificate that is trusted by nearly all potential visitors to their web site.

The policies and processes a provider uses to decide which certificate authorities their software should trust are called root programs. The most influential root programs are:

- Microsoft Root Program
- Apple Root Program
- Mozilla Root Program
- Oracle Java root program
- Adobe AATL Adobe Approved Trust List and EUTL root programs (used for document signing)

Browsers other than Firefox generally use the operating system's facilities to decide which certificate authorities are trusted. So, for instance, Chrome on Windows trusts the certificate authorities included in the Microsoft Root Program, while on macOS or iOS, Chrome trusts the certificate authorities in the Apple Root Program.[6] Edge and Safari use their respective operating system trust stores as well, but each is only available on a single OS. Firefox uses the Mozilla Root Program trust store on all platforms.

The Mozilla Root Program is operated publicly, and its certificate list is part of the open source Firefox web browser, so it is broadly used outside Firefox. For instance, while there is no common Linux Root Program, many Linux distributions, like Debian,[7] include a package that periodically copies the contents of the Firefox trust list, which is then used by applications.

Root programs generally provide a set of valid purposes with the certificates they include. For instance, some CAs may be considered trusted for issuing TLS server certificates, but not for code signing certificates. This is indicated with a set of trust bits in a root certificate storage system.

Certificates and website security

The most common use of certificates is for HTTPS-based web sites. A web browser validates that an HTTPS web server is authentic, so that the user can feel secure that his/her interaction with the web site has no eavesdroppers and that the web site is who it claims to be. This security is important for electronic commerce. In practice, a web site operator obtains a certificate by applying to a certificate authority with a certificate signing request. The certificate request is an electronic document that contains the web site name, company information and the public key. The certificate provider signs the request, thus producing a public certificate. During web browsing, this public certificate is served to any web browser that connects to the web site and proves to the web browser that the provider believes it has issued a certificate to the owner of the web site.

As an example, when a user connects to `https://www.example.com/` with their browser, if the browser does not give any certificate warning message, then the user can be theoretically sure that interacting with `https://www.example.com/` is equivalent to interacting with the entity in contact with the email address listed in the public registrar under "example.com", even though that email address may not be displayed anywhere on the web site. No other surety of any kind is implied. Further, the relationship between the purchaser of the certificate, the operator of the web site, and the generator of the web site content may be tenuous and is not guaranteed. At best, the certificate guarantees uniqueness of the web site, provided that the web site itself has not been compromised (hacked) or the certificate issuing process subverted.

A certificate provider can opt to issue three types of certificates, each requiring its own degree of vetting rigor. In order of increasing rigor (and naturally, cost) they are: Domain Validation, Organization Validation and Extended Validation. These rigors are loosely agreed upon by voluntary participants in the CA/Browser Forum.

Validation levels

Domain validation

A certificate provider will issue a domain-validated (DV) certificate to a purchaser if the purchaser can demonstrate one vetting criterion: the right to administratively manage the affected DNS domain(s).

Organization validation

A certificate provider will issue an organization validation (OV) class certificate to a purchaser if the purchaser can meet two criteria: the right to administratively manage the domain name in question, and perhaps, the organization's actual existence as a legal entity. A certificate provider publishes its OV vetting criteria through its certificate policy.

Extended validation

To acquire an Extended Validation (EV) certificate, the purchaser must persuade the certificate provider of its legal identity, including manual verification checks by a human. As with OV certificates, a certificate provider publishes its EV vetting criteria through its certificate policy.

Until 2019, major browsers such as Chrome and Firefox generally offered users a visual indication of the legal identity when a site presented an EV certificate. This was done by showing the legal name before the domain, and a bright green color to highlight the change. Most browsers deprecated this feature[8][9] providing no visual difference to the user on the type of certificate used. This change followed security concerns raised by forensic experts and successful attempts to purchase EV certificates to impersonate famous organizations, proving the inefficiency of these visual indicators and highlighting potential abuses[10].

Weaknesses

A web browser will give no warning to the user if a web site suddenly presents a different certificate, even if that certificate has a lower number of key bits, even if it has a different provider, and even if the previous certificate had an expiry date far into the future.[*citation needed*] Where certificate providers are under the jurisdiction of governments, those governments may have the freedom to order the provider to generate any certificate, such as for the purposes of law enforcement. Subsidiary wholesale certificate providers also have the freedom to generate any certificate.

All web browsers come with an extensive built-in list of trusted root certificates, many of which are controlled by organizations that may be unfamiliar to the user.[1] Each of these organizations is free to issue any certificate for any web site and have the guarantee that web browsers that include its root certificates will accept it as genuine. In this instance, end users must rely on the developer of the browser software to manage its built-in list of certificates and on the certificate providers to behave correctly and to inform the browser developer of problematic certificates. While uncommon, there have been incidents in which fraudulent certificates have been issued: in some cases, the browsers have detected the fraud; in others, some time passed before browser developers removed these certificates from their software.[11][12]

The list of built-in certificates is also not limited to those provided by the browser developer: users (and to a degree applications) are free to extend the list for special purposes such as for company intranets.[13] This means that if someone gains access to a machine and can install a new root certificate in the browser, that browser will recognize websites that use the inserted certificate as legitimate.

For provable security, this reliance on something external to the system has the consequence that any public key certification scheme has to rely on some special setup assumption, such as the existence of a certificate authority.[14]

Usefulness versus unsecured web sites

In spite of the limitations described above, certificate-authenticated TLS is considered mandatory by all security guidelines whenever a web site hosts confidential information or performs material transactions. This is because, in practice, in spite of the weaknesses described above, web sites secured by public key certificates are still more secure than unsecured http:// web sites.[15]

List of Unix Commands

This is a list of Unix commands as specified by IEEE Std 1003.1-2008, which is part of the Single UNIX Specification (SUS). These commands can be found on Unix operating systems and most Unix-like operating systems.

IEEE Std 1003.1-2008 utilities

Name	Category	Description
admin	SCCS	Create and administer SCCS files
alias	Misc	Define or display aliases
ar	Misc	Create and maintain library archives
asa	Text processing	Interpret carriage-control characters
at	Process management	Execute commands at a later time
awk	Text processing	Pattern scanning and processing language
basename	Filesystem	Return non-directory portion of a pathname; see also dirname
batch	Process management	Schedule commands to be executed in a batch queue
bc	Misc	Arbitrary-precision arithmetic language
bg	Process management	Run jobs in the background
cc/c99	C programming	Compile standard C programs

Name	Category	Description
cal	Misc	Print a calendar
cat	Filesystem	Concatenate and print files
cd	Filesystem	Change the working directory
cflow	C programming	Generate a C-language call graph
chgrp	Filesystem	Change the file group ownership
chmod	Filesystem	Change the file modes/attributes/permissions
chown	Filesystem	Change the file ownership
cksum	Filesystem	Write file checksums and sizes
cmp	Filesystem	Compare two files; see also diff
comm	Text processing	Select or reject lines common to two files
command	Shell programming	Execute a simple command
compress	Filesystem	Compress data
cp	Filesystem	Copy files
crontab	Misc	Schedule periodic background work
csplit	Text processing	Split files based on context
ctags	C programming	Create a tags file
cut	Text processing	Cut out selected fields of each line of a file
cxref	C programming	Generate a C-language program cross-reference table
date	Misc	Display the date and time
dd	Filesystem	Convert and copy a file
delta	SCCS	Make a delta (change) to an SCCS file
df	Filesystem	Report free disk space
diff	Text processing	Compare two files; see also cmp
dirname	Filesystem	Return the directory portion of a pathname; see also basename
du	Filesystem	Estimate file space usage
echo	Shell programming	Write arguments to standard output
ed	Text processing	The standard text editor
env	Misc	Set the environment for command invocation
ex	Text processing	Text editor
expand	Text processing	Convert tabs to spaces
expr	Shell programming	Evaluate arguments as an expression
false	Shell programming	Return false value
fc	Misc	Process the command history list
fg	Process management	Run jobs in the foreground
file	Filesystem	Determine file type
find	Filesystem	Find files

Name	Category	Description
fold	Text processing	Filter for folding lines
fort77	FORTRAN77 programming	FORTRAN compiler
fuser	Process management	List process IDs of all processes that have one or more files open
gencat	Misc	Generate a formatted message catalog
get	SCCS	Get a version of an SCCS file
getconf	Misc	Get configuration values
getopts	Shell programming	Parse utility options
grep	Misc	Search text for a pattern
hash	Misc	Hash database access method
head	Text processing	Copy the first part of files
iconv	Text processing	Codeset conversion
id	Misc	Return user identity
ipcrm	Misc	Remove a message queue, semaphore set, or shared memory segment identifier
ipcs	Misc	Report interprocess communication facilities status
jobs	Process management	Display status of jobs in the current session
join	Text processing	Merges two sorted text files based on the presence of a common field
kill	Process management	Terminate or signal processes
lex	C programming	Generate programs for lexical tasks
link	Filesystem	Create a hard link to a file
ln	Filesystem	Link files
locale	Misc	Get locale-specific information
localedef	Misc	Define locale environment
logger	Shell programming	Log messages
logname	Misc	Return the user's login name
lp	Text processing	Send files to a printer
ls	Filesystem	List directory contents
m4	Misc	Macro processor
mailx	Misc	Process messages
make	Programming	Maintain, update, and regenerate groups of programs
man	Misc	Display system documentation
mesg	Misc	Permit or deny messages
mkdir	Filesystem	Make directories
mkfifo	Filesystem	Make FIFO special files
more	Text processing	Display files on a page-by-page basis

Name	Category	Description
mv	Filesystem	Move or rename files
newgrp	Misc	Change to a new group
nice	Process management	Invoke a utility with an altered nice value
nl	Text processing	Line numbering filter
nm	C programming	Write the name list of an object file
nohup	Process management	Invoke a utility immune to hangups
od	Misc	Dump files in various formats
paste	Text processing	Merge corresponding or subsequent lines of files
patch	Text processing	Apply changes to files
pathchk	Filesystem	Check pathnames
pax	Misc	Portable archive interchange
pr	Text processing	Print files
printf	Shell programming	Write formatted output
prs	SCCS	Print an SCCS file
ps	Process management	Report process status
pwd	Filesystem	Print working directory
qalter	Batch utilities	Alter batch job
qdel	Batch utilities	Delete batch jobs
qhold	Batch utilities	Hold batch jobs
qmove	Batch utilities	Move batch jobs
qmsg	Batch utilities	Send message to batch jobs
qrerun	Batch utilities	Rerun batch jobs
qrls	Batch utilities	Release batch jobs
qselect	Batch utilities	Select batch jobs
qsig	Batch utilities	Signal batch jobs
qstat	Batch utilities	Show status of batch jobs
qsub	Batch utilities	Submit a script
read	Shell programming	Read a line from standard input
renice	Process management	Set nice values of running processes
rm	Filesystem	Remove directory entries
rmdel	SCCS	Remove a delta from an SCCS file
rmdir	Filesystem	Remove directories, if they are empty.
sact	SCCS	Print current SCCS file-editing activity
sccs	SCCS	Front end for the SCCS subsystem
sed	Text processing	Stream editor
sh	Shell programming	Shell, the standard command language interpreter

Name	Category	Description
sleep	Shell programming	Suspend execution for an interval
sort	Text processing	Sort, merge, or sequence check text files
split	Misc	Split files into pieces
strings	C programming	Find printable strings in files
strip	C programming	Remove unnecessary information from executable files
stty	Misc	Set the options for a terminal
tabs	Misc	Set terminal tabs
tail	Text processing	Copy the last part of a file
talk	Misc	Talk to another user
tee	Shell programming	Duplicate the standard output
test	Shell programming	Evaluate expression
time	Process management	Time a simple command
touch	Filesystem	Change file access and modification times
tput	Misc	Change terminal characteristics
tr	Text processing	Translate characters
true	Shell programming	Return true value
tsort	Text processing	Topological sort
tty	Misc	Return user's terminal name
type	Misc	Displays how a name would be interpreted if used as a command
ulimit	Misc	Set or report file size limit
umask	Misc	Get or set the file mode creation mask
unalias	Misc	Remove alias definitions
uname	Misc	Return system name
uncompress	Misc	Expand compressed data
unexpand	Text processing	Convert spaces to tabs
unget	SCCS	Undo a previous get of an SCCS file
uniq	Text processing	Report or filter out repeated lines in a file
unlink	Filesystem	Call the unlink function
uucp	Network	System-to-system copy
uudecode	Network	Decode a binary file
uuencode	Network	Encode a binary file
uustat	Network	uucp status inquiry and job control
uux	Process management	Remote command execution
val	SCCS	Validate SCCS files
vi	Text processing	Screen-oriented (visual) display editor
wait	Process management	Await process completion

Name	Category	Description
wc	Text processing	Line, word and byte or character count
what	SCCS	Identify SCCS files
who	System administration	Display who is on the system
write	Misc	Write to another user's terminal
xargs	Shell programming	Construct argument lists and invoke utility
yacc	C programming	Yet another compiler compiler
zcat	Text processing	Expand and concatenate data

Social engineering (security), References

1. *Anderson, Ross J. (2008). Security engineering: a guide to building dependable distributed systems (2nd ed.). Indianapolis, IN: Wiley. p. 1040. ISBN 978-0-470-06852-6.* Chapter 2, page 17
2. *"Social Engineering Defined". Security Through Education. Retrieved 3 October 2018.*
3. Lim, Joo S., et al. "Exploring the Relationship between Organizational Culture and Information Security Culture." Australian Information Security Management Conference.
4. Anderson, D., Reimers, K. and Barretto, C. (March 2014). Post-Secondary Education Network Security: Results of Addressing the End-User Challenge.publication date 11 March 2014 publication description INTED2014 (International Technology, Education, and Development Conference)
5. *Schlienger, Thomas; Teufel, Stephanie (2003). "Information security culture-from analysis to change". South African Computer Journal. 31: 46–52.*
6. Jaco, K: "CSEPS Course Workbook" (2004), unit 3, Jaco Security Publishing.
7. *Hatfield, Joseph M (June 2019). "Virtuous human hacking: The ethics of social engineering in penetration-testing". Computers & Security. 83: 354–366. doi:10.1016/j.cose.2019.02.012.*
8. The story of HP pretexting scandal with discussion is available at *Davani, Faraz (14 August 2011). "HP Pretexting Scandal by Faraz Davani". Retrieved 15 August 2011 – via Scribd.*
9. "Pretexting: Your Personal Information Revealed", Federal Trade Commission
10. *Fagone, Jason (24 November 2015). "The Serial Swatter". The New York Times. Retrieved 25 November 2015.*
11. *"The Real Dangers of Spear-Phishing Attacks". FireEye. 2016. Retrieved 9 October 2016.*
12. *"Chinese Espionage Campaign Compromises Forbes.com to Target US Defense, Financial Services Companies in Watering Hole Style Attack". invincea.com. 10 February 2015. Retrieved 23 February 2017.*
13. *"Social Engineering, the USB Way". Light Reading Inc. 7 June 2006. Archived from the original on 13 July 2006. Retrieved 23 April 2014.*
14. *"Archived copy" (PDF). Archived from the original (PDF) on 11 October 2007. Retrieved 2 March 2012.*
15. *Conklin, Wm. Arthur; White, Greg; Cothren, Chuck; Davis, Roger; Williams, Dwayne (2015). Principles of Computer Security, Fourth Edition (Official Comptia Guide). New York: McGraw-Hill Education. pp. 193–194. ISBN 978-0071835978.*
16. *Raywood, Dan (4 August 2016). "#BHUSA Dropped USB Experiment Detailed". info security. Retrieved 28 July 2017.*
17. *Leyden, John (18 April 2003). "Office workers give away passwords". The Register. Retrieved 11 April 2012.*
18. *"Passwords revealed by sweet deal". BBC News. 20 April 2004. Retrieved 11 April 2012.*
19. Treglia, J., & Delia, M. (2017). Cyber Security Inoculation. Presented at NYS Cyber Security Conference, Empire State Plaza Convention Center, Albany, NY, 3–4 June.
20. Mitnick, K., & Simon, W. (2005). "The Art of Intrusion". Indianapolis, IN: Wiley Publishing.
21. Allsopp, William. Unauthorised access: Physical penetration testing for it security teams. Hoboken, NJ: Wiley, 2009. 240–241.
22. *"social engineering – GW Information Security Blog". blogs.gwu.edu. Retrieved 18 February 2020.*
23. *Salinger, Lawrence M. (2005). Encyclopedia of White-Collar & Corporate Crime. SAGE. ISBN 978-0-7619-3004-4.*
24. *"How Frank Abagnale Would Swindle You". U.S. News. 17 December 2019. Archived from the original on 28 April 2013. Retrieved 17 December 2019.*
25. *"Kevin Mitnick sentenced to nearly four years in prison; computer hacker ordered to pay restitution to victim companies whose systems were compromised" (Press release). United States Attorney's Office, Central District of California. 9 August 1999. Archived from the original on 13 June 2013.*
26. *"DEF CON III Archives – Susan Thunder Keynote". DEF CON. Retrieved 12 August 2017.*
27. *"Archived copy". Archived from the original on 17 April 2001. Retrieved 6 January 2007.*
28. *Hafner, Katie (August 1995). "Kevin Mitnick, unplugged". Esquire. 124 (2): 80(9).*
29. *"Wired 12.02: Three Blind Phreaks". Wired. 14 June 1999. Retrieved 11 April 2012.*
30. *"43 Best Social Engineering Books of All Time". BookAuthority. Retrieved 22 January 2020.*
31. \ *(31 August 2018). "Bens Book of the Month Review of Social Engineering The Science of Human Hacking". RSA Conference. Retrieved 22 January 2020.*
32. *"Book Review: Social Engineering: The Science of Human Hacking". The Ethical Hacker Network. 26 July 2018. Retrieved 22 January 2020.*
33. *Hadnagy, Christopher; Fincher, Michele (22 January 2020). "Phishing Dark Waters: The Offensive and Defensive Sides of Malicious E-mails". ISACA. Retrieved 22 January 2020.*
34. *"WTVR:"Protect Your Kids from Online Threats"*
35. *Larson, Selena (14 August 2017). "Hacker creates organization to unmask child predators". CNN. Retrieved 14 November 2019.*
36. Restatement 2d of Torts § 652C.
37. *"Congress outlaws pretexting". 109th Congress (2005–2006) H.R.4709 – Telephone Records and Privacy Protection Act of 2006. 2007.*
38. Mitnick, K (2002): "The Art of Deception", p. 103 Wiley Publishing Ltd: Indianapolis, Indiana; United States of America. ISBN 0-471-23712-4
39. HP chairman: Use of pretexting 'embarrassing' Stephen Shankland, 8 September 2006 1:08 PM PDT *CNET News.com*
40. *"Calif. court drops charges against Dunn". CNET. 14 March 2007. Retrieved 11 April 2012.*
41. *"What is Social Engineering | Attack Techniques & Prevention Methods | Imperva". Learning Center. Retrieved 18 February 2020.*
42. *"Amazon.fr: Maxime Frantini: Livres, Biographie, écrits, livres audio, Kindle". Retrieved 30 November 2016.*
43. *"Analyzing the Hacks: The Girl in the Spider's Web Explained". WonderHowTo. Retrieved 13 December 2019.*

Malware, References

1. *"Defining Malware: FAQ". technet.microsoft.com. Retrieved 10 September 2009.*
2. *"An Undirected Attack Against Critical Infrastructure" (PDF). United States Computer Emergency Readiness Team(Us-cert.gov). Retrieved 28 September 2014.*
3. *Klein, Tobias (11 October 2011). A Bug Hunter's Diary: A Guided Tour Through the Wilds of Software Security. No Starch Press. ISBN 978-1-59327-415-3.*
4. *Russinovich, Mark (31 October 2005). "Sony, Rootkits and Digital Rights Management Gone Too Far". Mark's Blog. Microsoft MSDN. Retrieved 29 July 2009.*
5. *"Protect Your Computer from Malware". OnGuardOnline.gov. 11 October 2012. Retrieved 26 August 2013.*
6. *Tipton, Harold F. (26 December 2002). Information Security Management Handbook. CRC Press. ISBN 978-1-4200-7241-9.*
7. *"Malware". FEDERAL TRADE COMMISSION- CONSUMER INFORMATION. Retrieved 27 March 2014.*
8. *Hernandez, Pedro. "Microsoft Vows to Combat Government Cyber-Spying". eWeek. Retrieved 15 December 2013.*
9. *Kovacs, Eduard. "MiniDuke Malware Used Against European Government Organizations". Softpedia. Retrieved 27 February 2013.*
10. *"Malware Revolution: A Change in Target". March 2007.*
11. *"Child Porn: Malware's Ultimate Evil". November 2009.*
12. PC World – Zombie PCs: Silent, Growing Threat.
13. *"Peer To Peer Information". NORTH CAROLINA STATE UNIVERSITY. Retrieved 25 March 2011.*
14. *Richardson, Ronny; North, Max (1 January 2017). "Ransomware: Evolution, Mitigation and Prevention". International Management Review. 13 (1): 10–21.*
15. *Fruhlinger, Josh (1 August 2017). "The 5 biggest ransomware attacks of the last 5 years". CSO. Retrieved 23 March 2018.*
16. *"Another way Microsoft is disrupting the malware ecosystem". Archived from the original on 20 September 2015. Retrieved 18 February 2015.*
17. *"Shamoon is latest malware to target energy sector". Retrieved 18 February 2015.*
18. *"Computer-killing malware used in Sony attack a wake-up call". Retrieved 18 February 2015.*
19. *"computer virus – Encyclopædia Britannica". Britannica.com. Retrieved 28 April 2013.*
20. *"All about Malware and Information Privacy - TechAcute". techacute.com. 31 August 2014.*
21. *"What are viruses, worms, and Trojan horses?". Indiana University. The Trustees of Indiana University. Retrieved 23 February 2015.*
22. *Peter Szor (3 February 2005). The Art of Computer Virus Research and Defense. Pearson Education. p. 204. ISBN 978-0-672-33390-3.*
23. *"Rise of Android Ransomware, research" (PDF). ESET.*
24. *"State of Malware, research" (PDF). Malwarebytes.*
25. *Landwehr, C. E; A. R Bull; J. P McDermott; W. S Choi (1993). A taxonomy of computer program security flaws, with examples. DTIC Document. Retrieved 5 April 2012.*
26. *"Trojan Horse Definition". Retrieved 5 April 2012.*
27. *"Trojan horse". Webopedia. Retrieved 5 April 2012.*
28. *"What is Trojan horse? – Definition from Whatis.com". Retrieved 5 April 2012.*
29. *"Trojan Horse: [coined By MIT-hacker-turned-NSA-spook Dan Edwards] N." Archived from the original on 5 July 2017. Retrieved 5 April 2012.*
30. *"What is the difference between viruses, worms, and Trojan horses?". Symantec Corporation. Retrieved 10 January 2009.*
31. *"VIRUS-L/comp.virus Frequently Asked Questions (FAQ) v2.00 (Question B3: What is a Trojan horse?)". 9 October 1995. Retrieved 13 September 2012.*
32. *"Proton Mac Trojan Has Apple Code Signing Signatures Sold to Customers for $50k". AppleInsider.*
33. *"Non-Windows Malware". Betanews. 24 August 2017.*
34. *McDowell, Mindi. "Understanding Hidden Threats: Rootkits and Botnets". US-CERT. Retrieved 6 February 2013.*
35. *"Catb.org". Catb.org. Retrieved 15 April 2010.*
36. *Vincentas (11 July 2013). "Malware in SpyWareLoop.com". Spyware Loop. Retrieved 28 July 2013.*
37. *Staff, SPIEGEL (29 December 2013). "Inside TAO: Documents Reveal Top NSA Hacking Unit". Spiegel Online. SPIEGEL. Retrieved 23 January 2014.*
38. *Edwards, John. "Top Zombie, Trojan Horse and Bot Threats". IT Security. Archived from the original on 9 February 2017. Retrieved 25 September 2007.*
39. *Appelbaum, Jacob (29 December 2013). "Shopping for Spy Gear:Catalog Advertises NSA Toolbox". Spiegel Online. SPIEGEL. Retrieved 29 December 2013.*
40. *"Evasive malware goes mainstream - Help Net Security". net-security.org. 22 April 2015.*
41. *Kirat, Dhilung; Vigna, Giovanni; Kruegel, Christopher (2014). Barecloud: bare-metal analysis-based evasive malware detection. ACM. pp. 287–301. ISBN 978-1-931971-15-7.* Freely accessible at: *"Barecloud: bare-metal analysis-based evasive malware detection" (PDF).*
42. The Four Most Common Evasive Techniques Used by Malware. 27 April 2015.
43. *Young, Adam; Yung, Moti (1997). "Deniable Password Snatching: On the Possibility of Evasive Electronic Espionage". Symp. on Security and Privacy. IEEE. pp. 224–235. ISBN 0-8186-7828-3.*
44. *Casey, Henry T. (25 November 2015). "Latest adware disables antivirus software". Tom's Guide. Yahoo.com. Retrieved 25 November 2015.*
45. *Cabaj, Krzysztof; Caviglione, Luca; Mazurczyk, Wojciech; Wendzel, Steffen; Woodward, Alan; Zander, Sebastian (May 2018). "The New Threats of Information Hiding: The Road Ahead". IT Professional. 20 (3): 31–39. arXiv:1801.00694. doi:10.1109/MITP.2018.032501746. S2CID 22328658.*
46. *"Penn State WebAccess Secure Login". webaccess.psu.edu. doi:10.1145/3365001. Retrieved 29 February 2020.*
47. *"Malware Dynamic Analysis Evasion Techniques: A Survey". ResearchGate. Retrieved 29 February 2020.*

48. *"Global Web Browser... Security Trends" (PDF). Kaspersky lab. November 2012.*
49. *Rashid, Fahmida Y. (27 November 2012). "Updated Browsers Still Vulnerable to Attack if Plugins Are Outdated". pcmag.com. Archived from the original on 9 April 2016. Retrieved 17 January 2013.*
50. *Danchev, Dancho (18 August 2011). "Kaspersky: 12 different vulnerabilities detected on every PC". pcmag.com.*
51. *"Adobe Security bulletins and advisories". Adobe.com. Retrieved 19 January 2013.*
52. *Rubenking, Neil J. "Secunia Personal Software Inspector 3.0 Review & Rating". PCMag.com. Retrieved 19 January 2013.*
53. *"USB devices spreading viruses". CNET. CBS Interactive. Retrieved 18 February 2015.*
54. https://enterprise.verizon.com/resources/reports/DBIR_2018_Report.pdf
55. *Fruhlinger, Josh (10 October 2018). "Top cybersecurity facts, figures and statistics for 2018". CSO Online. Retrieved 20 January 2020.*
56. "LNCS 3786 – Key Factors Influencing Worm Infection", U. Kanlayasiri, 2006, web (PDF): SL40-PDF.
57. *"How Antivirus Software Works?". Retrieved 16 October 2015.*
58. *Souppaya, Murugiah; Scarfone, Karen (July 2013). "Guide to Malware Incident Prevention and Handling for Desktops and Laptops". National Institute of Standards and Technology. doi:10.6028/nist.sp.800-83r1.*
59. *"Microsoft Security Essentials". Microsoft. Retrieved 21 June 2012.*
60. *"Malicious Software Removal Tool". Microsoft. Archived from the original on 21 June 2012. Retrieved 21 June 2012.*
61. *"Windows Defender". Microsoft. Archived from the original on 22 June 2012. Retrieved 21 June 2012.*
62. *Rubenking, Neil J. (8 January 2014). "The Best Free Antivirus for 2014". pcmag.com.*
63. *"Free antivirus profiles in 2018". antivirusgratis.org. Archived from the original on 10 August 2018. Retrieved 13 February 2020.*
64. *"Quickly identify malware running on your PC". techadvisor.co.uk.*
65. *"How do I remove a computer virus?". Microsoft. Retrieved 26 August 2013.*
66. *"Microsoft Safety Scanner". Microsoft. Retrieved 26 August 2013.*
67. *"An example of a website vulnerability scanner". Unmaskparasites.com. Retrieved 19 January 2013.*
68. *"Redleg's File Viewer. Used to check a webpage for malicious redirects or malicious HTML coding". Aw-snap.info. Retrieved 19 January 2013.*
69. *"Example Google.com Safe Browsing Diagnostic page". Retrieved 19 January 2013.*
70. *"Safe Browsing (Google Online Security Blog)". Retrieved 21 June 2012.*
71. *"Wordpress malware redirect". wphackedhelp.com. 23 May 2018. Retrieved 20 February 2020.*
72. M. Guri, G. Kedma, A. Kachlon and Y. Elovici, "AirHopper: Bridging the air-gap between isolated networks and mobile phones using radio frequencies," *Malicious and Unwanted Software: The Americas (MALWARE), 2014 9th International Conference on, Fajardo, PR, 2014, pp. 58-67.*
73. M. Guri, M. Monitz, Y. Mirski and Y. Elovici, "BitWhisper: Covert Signaling Channel between Air-Gapped Computers Using Thermal Manipulations," *2015 IEEE 28th Computer Security Foundations Symposium, Verona, 2015, pp. 276-289.*
74. GSMem: Data Exfiltration from Air-Gapped Computers over GSM Frequencies. Mordechai Guri, Assaf Kachlon, Ofer Hasson, Gabi Kedma, Yisroel Mirsky, and Yuval Elovici, *Ben-Gurion University of the Negev; USENIX Security Symposium 2015*
75. *Hanspach, Michael; Goetz, Michael; Daidakulov, Andrey; Elovici, Yuval (2016). "Fansmitter: Acoustic Data Exfiltration from (Speakerless) Air-Gapped Computers". arXiv:1606.05915 [cs.CR].*
76. *Vincentas (11 July 2013). "Grayware in SpyWareLoop.com". Spyware Loop. Archived from the original on 15 July 2014. Retrieved 28 July 2013.*
77. *"Threat Encyclopedia – Generic Grayware". Trend Micro. Retrieved 27 November 2012.*
78. *"Rating the best anti-malware solutions". Arstechnica. 15 December 2009. Retrieved 28 January 2014.*
79. *"PUP Criteria". malwarebytes.org. Retrieved 13 February 2015.*
80. *"Boot sector virus repair". Antivirus.about.com. 10 June 2010. Archived from the original on 12 January 2011. Retrieved 27 August 2010.*
81. *Avoine, Gildas; Pascal Junod; Philippe Oechslin (2007). Computer system security: basic concepts and solved exercises. EFPL Press. p. 20. ISBN 978-1-4200-4620-5.* The first PC virus is credited to two brothers, Basit Farooq Alvi and Amjad Farooq Alvi, from Pakistan
82. *William A Hendric (4 September 2014). "Computer Virus history". The Register. Retrieved 29 March 2015.*
83. *"Cryptomining Worm MassMiner Exploits Multiple Vulnerabilities - Security Boulevard". Security Boulevard. 2 May 2018. Retrieved 9 May 2018.*
84. *"Malware: Types, Protection, Prevention, Detection & Removal - Ultimate Guide". EasyTechGuides.*
85. *"Beware of Word Document Viruses". us.norton.com. Retrieved 25 September 2017.*
86. John von Neumann, "Theory of Self-Reproducing Automata", Part 1: Transcripts of lectures given at the University of Illinois, December 1949, Editor: A. W. Burks, University of Illinois, USA, 1966.
87. Fred Cohen, "Computer Viruses", PhD Thesis, University of Southern California, ASP Press, 1988.
88. *Young, Adam; Yung, Moti (2004). Malicious cryptography - exposing cryptovirology. Wiley. pp. 1 392. ISBN 978-0-7645-4975-5.*

Security testing, References

1. M Martellini, & Malizia, A. (2017). Cyber and chemical, biological, radiological, nuclear, explosives challenges : threats and counter efforts. Springer.
2. "Introduction to Information Security" US-CERT https://www.us-cert.gov/security-publications/introduction-information-security

Vulnerability (computing), References

1. *"Vulnerability Management Life Cycle | NPCR | CDC". www.cdc.gov. 2019-03-12. Retrieved 2020-07-04.*
2. ISO/IEC, "Information technology -- Security techniques-Information security risk management" ISO/IEC FIDIS 27005:2008
3. British Standard Institute, Information technology -- Security techniques -- Management of information and communications technology security -- Part 1: Concepts and models for information and communications technology security management BS ISO/IEC 13335-1-2004
4. Internet Engineering Task Force RFC 4949 Internet Security Glossary, Version 2
5. *"CNSS Instruction No. 4009" (PDF). 26 April 2010. Archived from the original (PDF) on 2013-06-28.*
6. *"FISMApedia". fismapedia.org.*
7. *"Term:Vulnerability". fismapedia.org.*
8. NIST SP 800-30 Risk Management Guide for Information Technology Systems
9. *"Glossary". europa.eu.*
10. Technical Standard Risk Taxonomy ISBN 1-931624-77-1 Document Number: C081 Published by The Open Group, January 2009.
11. "An Introduction to Factor Analysis of Information Risk (FAIR)", Risk Management Insight LLC, November 2006 Archived 2014-11-18 at the Wayback Machine;
12. Matt Bishop and Dave Bailey. A Critical Analysis of Vulnerability Taxonomies. Technical Report CSE-96-11, Department of Computer Science at the University of California at Davis, September 1996
13. Schou, Corey (1996). Handbook of INFOSEC Terms, Version 2.0. CD-ROM (Idaho State University & Information Systems Security Organization)
14. NIATEC Glossary
15. ISACA THE RISK IT FRAMEWORK (registration required) Archived July 5, 2010, at the Wayback Machine
16. *Wright, Joe; Harmening, Jim (2009). "15". In Vacca, John (ed.). Computer and Information Security Handbook. Morgan Kaufmann Publications. Elsevier Inc. p. 257. ISBN 978-0-12-374354-1.*
17. *Kakareka, Almantas (2009). "23". In Vacca, John (ed.). Computer and Information Security Handbook. Morgan Kaufmann Publications. Elsevier Inc. p. 393. ISBN 978-0-12-374354-1.*
18. *Krsul, Ivan (April 15, 1997). "Technical Report CSD-TR-97-026". The COAST Laboratory Department of Computer Sciences, Purdue University. CiteSeerX 10.1.1.26.5435.*
19. *Pauli, Darren (16 January 2017). "Just give up: 123456 is still the world's most popular password". The Register. Retrieved 2017-01-17.*
20. *"The Six Dumbest Ideas in Computer Security". ranum.com.*
21. *"The Web Application Security Consortium / Web Application Security Statistics". webappsec.org.*
22. Ross Anderson. Why Cryptosystems Fail. Technical report, University Computer Laboratory, Cam- bridge, January 1994.
23. Neil Schlager. When Technology Fails: Significant Technological Disasters, Accidents, and Failures of the Twentieth Century. Gale Research Inc., 1994.
24. Hacking: The Art of Exploitation Second Edition
25. *Kiountouzis, E. A.; Kokolakis, S. A. Information systems security: facing the information society of the 21st century. London: Chapman & Hall, Ltd. ISBN 0-412-78120-4.*
26. *Rasmussen, Jeremy (February 12, 2018). "Best Practices for Cybersecurity: Stay Cyber SMART". Tech Decisions. Retrieved September 18, 2020.*
27. *Bavisi, Sanjay (2009). "22". In Vacca, John (ed.). Computer and Information Security Handbook. Morgan Kaufmann Publications. Elsevier Inc. p. 375. ISBN 978-0-12-374354-1.*
28. *"The new era of vulnerability disclosure - a brief chat with HD Moore". The Tech Herald. Archived from the original on 2010-08-26. Retrieved 2010-08-24.*
29. *Betz, Chris (11 Jan 2015). "A Call for Better Coordinated Vulnerability Disclosure - MSRC - Site Home - TechNet Blogs". blogs.technet.com. Retrieved 12 January 2015.*
30. *"Category:Vulnerability". owasp.org.*
31. *David Harley (10 March 2015). "Operating System Vulnerabilities, Exploits and Insecurity". Retrieved 15 January 2019.*
32. Most laptops vulnerable to attack via peripheral devices. http://www.sciencedaily.com/releases/2019/02/190225192119.htm Source: University of Cambridge]
33. Exploiting Network Printers. Institute for IT-Security, Ruhr University Bochum
34. [1] Archived October 21, 2007, at the Wayback Machine
35. *"Jesse Ruderman » Race conditions in security dialogs". squarefree.com.*
36. *"lcamtuf's blog". lcamtuf.blogspot.com.*
37. *"Warning Fatigue". freedom-to-tinker.com.*

Computer security, References

1. *Schatz, Daniel; Bashroush, Rabih; Wall, Julie (2017). "Towards a More Representative Definition of Cyber Security". Journal of Digital Forensics, Security and Law. 12 (2). ISSN 1558-7215.*
2. "Reliance spells end of road for ICT amateurs", 7 May 2013, The Australian
3. *Stevens, Tim (11 June 2018). "Global Cybersecurity: New Directions in Theory and Methods" (PDF). Politics and Governance. 6 (2): 1–4. doi:10.17645/pag.v6i2.1569.*

4. "Computer Security and Mobile Security Challenges". researchgate.net. 3 December 2015. Archived from the original on 12 October 2016. Retrieved 4 August 2016.
5. "Ghidra".
6. "Syzbot: Google Continuously Fuzzing The Linux Kernel".
7. "Distributed Denial of Service Attack". csa.gov.sg. Archived from the original on 6 August 2016. Retrieved 12 November 2014.
8. "Multi-Vector Attacks Demand Multi-Vector Protection". MSSP Alert. 24 July 2018.
9. Millman, Renee (15 December 2017). "New polymorphic malware evades three quarters of AV scanners". SC Magazine UK.
10. "Identifying Phishing Attempts". Case. Archived from the original on 13 September 2015. Retrieved 4 July 2016.
11. "Phishers send fake invoices". Consumer Information. 23 February 2018. Retrieved 17 February 2020.
12. Eilam, Eldad (2005). Reversing: secrets of reverse engineering. John Wiley & Sons. ISBN 978-0-7645-7481-8.
13. Arcos Sergio. "Social Engineering" (PDF). Archived (PDF) from the original on 3 December 2013.
14. Scannell, Kara (24 February 2016). "CEO email scam costs companies $2bn". Financial Times (25 Feb 2016). Archived from the original on 23 June 2016. Retrieved 7 May 2016.
15. "Bucks leak tax info of players, employees as result of email scam". Associated Press. 20 May 2016. Archived from the original on 20 May 2016. Retrieved 20 May 2016.
16. "What is Spoofing? – Definition from Techopedia". Archived from the original on 30 June 2016.
17. Butterfield, Andrew; Ngondi, Gerard Ekembe, eds. (21 January 2016). spoofing. Oxford Reference. Oxford University Press. doi:10.1093/acref/9780199688975.001.0001. ISBN 9780199688975. Retrieved 8 October 2017.
18. Marcel, Sébastien; Nixon, Mark; Li, Stan, eds. (2014). Handbook of Biometric Anti-Spoofing: Trusted Biometrics under Spoofing Attacks. Advances in Computer Vision and Pattern Recognition. London: Springer. doi:10.1007/978-1-4471-6524-8. ISBN 978-1-4471-6524-8. ISSN 2191-6594. LCCN 2014942635. S2CID 27594864.
19. Gallagher, Sean (14 May 2014). "Photos of an NSA "upgrade" factory show Cisco router getting implant". Ars Technica. Archived from the original on 4 August 2014. Retrieved 3 August 2014.
20. Bendovschi, Andreea (2015). "Cyber-Attacks – Trends, Patterns and Security Countermeasures" (PDF). ELSEVIER (2015): 8.
21. Lim, Joo S., et al. "Exploring the Relationship between Organizational Culture and Information Security Culture." Australian Information Security Management Conference.
22. K. Reimers, D. Andersson (2017) POST-SECONDARY EDUCATION NETWORK SECURITY: THE END USER CHALLENGE AND EVOLVING THREATS, ICERI2017 Proceedings, pp. 1787-1796.
23. Schlienger, Thomas; Teufel, Stephanie (2003). "Information security culture-from analysis to change". South African Computer Journal. **31**: 46–52.
24. Lin, Tom C. W. (3 July 2017). "The New Market Manipulation". Emory Law Journal. **66**: 1253. SSRN 2996896.
25. Lin, Tom C. W. (2016). "Financial Weapons of War". Minnesota Law Review. SSRN 2765010.
26. Pagliery, Jose (18 November 2014). "Hackers attacked the U.S. energy grid 79 times this year". CNN Money. Cable News Network. Archived from the original on 18 February 2015. Retrieved 16 April 2015.
27. P. G. Neumann, "Computer Security in Aviation," presented at International Conference on Aviation Safety and Security in the 21st Century, White House Commission on Safety and Security, 1997.
28. J. Zellan, Aviation Security. Hauppauge, NY: Nova Science, 2003, pp. 65–70.
29. "Air Traffic Control Systems Vulnerabilities Could Make for Unfriendly Skies [Black Hat] - SecurityWeek.Com". Archived from the original on 8 February 2015.
30. "Hacker Says He Can Break Into Airplane Systems Using In-Flight Wi-Fi". NPR.org. 4 August 2014. Archived from the original on 8 February 2015.
31. Jim Finkle (4 August 2014). "Hacker says to show passenger jets at risk of cyber attack". Reuters. Archived from the original on 13 October 2015.
32. "Pan-European Network Services (PENS) - Eurocontrol.int". Archived from the original on 12 December 2016.
33. "Centralised Services: NewPENS moves forward - Eurocontrol.int". 17 January 2016. Archived from the original on 19 March 2017.
34. "NextGen Data Communication". FAA. Archived from the original on 13 March 2015. Retrieved 15 June 2017.
35. "Is Your Watch Or Thermostat A Spy? Cybersecurity Firms Are On It". NPR.org. 6 August 2014. Archived from the original on 11 February 2015.
36. Melvin Backman (18 September 2014). "Home Depot: 56 million cards exposed in breach". CNNMoney. Archived from the original on 18 December 2014.
37. "Staples: Breach may have affected 1.16 million customers' cards". Fortune.com. 19 December 2014. Archived from the original on 21 December 2014. Retrieved 21 December 2014.
38. CNNMoney Staff (19 December 2013). "Target: 40 million credit cards compromised". CNN. Archived from the original on 1 December 2017. Retrieved 29 November 2017.
39. Cowley, Stacy (2 October 2017). "2.5 Million More People Potentially Exposed in Equifax Breach". The New York Times. Archived from the original on 1 December 2017. Retrieved 29 November 2017.
40. Wakabayashi, Daisuke; Shane, Scott (27 September 2017). "Twitter, With Accounts Linked to Russia, to Face Congress Over Role in Election". The New York Times. Archived from the original on 2 November 2017. Retrieved 29 November 2017.
41. Jim Finkle (23 April 2014). "Exclusive: FBI warns healthcare sector vulnerable to cyber attacks". Reuters. Archived from the original on 4 June 2016. Retrieved 23 May 2016.
42. Seals, Tara (6 November 2015). "Lack of Employee Security Training Plagues US Businesses". Infosecurity Magazine. Archived from the original on 9 November 2017. Retrieved 8 November 2017.
43. Bright, Peter (15 February 2011). "Anonymous speaks: the inside story of the HBGary hack". Arstechnica.com. Archived from the original on 27 March 2011. Retrieved 29 March 2011.
44. Anderson, Nate (9 February 2011). "How one man tracked down Anonymous—and paid a heavy price". Arstechnica.com. Archived from the original on 29 March 2011. Retrieved 29 March 2011.
45. Palilery, Jose (24 December 2014). "What caused Sony hack: What we know now". CNN Money. Archived from the original on 4 January 2015. Retrieved 4 January 2015.
46. James Cook (16 December 2014). "Sony Hackers Have Over 100 Terabytes Of Documents. Only Released 200 Gigabytes So Far". Business Insider. Archived from the original on 17 December 2014. Retrieved 18 December 2014.
47. Timothy B. Lee (18 January 2015). "The next frontier of hacking: your car". Vox. Archived from the original on 17 March 2017.
48. Tracking & Hacking: Security & Privacy Gaps Put American Drivers at Risk (PDF) (Report). 6 February 2015. Archived (PDF) from the original on 9 November 2016. Retrieved 4 November 2016.
49. Staff, AOL. "Cybersecurity expert: It will take a 'major event' for companies to take this issue seriously". AOL.com. Archived from the original on 20 January 2017. Retrieved 22 January 2017.
50. "The problem with self-driving cars: who controls the code?". The Guardian. 23 December 2015. Archived from the original on 16 March 2017. Retrieved 22 January 2017.
51. Stephen Checkoway; Damon McCoy; Brian Kantor; Danny Anderson; Hovav Shacham; Stefan Savage; Karl Koscher; Alexei Czeskis; Franziska Roesner; Tadayoshi Kohno (2011). Comprehensive Experimental Analyses of Automotive Attack Surfaces (PDF). SEC'11 Proceedings of the 20th USENIX conference on Security. Berkeley, CA, US: USENIX Association. p. 6. Archived (PDF) from the original on 21 February 2015.
52. Greenberg, Andy (21 July 2015). "Hackers Remotely Kill a Jeep on the Highway—With Me in It". Wired. Archived from the original on 19 January 2017. Retrieved 22 January 2017.
53. "Hackers take control of car, drive it into a ditch". The Independent. 22 July 2015. Archived from the original on 2 February 2017. Retrieved 22 January 2017.
54. Staff, Our Foreign (21 September 2016). "Tesla fixes software bug that allowed Chinese hackers to control car remotely". The Telegraph. Archived from the original on 2 February 2017. Retrieved 22 January 2017.
55. Kang, Cecilia (19 September 2016). "Self-Driving Cars Gain Powerful Ally: The Government". The New York Times. Archived from the original on 14 February 2017. Retrieved 22 January 2017.
56. "Federal Automated Vehicles Policy" (PDF). Archived (PDF) from the original on 21 January 2017. Retrieved 22 January 2017.
57. "Gary McKinnon profile: Autistic 'hacker' who started writing computer programs at 14". The Daily Telegraph. London. 23 January 2009. Archived from the original on 2 June 2010.
58. "Gary McKinnon extradition ruling due by 16 October". BBC News. 6 September 2012. Archived from the original on 6 September 2012. Retrieved 25 September 2012.
59. Law Lords Department (30 July 2008). "House of Lords – Mckinnon V Government of The United States of America and Another". Publications.parliament.uk. Archived from the original on 7 March 2009. Retrieved 30 January 2010. 15. … alleged to total over $700,000
60. "NSA Accessed Mexican President's Email" Archived 6 November 2015 at the Wayback Machine, 20 October 2013, Jens Glüsing, Laura Poitras, Marcel Rosenbach and Holger Stark, spiegel.de
61. Sanders, Sam (4 June 2015). "Massive Data Breach Puts 4 Million Federal Employees' Records At Risk". NPR. Archived from the original on 5 June 2015. Retrieved 5 June 2015.
62. Liptak, Kevin (4 June 2015). "U.S. government hacked; feds think China is the culprit". CNN. Archived from the original on 6 June 2015. Retrieved 5 June 2015.
63. Sean Gallagher. "Encryption "would not have helped" at OPM, says DHS official". Archived from the original on 24 June 2017.
64. Davis, Michelle R. (19 October 2015). "Schools Learn Lessons From Security Breaches". Education Week. Archived from the original on 10 June 2016. Retrieved 23 May 2016.
65. "Internet of Things Global Standards Initiative". ITU. Archived from the original on 26 June 2015. Retrieved 26 June 2015.
66. Singh, Jatinder; Pasquier, Thomas; Bacon, Jean; Ko, Hajoon; Eyers, David (2015). "Twenty Cloud Security Considerations for Supporting the Internet of Things". IEEE Internet of Things Journal. **3** (3): 269–284. doi:10.1109/JIOT.2015.2460333. S2CID 4732406.
67. Chris Clearfield. "Why The FTC Can't Regulate The Internet Of Things". Forbes. Archived from the original on 27 June 2015. Retrieved 26 June 2015.
68. "Internet of Things: Science Fiction or Business Fact?" (PDF). Harvard Business Review. Retrieved 4 November 2016.
69. Ovidiu Vermesan; Peter Friess. "Internet of Things: Converging Technologies for Smart Environments and Integrated Ecosystems" (PDF). River Publishers. Archived (PDF) from the original on 12 October 2016. Retrieved 4 November 2016.
70. Christopher Clearfield "Rethinking Security for the Internet of Things" Harvard Business Review Blog, 26 June 2013 Archived 20 September 2013 at the Wayback Machine/
71. "Hotel room burglars exploit critical flaw in electronic door locks". Ars Technica. 26 November 2012. Archived from the original on 14 May 2016. Retrieved 23 May 2016.
72. "Hospital Medical Devices Used As Weapons In Cyberattacks". Dark Reading. Archived from the original on 29 May 2016. Retrieved 23 May 2016.
73. Jeremy Kirk (17 October 2012). "Pacemaker hack can deliver deadly 830-volt jolt". Computerworld. Archived from the original on 4 June 2016. Retrieved 23 May 2016.
74. News, Kaiser Health (17 November 2014). "How Your Pacemaker Will Get Hacked". The Daily Beast. Archived from the original on 20 May 2016. Retrieved 23 May 2016.
75. Leetaru, Kalev. "Hacking Hospitals And Holding Hostages: Cybersecurity In 2016". Forbes. Archived from the original on 29 December 2016. Retrieved 29 December 2016.
76. "Cyber-Angriffe: Krankenhäuser rücken ins Visier der Hacker". Wirtschafts Woche. Archived from the original on 29 December 2016. Retrieved 29 December 2016.
77. "Hospitals keep getting attacked by ransomware—Here's why". Business Insider. Archived from the original on 29 December 2016. Retrieved 29 December 2016.
78. "MedStar Hospitals Recovering After 'Ransomware' Hack". NBC News. Archived from the original on 29 December 2016. Retrieved 29 December 2016.
79. Pauli, Darren. "US hospitals hacked with ancient exploits". The Register. Archived from the original on 16 November 2016. Retrieved 29 December 2016.
80. Pauli, Darren. "Zombie OS lurches through Royal Melbourne Hospital spreading virus". The Register. Archived from the original on 29 December 2016. Retrieved 29 December 2016.
81. "Hacked Lincolnshire hospital computer systems 'back up'". BBC News. 2 November 2016. Archived from the original on 29 December 2016. Retrieved 29 December 2016.
82. "Lincolnshire operations cancelled after network attack". BBC News. 31 October 2016. Archived from the original on 29 December 2016. Retrieved 29 December 2016.
83. "Legion cyber-attack: Next dump is sansad.nic.in, say hackers". The Indian Express. 12 December 2016. Archived from the original on 29 December 2016. Retrieved 29 December 2016.
84. "Former New Hampshire Psychiatric Hospital Patient Accused Of Data Breach". CBS Boston. 27 December 2016. Archived from the original on 29 September 2017. Retrieved 29 December 2016.
85. "Texas Hospital hacked, affects nearly 30,000 patient records". Healthcare IT News. 4 November 2016. Archived from the original on 29 December 2016. Retrieved 29 December 2016.
86. Becker, Rachel (27 December 2016). "New cybersecurity guidelines for medical devices tackle evolving threats". The Verge. Archived from the original on 28 December 2016. Retrieved 29 December 2016.
87. "Postmarket Management of Cybersecurity in Medical Devices" (PDF). 28 December 2016. Archived (PDF) from the original on 29 December 2016. Retrieved 29 December 2016.
88. Brandt, Jaclyn (18 June 2018). "D.C. distributed energy proposal draws concerns of increased cybersecurity risks". Daily Energy Insider. Retrieved 4 July 2018.
89. Cashell, B., Jackson, W. D., Jickling, M., & Webel, B. (2004). The Economic Impact of Cyber-Attacks. Congressional Research Service, Government and Finance Division. Washington DC: The Library of Congress.
90. Gordon, Lawrence; Loeb, Martin (November 2002). "The Economics of Information Security Investment". ACM Transactions on Information and System Security. **5** (4): 438–457. doi:10.1145/581271.581274. S2CID 1500788.
91. Chermick, Steven; Freilich, Joshua; Holt, Thomas (April 2017). "Exploring the Subculture of Ideologically Motivated Cyber-Attackers". Journal of Contemporary Criminal Justice. **33** (3): 212–233.

doi:10.1177/1043986217699100. S2CID 152277480.

92. RFC 2828 Internet Security Glossary
93. CNSS Instruction No. 4009 Archived 27 February 2012 at the Wayback Machine dated 26 April 2010
94. "InfosecToday Glossary" (PDF). Archived (PDF) from the original on 20 November 2014.
95. Definitions: IT Security Architecture Archived 15 March 2014 at the Wayback Machine. SecurityArchitecture.org, Jan, 2006
96. Jannsen, Cory. "Security Architecture". Techopedia. Janalta Interactive Inc. Archived from the original on 3 October 2014. Retrieved 9 October 2014.
97. Woodie, Alex (9 May 2016). "Why ONI May Be Our Best Hope for Cyber Security Now". Archived from the original on 20 August 2016. Retrieved 13 July 2016.
98. "Firms lose more to electronic than physical theft". Reuters. 18 October 2010. Archived from the original on 25 September 2015.
99. Walkowski, Debbie (9 July 2019). "What Is The CIA Triad?". F5 Labs. Retrieved 25 February 2020.
100. "Knowing Value of Data Assets is Crucial to Cybersecurity Risk Management | SecurityWeek.Com". www.securityweek.com. Retrieved 25 February 2020.
101. Foreman, P: Vulnerability Management, page 1. Taylor & Francis Group, 2010. ISBN 978-1-4398-0150-5
102. Academy, Cisco Networking (17 June 2018). CCNA Cybersecurity Operations Companion Guide. Cisco Press. ISBN 978-0-13-516624-6.
103. Alan Calder and Geraint Williams (2014). PCI DSS: A Pocket Guide, 3rd Edition. ISBN 978-1-84928-554-4. network vulnerability scans at least quarterly and after any significant change in the network
104. Harrison, J. (2003). "Formal verification at Intel". 18th Annual IEEE Symposium of Logic in Computer Science, 2003. Proceedings. pp. 45–54. doi:10.1109/LICS.2003.1210044. ISBN 978-0-7695-1884-8. S2CID 44585546.
105. Umrigar, Zerksis D.; Pitchumani, Vijay (1983). "Formal verification of a real-time hardware design". Proceeding DAC '83 Proceedings of the 20th Design Automation Conference. IEEE Press. pp. 221–7. ISBN 978-0-8186-0026-5.
106. "Abstract Formal Specification of the seL4/ARMv6 API" (PDF). Archived from the original (PDF) on 21 May 2015. Retrieved 19 May 2015.
107. Christoph Baumann, Bernhard Beckert, Holger Blasum, and Thorsten Bormer Ingredients of Operating System Correctness? Lessons Learned in the Formal Verification of PikeOS Archived 19 July 2011 at the Wayback Machine
108. "Getting it Right" Archived 4 May 2013 at the Wayback Machine by Jack Ganssle
109. Treglia, J., & Delia, M. (2017). Cyber Security Inoculation. Presented at NYS Cyber Security Conference, Empire State Plaza Convention Center, Albany, NY, 3–4 June.
110. Villasenor, John (2010). "The Hacker in Your Hardware: The Next Security Threat". Scientific American. 303 (2): 82–88. Bibcode:2010SciAm.303b..82V. doi:10.1038/scientificamerican0810-82. PMID 20684377.
111. Waksman, Adam; Sethumadhavan, Simha (2010), "Tamper Evident Microprocessors" (PDF), Proceedings of the IEEE Symposium on Security and Privacy, Oakland, California, archived from the original (PDF) on 21 September 2013, retrieved 27 August 2019
112. "Token-based authentication". SafeNet.com. Archived from the original on 20 March 2014. Retrieved 20 March 2014.
113. "Lock and protect your Windows PC". TheWindowsClub.com. 10 February 2010. Archived from the original on 20 March 2014. Retrieved 20 March 2014.
114. James Greene (2012). "Intel Trusted Execution Technology: White Paper" (PDF). Intel Corporation. Archived (PDF) from the original on 11 June 2014. Retrieved 18 December 2013.
115. "SafeNet ProtectDrive 8.4". SCMagazine.com. 4 October 2008. Archived from the original on 20 March 2014. Retrieved 20 March 2014.
116. "Secure Hard Drives: Lock Down Your Data". PCMag.com. 11 May 2009. Archived from the original on 21 June 2017.
117. NIST 800-124 https://www.nist.gov/publications/guidelines-managing-security-mobile-devices-enterprise
118. "Forget IDs, use your phone as credentials". Fox Business Network. 4 November 2013. Archived from the original on 20 March 2014. Retrieved 20 March 2014.
119. Lipner, Steve (2015). "The Birth and Death of the Orange Book". IEEE Annals of the History of Computing. 37 (2): 19–31. doi:10.1109/MAHC.2015.27. S2CID 16625319.
120. Kelly Jackson Higgins (18 November 2008). "Secure OS Gets Highest NSA Rating, Goes Commercial". Dark Reading. Archived from the original on 3 December 2013. Retrieved 1 December 2013.
121. "Board or bored? Lockheed Martin gets into the COTS hardware biz". VITA Technologies Magazine. 10 December 2010. Archived from the original on 2 May 2012. Retrieved 9 March 2012.
122. Sanghavi, Alok (21 May 2010). "What is formal verification?". EE Times_Asia.
123. Yuanzhong Xu; Alan M. Dunn; Owen S. Hofmann; Michael Z. Lee; Syed Akbar Mehdi; Emmett Witchel (23 November 2014). "Application-Defined Decentralized Access Control". Proceedings of the Usenix ... Annual Technical Conference. Usenix Technical Conference. 2014: 395–408. PMC 4241348. PMID 25426493.
124. "Studies prove once again that users are the weakest link in the security chain". CSO Online. 22 January 2014. Retrieved 8 October 2018.
125. "The Role of Human Error in Successful Security Attacks". IBM Security Intelligence. 2 September 2014. Retrieved 8 October 2018.
126. "90% of security incidents trace back to PEBKAC and ID10T errors". Computerworld. 15 April 2015. Retrieved 8 October 2018.
127. "Protect your online banking with 2FA". NZ Bankers Association. Retrieved 7 September 2019.
128. Security Intelligence Index.pdf "IBM Security Services 2014 Cyber Security Intelligence Index" Check |url= value (help) (PDF). 2014. Retrieved 9 October 2020.
129. Caldwell, Tracey (12 February 2013). "Risky business: why security awareness is crucial for employees". The Guardian. Retrieved 8 October 2018.
130. "Developing a Security Culture". CPNI - Centre for the Protection of National Infrastructure.
131. "Cyber Hygiene — ENISA". Retrieved 27 September 2018.
132. Kuchler, Hannah (27 April 2015). "Security execs call on companies to improve 'cyber hygiene'". Financial Times. Retrieved 27 September 2018.
133. "From AI to Russia, Here's How Estonia's President Is Planning for the Future". WIRED. Retrieved 28 September 2018.
134. "Professor Len Adleman explains how he coined the term "computer virus"". WeLiveSecurity. 1 November 2017. Retrieved 28 September 2018.
135. "Statement of Dr. Vinton G. Cerf". www.jec.senate.gov. Retrieved 28 September 2018.
136. Anna, Eshoo (22 May 2018). "Text - H.R.3010 - 115th Congress (2017-2018): Promoting Good Cyber Hygiene Act of 2017". www.congress.gov. Retrieved 28 September 2018.
137. "Analysis | The Cybersecurity 202: Agencies struggling with basic cybersecurity despite Trump's pledge to prioritize it". Washington Post. Retrieved 28 September 2018.
138. "Protected Voices". Federal Bureau of Investigation. Retrieved 28 September 2018.
139. Kaljulaid, Kersti (16 October 2017). "President of the Republic at the Aftenposten's Technology Conference". Retrieved 27 September 2018.
140. Jonathan Zittrain, 'The Future of The Internet', Penguin Books, 2008
141. Information Security Archived 6 March 2016 at the Wayback Machine. United States Department of Defense, 1986
142. "THE TJX COMPANIES, INC. VICTIMIZED BY COMPUTER SYSTEMS INTRUSION; PROVIDES INFORMATION TO HELP PROTECT CUSTOMERS" (Press release). The TJX Companies, Inc. 17 January 2007. Archived from the original on 27 September 2012. Retrieved 12 December 2009.
143. Largest Customer Info Breach Grows Archived 28 September 2007 at the Wayback Machine. MyFox Twin Cities, 29 March 2007.
144. "The Stuxnet Attack On Iran's Nuclear Plant Was 'Far More Dangerous' Than Previously Thought". Business Insider. 20 November 2013. Archived from the original on 9 May 2014.
145. Reals, Tucker (24 September 2010). "Stuxnet Worm a U.S. Cyber-Attack on Iran Nukes?". CBS News. Archived from the original on 16 October 2013.
146. Kim Zetter (17 February 2011). "Cyberwar Issues Likely to Be Addressed Only After a Catastrophe". Wired. Archived from the original on 18 February 2011. Retrieved 18 February 2011.
147. Chris Carroll (18 October 2011). "Cone of silence surrounds U.S. cyberwarfare". Stars and Stripes. Archived from the original on 7 March 2012. Retrieved 30 October 2011.
148. John Bumgarner (27 April 2010). "Computers as Weapons of War" (PDF). IO Journal. Archived from the original (PDF) on 19 December 2011. Retrieved 30 October 2011.
149. Greenwald, Glenn (6 June 2013). "NSA collecting phone records of millions of Verizon customers daily". The Guardian. Archived from the original on 16 August 2013. Retrieved 16 August 2013. Exclusive: Top secret court order requiring Verizon to hand over all call data shows scale of domestic surveillance under Obama
150. Seipel, Hubert. "Transcript: ARD interview with Edward Snowden". La Foundation Courage. Archived from the original on 14 July 2014. Retrieved 11 June 2014.
151. Newman, Lily Hay (9 October 2013). "Can You Trust NIST?". IEEE Spectrum. Archived from the original on 1 February 2016.
152. "NIST Removes Cryptography Algorithm from Random Number Generator Recommendations". National Institute of Standards and Technology. 21 April 2014.
153. "New Snowden Leak: NSA Tapped Google, Yahoo Data Centers" Archived 9 July 2014 at the Wayback Machine, 31 Oct 2013, Lorenzo Franceschi-Bicchierai, mashable.com
154. Michael Riley; Ben Elgin; Dune Lawrence; Carol Matlack. "Target Missed Warnings in Epic Hack of Credit Card Data – Businessweek". Businessweek.com. Archived from the original on 27 January 2015.
155. "Home Depot says 53 million emails stolen". CNET. CBS Interactive. 6 November 2014. Archived from the original on 9 December 2014.
156. "Millions more Americans hit by government personnel data hack". Reuters. 9 July 2017. Archived from the original on 28 February 2017. Retrieved 25 February 2017.
157. Barrett, Devlin. "U.S. Suspects Hackers in China Breached About four (4) Million People's Records, Officials Say". The Wall Street Journal. Archived from the original on 4 June 2015.
158. Risen, Tom (5 June 2015). "China Suspected in Theft of Federal Employee Records". US News & World Report. Archived from the original on 6 June 2015.
159. Zengerle, Patricia (19 July 2015). "Estimate of Americans hit by government personnel data hack skyrockets". Reuters. Archived from the original on 10 July 2015.
160. Sanger, David (5 June 2015). "Hacking Linked to China Exposes Millions of U.S. Workers". New York Times. Archived from the original on 5 June 2015.
161. Mansfield-Devine, Steve (1 September 2015). "The Ashley Madison affair". Network Security. 2015 (9): 8–16. doi:10.1016/S1353-4858(15)30080-5.
162. "Mikko Hypponen: Fighting viruses, defending the net". TED. Archived from the original on 16 January 2013.
163. "Mikko Hypponen – Behind Enemy Lines". Hack In The Box Security Conference. Archived from the original on 25 November 2016.
164. "Ensuring the Security of Federal Information Systems and Cyber Critical Infrastructure and Protecting the Privacy of Personally Identifiable Information". Government Accountability Office. Archived from the original on 19 November 2015. Retrieved 3 November 2015.
165. King, Georgia (23 May 2018). "The Venn diagram between libertarians and crypto bros is so close it's basically a circle". Quartz.
166. Kirby, Carrie (24 June 2011). "Former White House aide backs some Net regulation / Clarke says government, industry deserve 'F' in cyber security". The San Francisco Chronicle.
167. McCarthy, Daniel (11 June 2018). "Privatizing Political Authority: Cybersecurity, Public-Private Partnerships, and the Reproduction of Liberal Political Order". Politics and Governance. 6 (2): 5–12. doi:10.17645/pag.v6i2.1335.
168. "It's Time to Treat Cybersecurity as a Human Rights Issue". Human Rights Watch. Retrieved 26 May 2020.
169. "FIRST Mission". FIRST. Retrieved 6 July 2018.
170. "FIRST Members". FIRST. Retrieved 6 July 2018.
171. "European council". Archived from the original on 3 December 2014.
172. "MAAWG". Archived from the original on 23 September 2014.
173. "MAAWG". Archived from the original on 17 October 2014.
174. "Government of Canada Launches Canada's Cyber Security Strategy". Market Wired. 3 October 2010. Archived from the original on 2 November 2014. Retrieved 1 November 2014.
175. "Canada's Cyber Security Strategy". Public Safety Canada. Government of Canada. Archived from the original on 2 November 2014. Retrieved 1 November 2014.
176. "Action Plan 2010–2015 for Canada's Cyber Security Strategy". Public Safety Canada. Government of Canada. Archived from the original on 2 November 2014. Retrieved 3 November 2014.
177. "Cyber Incident Management Framework For Canada". Public Safety Canada. Government of Canada. Archived from the original on 2 November 2014. Retrieved 3 November 2014.
178. "Action Plan 2010–2015 for Canada's Cyber Security Strategy". Public Safety Canada. Government of Canada. Archived from the original on 2 November 2014. Retrieved 1 November 2014.
179. "Canadian Cyber Incident Response Centre". Public Safety Canada. Archived from the original on 8 October 2014. Retrieved 1 November 2014.
180. "Cyber Security Bulletins". Public Safety Canada. Archived from the original on 8 October 2014. Retrieved 1 November 2014.
181. "Report a Cyber Security Incident". Public Safety Canada. Government of Canada. Archived from the original on 11 November 2014. Retrieved 3 November 2014.
182. "Government of Canada Launches Cyber Security Awareness Month With New Public Awareness Partnership". Market Wired. Government of Canada. 27 September 2012. Archived from the original

on 3 November 2014. Retrieved 3 November 2014.
183. "Cyber Security Cooperation Program". Public Safety Canada. Archived from the original on 2 November 2014. Retrieved 1 November 2014.
184. "Cyber Security Cooperation Program". Public Safety Canada. 16 December 2015. Archived from the original on 2 November 2014.
185. "GetCyberSafe". Get Cyber Safe. Government of Canada. Archived from the original on 11 November 2014. Retrieved 3 November 2014.
186. "6.16 Internet security: National IT independence and China's cyber policy," in: Sebastian Heilmann, editor, ["Archived copy". Archived from the original on 23 March 2017. Retrieved 11 May 2017. China's Political System], Lanham, Boulder, New York, London: Rowman & Littlefield Publishers (2017) ISBN 978-1442277342
187. "Need for proper structure of PPPs to address specific cyberspace risks". Archived from the original on 13 November 2017.
188. "National Cyber Safety and Security Standards(NCSSS)–Home". www.ncdrc.res.in.
189. "South Korea seeks global support in cyber attack probe". BBC Monitoring Asia Pacific. 7 March 2011.
190. Kwanwoo Jun (23 September 2013). "Seoul Puts a Price on Cyberdefense". Wall Street Journal. Dow Jones & Company, Inc. Archived from the original on 25 September 2013. Retrieved 24 September 2013.
191. "Text of H.R.4962 as Introduced in House: International Cybercrime Reporting and Cooperation Act – U.S. Congress". OpenCongress. Archived from the original on 28 December 2010. Retrieved 25 September 2013.
192. [1] Archived 20 January 2012 at the Wayback Machine
193. "National Cyber Security Division". U.S. Department of Homeland Security. Archived from the original on 11 June 2008. Retrieved 14 June 2008.
194. "FAQ: Cyber Security R&D Center". U.S. Department of Homeland Security S&T Directorate. Archived from the original on 6 October 2008. Retrieved 14 June 2008.
195. AFP-JiJi, "U.S. boots up cybersecurity center", 31 October 2009.
196. "Federal Bureau of Investigation – Priorities". Federal Bureau of Investigation. Archived from the original on 11 July 2016.
197. "Internet Crime Complaint Center (IC3) – Home". Archived from the original on 20 November 2011.
198. "Infragard, Official Site". Infragard. Archived from the original on 9 September 2010. Retrieved 10 September 2010.
199. "Robert S. Mueller, III – InfraGard Interview at the 2005 InfraGard Conference". Infragard (Official Site) – "Media Room". Archived from the original on 17 June 2011. Retrieved 9 December 2009.
200. "CCIPS". 25 March 2015. Archived from the original on 23 August 2006.
201. "A Framework for a Vulnerability Disclosure Program for Online Systems". Cybersecurity Unit, Computer Crime & Intellectual Property Section Criminal Division U.S. Department of Justice. July 2017. Retrieved 9 July 2018.
202. "Mission and Vision". www.cybercom.mil. Retrieved 20 June 2020.
203. "Speech". Defense.gov. Archived from the original on 15 April 2010. Retrieved 10 July 2010.
204. Shachtman, Noah. "Military's Cyber Commander Swears: "No Role" in Civilian Networks" Archived 6 November 2010 at the Wayback Machine, The Brookings Institution Archived 10 February 2006 at the Wayback Machine, 23 September 2010.
205. "FCC Cybersecurity". FCC. Archived from the original on 27 May 2010. Retrieved 3 December 2014.
206. "Cybersecurity for Medical Devices and Hospital Networks: FDA Safety Communication". Archived from the original on 28 May 2016. Retrieved 23 May 2016.
207. "Automotive Cybersecurity – National Highway Traffic Safety Administration (NHTSA)". Archived from the original on 25 May 2016. Retrieved 23 May 2016.
208. Air Traffic Control: FAA Needs a More Comprehensive Approach to Address Cybersecurity As Agency Transitions to NextGen (Report). U. S. Government Accountability Office. 14 April 2015. Archived from the original on 13 June 2016. Retrieved 23 May 2016.
209. Aliya Sternstein (4 March 2016). "FAA Working on New Guidelines for Hack-Proof Planes". Nextgov. Archived from the original on 19 May 2016. Retrieved 23 May 2016.
210. Bart Elias (18 June 2015). "Protecting Civil Aviation from Cyberattacks" (PDF). Archived (PDF) from the original on 17 October 2016. Retrieved 4 November 2016.
211. Verton, Dan (28 January 2004). "DHS launches national cyber alert system". Computerworld. IDG. Archived from the original on 31 August 2005. Retrieved 15 June 2008.
212. Clayton, Mark (7 March 2011). "The new cyber arms race". The Christian Science Monitor. Archived from the original on 16 April 2015. Retrieved 16 April 2015.
213. Nakashima, Ellen (13 September 2016). "Obama to be urged to split cyberwar command from NSA". The Washington Post. Archived from the original on 12 October 2016. Retrieved 15 June 2017.
214. Overland, Indra (1 March 2019). "The geopolitics of renewable energy: Debunking four emerging myths". Energy Research & Social Science. 49: 36–40. doi:10.1016/j.erss.2018.10.018. ISSN 2214-6296.
215. Maness, Ryan C.; Valeriano, Brandon (11 June 2018). "How We Stopped Worrying about Cyber Doom and Started Collecting Data". Politics and Governance. 6 (2): 49–60. doi:10.17645/pag.v6i2.1368. ISSN 2183-2463.
216. Maness, Ryan C.; Valeriano, Brandon (25 March 2015). "The Impact of Cyber Conflict on International Interactions". Armed Forces & Society. 42 (2): 301–323. doi:10.1177/0095327x15572997. ISSN 0095-327X. S2CID 146145942.
217. Bullard, Brittany (16 November 2016). Style and Statistics: The Art of Retail Analytics (1 ed.). Wiley. doi:10.1002/9781119271260.ch8. ISBN 978-1-119-27031-7.
218. Oltsik, Jon (18 March 2016). "Cybersecurity Skills Shortage Impact on Cloud Computing". Network World. Archived from the original on 23 March 2016. Retrieved 23 March 2016.
219. de Silva, Richard (11 October 2011). "Government vs. Commerce: The Cyber Security Industry and You (Part One)". Defence IQ. Archived from the original on 24 April 2014. Retrieved 24 April 2014.
220. "Department of Computer Science". Archived from the original on 3 June 2013. Retrieved 30 April 2013.
221. "(Information for) Students". NICCS (US National Initiative for Cybercareers and Studies). Archived from the original on 23 February 2014. Retrieved 24 April 2014.
222. "Current Job Opportunities at DHS". U.S. Department of Homeland Security. Archived from the original on 2 May 2013. Retrieved 5 May 2013.
223. "Cybersecurity Training & Exercises". U.S. Department of Homeland Security. 12 May 2010. Archived from the original on 7 January 2015. Retrieved 9 January 2015.
224. "Cyber Security Awareness Free Training and Webcasts". MS-ISAC (Multi-State Information Sharing & Analysis Center). Archived from the original on 6 January 2015. Retrieved 9 January 2015.
225. "DoD Approved 8570 Baseline Certifications". iase.disa.mil. Archived from the original on 21 October 2016. Retrieved 19 June 2017.
226. https://assets.publishing.service.gov.uk/government/uploads/system/uploads/attachment_data/file/386093/The_UK_Cyber_Security_Strategy_Report_on_Progress_and_Forward_Plans_-_De____.pdf
227. "Cyber skills for a vibrant and secure UK".
228. "Confidentiality". Retrieved 31 October 2011.
229. "Data Integrity". Archived from the original on 6 November 2011. Retrieved 31 October 2011.
230. "Endpoint Security". Archived from the original on 16 March 2014. Retrieved 15 March 2014.

Information security, References

1. Cherdantseva Y. and Hilton J.: "Information Security and Information Assurance. The Discussion about the Meaning, Scope and Goals". In: Organizational, Legal, and Technological Dimensions of Information System Administrator. Almeida F., Portela, I. (eds.). IGI Global Publishing. (2013)
2. ISO/IEC 27000:2009 (E). (2009). Information technology – Security techniques – Information security management systems – Overview and vocabulary. ISO/IEC.
3. Committee on National Security Systems: National Information Assurance (IA) Glossary, CNSS Instruction No. 4009, 26 April 2010.
4. ISACA. (2008). Glossary of terms, 2008. Retrieved from http://www.isaca.org/Knowledge-Center/Documents/Glossary/glossary.pdf
5. Pipkin, D. (2000). Information security: Protecting the global enterprise. New York: Hewlett-Packard Company.
6. B., McDermott, E., & Geer, D. (2001). Information security is information risk management. In Proceedings of the 2001 Workshop on New Security Paradigms NSPW '01, (pp. 97 – 104). ACM. doi:10.1145/508171.508187
7. Anderson, J. M. (2003). "Why we need a new definition of information security". Computers & Security. 22 (4): 308–313. doi:10.1016/S0167-4048(03)00407-3.
8. Venter, H. S.; Eloff, J. H. P. (2003). "A taxonomy for information security technologies". Computers & Security. 22 (4): 299–307. doi:10.1016/S0167-4048(03)00406-1.
9. Samonas, S.; Coss, D. (2014). "The CIA Strikes Back: Redefining Confidentiality, Integrity and Availability in Security". Journal of Information System Security. 10 (3): 21–45. Archived from the original on 2018-09-22. Retrieved 2018-01-25.
10. "Gartner Says Digital Disruptors Are Impacting All Industries; Digital KPIs Are Crucial to Measuring Success". Gartner. 2 October 2017. Retrieved 25 January 2018.
11. "Gartner Survey Shows 42 Percent of CEOs Have Begun Digital Business Transformation". Gartner. 24 April 2017. Retrieved 25 January 2018.
12. "Information Security Qualifications Fact Sheet" (PDF). IT Governance. Retrieved 16 March 2018.
13. Stewart, James (2012). CISSP Study Guide. Canada: John Wiley & Sons, Inc. pp. 255–257. ISBN 978-1-118-31417-3.
14. Enge, Eric. "Stone Temple". Cell phones
15. Gordon, Lawrence; Loeb, Martin (November 2002). "The Economics of Information Security Investment". ACM Transactions on Information and System Security. 5 (4): 438–457. doi:10.1145/581271.581274. S2CID 1500788.
16. Stewart, James (2012). CISSP Certified Information Systems Security Professional Study Guide Sixth Edition. Canada: John Wiley & Sons, Inc. pp. 255–257. ISBN 978-1-118-31417-3.
17. Suetonius Tranquillus, Gaius (2008). Lives of the Caesars (Oxford World's Classics). New York: Oxford University Press. p. 28. ISBN 978-0-19-953756-3.
18. Singh, Simon (2000). The Code Book. Anchor. pp. 289–290. ISBN 978-0-385-49532-5.
19. Johnson, John (1997). The Evolution of British Sigint: 1653–1939. Her Majesty's Stationery Office. ASIN B00GYX1GX2.
20. Ruppert, K. (2011). "Official Secrets Act (1889; New 1911; Amended 1920, 1939, 1989)". In Hastedt, G.P. (ed.). Spies, Wiretaps, and Secret Operations: An Encyclopedia of American Espionage. 2. ABC-CLIO. pp. 589–590. ISBN 9781851098088.
21. Maer, Lucinda; Gay (30 December 2008). "Official Secrecy" (PDF). Federation of American Scientists.
22. "Official Secrets Act: what it covers; when it has been used, questioned". The Indian Express. 2019-03-08. Retrieved 2020-08-07.
23. Sebag–Montefiore, H. (2011). Enigma: The Battle for the Code. Orion. p. 576. ISBN 9781780221236.
24. "A Brief History of the Internet". www.usg.edu. Retrieved 2020-08-07.
25. DeNardis, L. (2007). "Chapter 24: A History of Internet Security". In de Leeuw, K.M.M.; Bergstra, J. (eds.). The History of Information Security: A Comprehensive Handbook. Elsevier. pp. 681–704. ISBN 9780080550589.
26. Perrin, Chad. "The CIA Triad". Retrieved 31 May 2012.
27. "Engineering Principles for Information Technology Security" (PDF). csrc.nist.gov.
28. A. J. Neumann, N. Statland and R. D. Webb (1977). "Post-processing audit tools and techniques" (PDF). US Department of Commerce, National Bureau of Standards. pp. 11-3--11-4.
29. "oecd.org" (PDF). Archived from the original (PDF) on May 16, 2011. Retrieved 2014-01-17.
30. Slade, Rob. "(ICS)2 Blog".
31. Aceituno, Vicente. "Open Information Security Maturity Model". Retrieved 12 February 2017.
32. http://www.dartmouth.edu/~gvc/ThreeTenetsSPIE.pdf
33. Hughes, Jeff; Cybenko, George (21 June 2018). "Quantitative Metrics and Risk Assessment: The Three Tenets Model of Cybersecurity". Technology Innovation Management Review. 3 (8).
34. Teplow, Lily. "Are Your Clients Falling for These IT Security Myths? [CHART]". continuum.net.
35. Beckers, K. (2015). Pattern and Security Requirements: Engineering-Based Establishment of Security Standards. Springer. p. 100. ISBN 9783319166643.

36. Andress, J. (2014). The Basics of Information Security: Understanding the Fundamentals of InfoSec in Theory and Practice. Syngress. p. 240. ISBN 9780128008126.
37. Boritz, J. Efrim (2005). "IS Practitioners' Views on Core Concepts of Information Integrity". International Journal of Accounting Information Systems. Elsevier. 6 (4): 260–279. doi:10.1016/j.accinf.2005.07.001.
38. Loukas, G.; Oke, G. (September 2010) [August 2009]. "Protection Against Denial of Service Attacks: A Survey" (PDF). Comput. J. 53 (7): 1020–1037. doi:10.1093/comjnl/bxp078. Archived from the original (PDF) on 2012-03-24. Retrieved 2015-08-28.
39. McCarthy, C. (2006). "Digital Libraries: Security and Preservation Considerations". In Bidgoli, H. (ed.). Handbook of Information Security, Threats, Vulnerabilities, Prevention, Detection, and Management. 3. John Wiley & Sons. pp. 49–76. ISBN 9780470051214.
40. Grama, J.L. (2014). Legal Issues in Information Security. Jones & Bartlett Learning. p. 550. ISBN 9781284151046.
41. ISACA (2006). CISA Review Manual 2006. Information Systems Audit and Control Association. p. 85. ISBN 978-1-933284-15-6.
42. Spagnoletti, Paolo; Resca A. (2008). "The duality of Information Security Management: fighting against predictable and unpredictable threats". Journal of Information System Security. 4 (3): 46–62.
43. Kiountouzis, E.A.; Kokolakis, S.A. (1996-05-31). Information systems security: facing the information society of the 21st century. London: Chapman & Hall, Ltd. ISBN 978-0-412-78120-9.
44. Newsome, B. (2013). A Practical Introduction to Security and Risk Management. SAGE Publications. p. 208. ISBN 9781483324852.
45. Whitman, M.E.; Mattord, H.J. (2016). Management of Information Security (5th ed.). Cengage Learning. p. 592. ISBN 9781305501256.
46. "NIST SP 800-30 Risk Management Guide for Information Technology Systems" (PDF). Retrieved 2014-01-17.
47. Johnson, L. (2015). Security Controls Evaluation, Testing, and Assessment Handbook. Syngress. p. 678. ISBN 9780128025642.
48. 44 U.S.C. § 3542(b)(1)
49. Ransome, J.; Misra, A. (2013). Core Software Security: Security at the Source. CRC Press. pp. 40–41. ISBN 9781466560956.
50. "Segregation of Duties Control matrix". ISACA. 2008. Archived from the original on 3 July 2011. Retrieved 2008-09-30.
51. Kakareka, A. (2013). "Chapter 31: What is Vulnerability Assessment?". In Vacca, J.R. (ed.). Computer and Information Security Handbook (2nd ed.). Elsevier. pp. 541–552. ISBN 9780123946126.
52. Bayuk, J. (2009). "Chapter 4: Information Classification". In Axelrod, C.W.; Bayuk, J.L.; Schutzer, D. (eds.). Enterprise Information Security and Privacy. Artech House. pp. 59–70. ISBN 9781596931916.
53. "Business Model for Information Security (BMIS)". ISACA. Retrieved 25 January 2018.
54. Akpeninor, James Ohwofasa (2013). Modern Concepts of Security. Bloomington, IN: AuthorHouse. p. 135. ISBN 978-1-4817-8232-6. Retrieved 18 January 2018.
55. "The Use of Audit Trails to Monitor Key Networks and Systems Should Remain Part of the Computer Security Material Weakness". www.treasury.gov. Retrieved 2017-10-06.
56. Vallabhaneni, S.R. (2008). Corporate Management, Governance, and Ethics Best Practices. John Wiley & Sons. p. 288. ISBN 9780470255803.
57. Shon Harris (2003). All-in-one CISSP Certification Exam Guide (2nd ed.). Emeryville, California: McGraw-Hill/Osborne. ISBN 978-0-07-222966-0.
58. "The Duty of Care Risk Analysis Standard". DoCRA. Archived from the original on 2018-08-14. Retrieved 2018-08-15.
59. Westby, J.R.; Allen, J.H. (August 2007). "Governing for Enterprise Security (GES) Implementation Guide" (PDF). Software Engineering Institute. Retrieved 25 January 2018.
60. "Iltanget.org". iltanet.org. 2015.
61. Leonard, Wills (2019). A Brief Guide to Handling a Cyber Incident. <http://search.ebscohost.com.rcbc.idm.oclc.org/login.aspx?direct=true&db=aph&AN=136883429&site=ehost-live>. pp. 17–18.
62. Erlanger, Leon (2002). Defensive Strategies. PC Magazine. p. 70.
63. "Computer Security Incident Handling Guide" (PDF). Nist.gov. 2012.
64. He, Ying (December 1, 2017). "Challenges of Information Security Incident Learning: An Industrial Case Study in a Chinese Healthcare Organization" (PDF). Informatics for Health and Social Care. 42 (4): 394–395. doi:10.1080/17538157.2016.1255629. PMID 28068150. S2CID 20139345.
65. Campbell, T. (2016). "Chapter 14: Secure Systems Development". Practical Information Security Management: A Complete Guide to Planning and Implementation. Apress. p. 218. ISBN 9781484216859.
66. Taylor, J. (2008). "Chapter 10: Understanding the Project Change Process". Project Scheduling and Cost Control: Planning, Monitoring and Controlling the Baseline. J. Ross Publishing. pp. 187–214. ISBN 9781932159110.
67. itpi.org Archived December 10, 2013, at the Wayback Machine
68. "book summary of The Visible Ops Handbook: Implementing ITIL in 4 Practical and Auditable Steps". wikisummaries.org. Retrieved 2016-06-22.
69. Hotchkiss, Stuart. Business Continuity Management : In Practice, British Informatics Society Limited, 2010. ProQuest Ebook Central, https://ebookcentral.proquest.com/lib/pensu/detail.action?docID=634527.
70. "The Disaster Recovery Plan". Sans Institute. Retrieved 7 February 2012.
71. "Data Protection Act 1998". legislation.gov.uk. The National Archives. Retrieved 25 January 2018.
72. "Computer Misuse Act 1990". legislation.gov.uk. The National Archives. Retrieved 25 January 2018.
73. "Directive 2006/24/EC of the European Parliament and of the Council of 15 March 2006". EUR-Lex. European Union. Retrieved 25 January 2018.
74. Codified at 20 U.S.C. § 1232g, with implementing regulations in title 34, part 99 of the Code of Federal Regulations
75. "Audit Booklet". Information Technology Examination Handbook. FFIEC. Retrieved 25 January 2018.
76. "Public Law 104 - 191 - Health Insurance Portability and Accountability Act of 1996". U.S. Government Publishing Office. Retrieved 25 January 2018.
77. "Public Law 106 - 102 - Gramm–Leach–Bliley Act of 1999" (PDF). U.S. Government Publishing Office. Retrieved 25 January 2018.
78. "Public Law 107 - 204 - Sarbanes-Oxley Act of 2002". U.S. Government Publishing Office. Retrieved 25 January 2018.
79. "Payment Card Industry (PCI) Data Security Standard: Requirements and Security Assessment Procedures - Version 3.2" (PDF). Security Standards Council. April 2016. Retrieved 25 January 2018.
80. "Security Breach Notification Laws". National Conference of State Legislatures. 12 April 2017. Retrieved 25 January 2018.
81. "Personal Information Protection and Electronic Documents Act" (PDF). Canadian Minister of Justice. Retrieved 25 January 2018.
82. "Regulation for the Assurance of Confidentiality in Electronic Communications" (PDF). Government Gazette of the Hellenic Republic. Hellenic Authority for Communication Security and Privacy. 17 November 2011. Retrieved 25 January 2018.
83. "Αριθμ. απόφ. 205/2013" (PDF). Government Gazette of the Hellenic Republic. Hellenic Authority for Communication Security and Privacy. 15 July 2013. Retrieved 25 January 2018.
84. https://securitycultureframework.net (09/04/2014). "Definition of Security Culture". The Security Culture Framework. Check date values in: |date= (help)
85. Roer, Kai; Petric, Gregor (2017). The 2017 Security Culture Report - In depth insights into the human factor. CLTRe North America, Inc. pp. 42–43. ISBN 978-1544933948.
86. Anderson, D., Reimers, K. and Barretto, C. (March 2014). Post-Secondary Education Network Security: Results of Addressing the End-User Challenge.publication date Mar 11, 2014 publication description INTED2014 (International Technology, Education, and Development Conference)
87. Schlienger, Thomas; Teufel, Stephanie (December 2003). "Information security culture - from analysis to change". South African Computer Society (SAICSIT). 2003 (31): 46–52. hdl:10520/EJC27949.
88. "IISP Skills Framework".
89. "BSI-Standards". BSI. Retrieved 29 November 2013.

Cloud computing, References

1. The NIST Definition of Cloud Computing NIST
2. Wang (2012). "Enterprise cloud service architectures". Information Technology and Management. 13 (4): 445–454. doi:10.1007/s10799-012-0139-4. S2CID 8251298.
3. "What is Cloud Computing?". Amazon Web Services. 2013-03-19. Retrieved 2013-03-20.
4. Baburajan, Rajani (2011-08-24). "The Rising Cloud Storage Market Opportunity Strengthens Vendors". It.tmcnet.com. Retrieved 2011-12-02.
5. Oestreich, Ken (2010-11-15). "Converged Infrastructure". CTO Forum. Thectoforum.com. Archived from the original on 2012-01-13. Retrieved 2011-12-02.
6. Ted Simpson, Jason Novak, Hands on Virtual Computing, 2017, ISBN 1337515744, p. 451
7. "Where's The Rub: Cloud Computing's Hidden Costs". 2014-02-27. Retrieved 2014-07-14.
8. "Cloud Computing: Clash of the clouds". The Economist. 2009-10-15. Retrieved 2009-11-03.
9. "Gartner Says Cloud Computing Will Be As Influential As E-business". Gartner. Retrieved 2010-08-22.
10. Gruman, Galen (2008-04-07). "What cloud computing really means". InfoWorld. Retrieved 2009-06-02.
11. Vaughan-Nichols, Steven J. "Microsoft developer reveals Linux is now more used on Azure than Windows Server". ZDNet. Retrieved 2019-07-02.
12. Kumar, Guddu (9 September 2019). "A Review on Data Protection of Cloud Computing Security, Benefits, Risks and Suggestions" (PDF). United International Journal for Research & Technology. 1 (2): 26. Retrieved 9 September 2019.
13. "Announcing Amazon Elastic Compute Cloud (Amazon EC2) – beta". 24 August 2006. Retrieved 31 May 2014.
14. Antonio Regalado (31 October 2011). "Who Coined 'Cloud Computing'?". Technology Review. MIT. Retrieved 31 July 2013.
15. "Internet History 1977".
16. "National Science Foundation, "Diagram of CSNET," 1981".
17. "What Is Cloud Computing?". PCMAG. Retrieved 2020-02-24.
18. AT&T (1993). "What Is The Cloud?". Retrieved 2017-10-26. You can think of our electronic meeting place as the Cloud. PersonaLink was built from the ground up to give handheld communicators and other devices easy access to a variety of services. [...] Telescript is the revolutionary software technology that makes intelligent assistance possible. Invented by General Magic, AT&T is the first company to harness Telescript, and bring its benefits to people everywhere. [...] Very shortly, anyone with a computer, a personal communicator, or television will be able to use intelligent assistance in the Cloud. And our new meeting place is open, so that anyone, whether individual, entrepreneur, or a multinational company, will be able to offer information, goods, and services.
19. Steven Levy (April 1994). "Bill and Andy's Excellent Adventure II". Wired.
20. White, J.E. "Network Specifications for Remote Job Entry and Remote Job Output Retrieval at UCSB". tools.ietf.org. Retrieved 2016-03-21.
21. Griffin, Ry'mone (2018-11-20). Internet Governance. Scientific e-Resources. ISBN 978-1-83947-395-1.
22. "July, 1993 meeting report from the IP over ATM working group of the IETF". CH: Switch. Archived from the original on 2012-07-10. Retrieved 2010-08-22.
23. Griffin, Ry'mone (2018-11-20). Internet Governance. Scientific e-Resources. ISBN 978-1-83947-395-1.
24. Corbató, Fernando J. "An Experimental Time-Sharing System". SJCC Proceedings. MIT. Archived from the original on 6 September 2009. Retrieved 3 July 2012.
25. Griffin, Ry'mone (2018-11-20). Internet Governance. Scientific e-Resources. ISBN 978-1-83947-395-1.
26. Levy, Steven (April 1994). "Bill and Andy's Excellent Adventure II". Wired.
27. Levy, Steven (2014-05-23). "Tech Time Warp of the Week: Watch AT&T Invent Cloud Computing in 1994". Wired. AT&T and the film's director, David Hoffman, pulled out the cloud metaphor–something that had long been used among networking and telecom types. [...]
"You can think of our electronic meeting place as the cloud," says the film's narrator, [...]
David Hoffman, the man who directed the film and shaped all that cloud imagery, was a General Magic employee.
28. "Introducing Google App Engine + our new blog". Google Developer Blog. 2008-04-07. Retrieved 2017-03-07.

29. Rochwerger, B.; Breitgand, D.; Levy, E.; Galis, A.; Nagin, K.; Llorente, I. M.; Montero, R.; Wolfsthal, Y.; Elmroth, E.; Caceres, J.; Ben-Yehuda, M.; Emmerich, W.; Galan, F. (2009). "The Reservoir model and architecture for open federated cloud computing". IBM Journal of Research and Development. 53 (4): 4:1–4:11. doi:10.1147/JRD.2009.5429058.
30. Keep an eye on cloud computing, Amy Schurr, Network World, 2008-07-08, citing the Gartner report, "Cloud Computing Confusion Leads to Opportunity". Retrieved 2009-09-11.
31. Gartner (2008-08-18). "Gartner Says Worldwide IT Spending on Pace to Surpass Trillion in 2008".
32. Program Solicitation NSF 08-560
33. "Windows Azure General Availability". The Official Microsoft Blog. Microsoft. 2010-02-01. Archived from the original on 2014-05-11. Retrieved 2015-05-03.
34. Milita Datta (August 9, 2016). "Apache CloudStack vs. OpenStack: Which Is the Best?". DZone · Cloud Zone.
35. "OpenNebula vs OpenStack". SoftwareInsider.[dead link]
36. Kostantos, Konstantinos, et al. "OPEN-source IaaS fit for purpose: a comparison between OpenNebula and OpenStack." International Journal of Electronic Business Management 11.3 (2013)
37. L. Albertson, "OpenStack vs. Ganeti", LinuxFest Northwest 2017
38. Qevani, Elton, et al. "What can OpenStack adopt from a Ganeti-based open-source IaaS?." Cloud Computing (CLOUD), 2014 IEEE 7th International Conference on. IEEE, 2014
39. Von Laszewski, Gregor, et al. "Comparison of multiple cloud frameworks.", IEEE 5th International Conference on Cloud Computing (CLOUD), 2012.
40. Diaz, Javier et al. " Abstract Image Management and Universal Image Registration for Cloud and HPC Infrastructures ", IEEE 5th International Conference on Cloud Computing (CLOUD), 2012
41. "Launch of IBM Smarter Computing". Archived from the original on 20 April 2013. Retrieved 1 March 2011.
42. "Launch of Oracle Cloud". Retrieved 28 February 2014.
43. "Oracle Cloud, Enterprise-Grade Cloud Solutions: SaaS, PaaS, and IaaS". Retrieved 12 October 2014.
44. "Larry Ellison Doesn't Get the Cloud: The Dumbest Idea of 2013". Forbes.com. Retrieved 12 October 2014.
45. "Oracle Disrupts Cloud Industry with End-to-End Approach". Forbes.com. Retrieved 12 October 2014.
46. "Google Compute Engine is now Generally Available with expanded OS support, transparent maintenance, and lower prices". Google Developers Blog. 2013-12-02. Retrieved 2017-03-07.
47. HAMDAQA, Mohammad (2012). Cloud Computing Uncovered: A Research Landscape (PDF). Elsevier Press. pp. 41–85. ISBN 978-0-12-396535-6.
48. "Distributed Application Architecture" (PDF). Sun Microsystem. Retrieved 2009-06-16.
49. Vaquero, Luis M.; Rodero-Merino, Luis; Caceres, Juan; Lindner, Maik (December 2008). "It's probable that you've misunderstood 'Cloud Computing' until now". Sigcomm Comput. Commun. Rev. TechPluto. 39 (1): 50–55. doi:10.1145/1496091.1496100. S2CID 207171174.
50. Danielson, Krissi (2008-03-26). "Distinguishing Cloud Computing from Utility Computing". Ebizq.net. Retrieved 2010-08-22.
51. "Recession Is Good For Cloud Computing – Microsoft Agrees". CloudAve. 2009-02-12. Retrieved 2010-08-22.
52. "Defining 'Cloud Services' and "Cloud Computing"". IDC. 2008-09-23. Archived from the original on 2010-07-22. Retrieved 2010-08-22.
53. "e-FISCAL project state of the art repository".
54. Farber, Dan (2008-06-25). "The new geek chic: Data centers". CNET News. Retrieved 2010-08-22.
55. "Jeff Bezos' Risky Bet". Business Week.
56. He, Sijin; Guo, L.; Guo, Y.; Ghanem, M. (June 2012). Improving Resource Utilisation in the Cloud Environment Using Multivariate Probabilistic Models. 2012 2012 IEEE 5th International Conference on Cloud Computing (CLOUD). pp. 574–581. doi:10.1109/CLOUD.2012.66. ISBN 978-1-4673-2892-0. S2CID 15374752.
57. He, Qiang, et al. "Formulating Cost-Effective Monitoring Strategies for Service-based Systems." (2013): 1–1.
58. Heather Smith (23 May 2013). Xero For Dummies. John Wiley & Sons. pp. 37–. ISBN 978-1-118-57252-8.
59. King, Rachael (2008-08-04). "Cloud Computing: Small Companies Take Flight". Bloomberg BusinessWeek. Retrieved 2010-08-22.
60. Mao, Ming; M. Humphrey (2012). A Performance Study on the VM Startup Time in the Cloud. Proceedings of 2012 IEEE 5th International Conference on Cloud Computing (Cloud2012). p. 423. doi:10.1109/CLOUD.2012.103. ISBN 978-1-4673-2892-0. S2CID 1285357.
61. Bruneo, Dario; Distefano, Salvatore; Longo, Francesco; Puliafito, Antonio; Scarpa, Marco (2013). "Workload-Based Software Rejuvenation in Cloud Systems". IEEE Transactions on Computers. 62 (6): 1072–1085. doi:10.1109/TC.2013.30. S2CID 23981532.
62. Kuperberg, Michael; Herbst, Nikolas; Kistowski, Joakim Von; Reussner, Ralf (2011). "Defining and Measuring Cloud Elasticity". KIT Software Quality Departement. doi:10.5445/IR/1000023476. Retrieved 13 August 2011.
63. "Economies of Cloud Scale Infrastructure". Cloud Slam 2011. Retrieved 13 May 2011.
64. He, Sijin; L. Guo; Y. Guo; C. Wu; M. Ghanem; R. Han (March 2012). Elastic Application Container: A Lightweight Approach for Cloud Resource Provisioning. 2012 IEEE 26th International Conference on Advanced Information Networking and Applications (AINA). pp. 15–22. doi:10.1109/AINA.2012.74. ISBN 978-1-4673-0714-7. S2CID 4863927.
65. Marston, Sean; Li, Zhi; Bandyopadhyay, Subhajyoti; Zhang, Juheng; Ghalsasi, Anand (2011-04-01). "Cloud computing – The business perspective". Decision Support Systems. 51 (1): 176–189. doi:10.1016/j.dss.2010.12.006.
66. Nouri, Seyed; Han, Li; Srikumar, Venugopal; Wenxia, Guo; MingYun, He; Wenhong, Tian (2019). "Autonomic decentralized elasticity based on a reinforcement learning controller for cloud applications". Future Generation Computer Systems. 94: 765–780. doi:10.1016/j.future.2018.11.049.
67. Mills, Elinor (2009-01-27). "Cloud computing security forecast: Clear skies". CNET News. Retrieved 2019-09-19.
68. Peter Mell; Timothy Grance (September 2011). The NIST Definition of Cloud Computing (Technical report). National Institute of Standards and Technology: U.S. Department of Commerce. doi:10.6028/NIST.SP.800-145. Special publication 800-145.
69. Duan, Yucong; Fu, Guohua; Zhou, Nianjun; Sun, Xiaobing; Narendra, Nanjangud; Hu, Bo (2015). "Everything as a Service (XaaS) on the Cloud: Origins, Current and Future Trends". 2015 IEEE 8th International Conference on Cloud Computing. IEEE. pp. 621–628. doi:10.1109/CLOUD.2015.88. ISBN 978-1-4673-7287-9. S2CID 8201466.
70. "ElasticHosts Blog". Elastichosts. 2014-04-01. Retrieved 2016-06-02.
71. Amies, Alex; Sluiman, Harm; Tong, Qiang Guo; Liu, Guo Ning (July 2012). "Infrastructure as a Service Cloud Concepts". Developing and Hosting Applications on the Cloud. IBM Press. ISBN 978-0-13-306684-5.
72. Griffin, Ry'mone (2018-11-20). Internet Governance. Scientific e-Resources. p. 111. ISBN 978-1-83947-395-1.
73. Boniface, M.; et al. (2010). Platform-as-a-Service Architecture for Real-Time Quality of Service Management in Clouds. 5th International Conference on Internet and Web Applications and Services (ICIW). Barcelona, Spain: IEEE. pp. 155–160. doi:10.1109/ICIW.2010.91.
74. "Integration Platform as a Service (iPaaS)". Gartner IT Glossary. Gartner.
75. Gartner; Massimo Pezzini; Paolo Malinverno; Eric Thoo. "Gartner Reference Model for Integration PaaS". Retrieved 16 January 2013.
76. Loraine Lawson. "IT Business Edge". Retrieved 6 July 2015.
77. Enterprise CIO Forum; Gabriel Lowy. "The Value of Data Platform-as-a-Service (dPaaS)". Archived from the original on 19 April 2015. Retrieved 6 July 2015.
78. "Definition of: SaaS". PC Magazine Encyclopedia. Ziff Davis. Retrieved 14 May 2014.
79. Hamdaqa, Mohammad. A Reference Model for Developing Cloud Applications (PDF).
80. Chou, Timothy. Introduction to Cloud Computing: Business & Technology.
81. "HVD: the cloud's silver lining" (PDF). Intrinsic Technology. Archived from the original (PDF) on 2 October 2012. Retrieved 30 August 2012.
82. Carney, Michael (2013-06-24). "AnyPresence partners with Heroku to beef up its enterprise mBaaS offering". PandoDaily. Retrieved 24 June 2013.
83. Alex Williams (11 October 2012). "Kii Cloud Opens Doors For Mobile Developer Platform With 25 Million End Users". TechCrunch. Retrieved 16 October 2012.
84. Aaron Tan (30 September 2012). "FatFractal ups the ante in backend-as-a-service market". Techgoondu.com. Retrieved 16 October 2012.
85. Dan Rowinski (9 November 2011). "Mobile Backend As A Service Parse Raises $5.5 Million in Series A Funding". ReadWrite. Retrieved 23 October 2012.
86. Pankaj Mishra (7 January 2014). "MobStac Raises $2 Million in Series B To Help Brands Leverage Mobile Commerce". TechCrunch. Retrieved 22 May 2014.
87. "built.io Is Building an Enterprise MBaas Platform for IoT". programmableweb. 2014-03-03. Retrieved 3 March 2014.
88. Miller, Ron (24 Nov 2015). "AWS Lambda Makes Serverless Applications A Reality". TechCrunch. Retrieved 10 July 2016.
89. "bliki: Serverless". martinfowler.com. Retrieved 2018-05-04.
90. Sbarski, Peter (2017-05-04). Serverless Architectures on AWS: With examples using AWS Lambda (1st ed.). Manning Publications. ISBN 9781617293825.
91. "Self-Run Private Cloud Computing Solution – GovConnection". govconnection.com. 2014. Retrieved April 15, 2014.
92. "Private Clouds Take Shape – Services – Business services – Informationweek". 2012-09-09. Archived from the original on 2012-09-09.
93. Haff, Gordon (2009-01-27). "Just don't call them private clouds". CNET News. Retrieved 2010-08-22.
94. "There's No Such Thing As A Private Cloud – Cloud-computing -". 2013-01-26. Archived from the original on 2013-01-26.
95. Rouse, Margaret. "What is public cloud?". Definition from Whatis.com. Retrieved 12 October 2014.
96. "FastConnect | Oracle Cloud Infrastructure". cloud.oracle.com. Retrieved 2017-11-15.
97. "What is hybrid cloud? - Definition from WhatIs.com". SearchCloudComputing. Retrieved 2019-08-10.
98. Butler, Brandon (2017-10-17). "What is hybrid cloud computing? The benefits of mixing private and public cloud services". Network World. Retrieved 2019-08-11.
99. "Mind the Gap: Here Comes Hybrid Cloud – Thomas Bittman". Thomas Bittman. Retrieved 22 April 2015.
100. "Business Intelligence Takes to Cloud for Small Businesses". CIO.com. 2014-06-04. Retrieved 2014-06-04.
101. Désiré Athow. "Hybrid cloud: is it right for your business?". TechRadar. Retrieved 22 April 2015.
102. Metzler, Jim; Taylor, Steve. (2010-08-23) "Cloud computing: Reality vs. fiction", Network World.
103. Rouse, Margaret. "Definition: Cloudbursting", May 2011. SearchCloudComputing.com.
104. "How Cloudbursting "Rightsizes" the Data Center". 2012-06-22.
105. Kaewkasi, Chanwit (3 May 2015). "Cross-Platform Hybrid Cloud with Docker".
106. Qiang, Li (2009). "Adaptive management of virtualized resources in cloud computing using feedback control". First International Conference on Information Science and Engineering.
107. Cunsolo, Vincenzo D.; Distefano, Salvatore; Puliafito, Antonio; Scarpa, Marco (2009). "Volunteer Computing and Desktop Cloud: The Cloud@Home Paradigm". 2009 Eighth IEEE International Symposium on Network Computing and Applications. pp. 134–139. doi:10.1109/NCA.2009.41. S2CID 15848602.
108. Rouse, Margaret. "What is a multi-cloud strategy". SearchCloudApplications. Retrieved 3 July 2014.
109. King, Rachel. "Pivotal's head of products: We're moving to a multi-cloud world". ZDnet. Retrieved 3 July 2014.
110. Multcloud manage multiple cloud accounts. Retrieved on 06 August 2014
111. Gall, Richard (2018-05-16). "Polycloud: a better alternative to cloud agnosticism". Packt Hub. Retrieved 2019-11-11.
112. Roh, Lucas (31 August 2016). "Is the Cloud Finally Ready for Big Data?". dataconomy.com. Retrieved 29 January 2018.
113. Yang, C.; Huang, Q.; Li, Z.; Liu, K.; Hu, F. (2017). "Big Data and cloud computing: innovation opportunities and challenges". International Journal of Digital Earth. 10 (1): 13–53. Bibcode:2017IJDE...10...13Y. doi:10.1080/17538947.2016.1239771. S2CID 8053067.
114. Netto, M.; Calheiros, R.; Rodrigues, E.; Cunha, R.; Buyya, R. (2018). "HPC Cloud for Scientific and Business Applications: Taxonomy, Vision, and Research Challenges". ACM Computing Surveys. 51 (1): 8:1–8:29. arXiv:1710.08731. doi:10.1145/3150224. S2CID 3604131.
115. Eadline, Douglas. "Moving HPC to the Cloud". Admin Magazine. Admin Magazine. Retrieved 30 March 2019.
116. "Penguin Computing On Demand (POD)". Retrieved 23 January 2018.

117. Niccolai, James (11 August 2009). "Penguin Puts High-performance Computing in the Cloud". PCWorld. IDG Consumer & SMB. Retrieved 6 June 2016.
118. "HPC in AWS". Retrieved 23 January 2018.
119. "Building GrepTheWeb in the Cloud, Part 1: Cloud Architectures". Developer.amazonwebservices.com. Archived from the original on 5 May 2009. Retrieved 22 August 2010.
120. "Cloud Computing Privacy Concerns on Our Doorstep".
121. Haghighat, Mohammad; Zonouz, Saman; Abdel-Mottaleb, Mohamed (2015). "CloudID: Trustworthy cloud-based and cross-enterprise biometric identification". Expert Systems with Applications. 42 (21): 7905–7916. doi:10.1016/j.eswa.2015.06.025.
122. Identity and access management in cloud environment: Mechanisms and challenges
123. "Google Drive, Dropbox, Box and iCloud Reach the Top 5 Cloud Storage Security Breaches List". psg.hitachi-solutions.com. Archived from the original on 2015-11-23. Retrieved 2015-11-22.
124. Maltais, Michelle (26 April 2012). "Who owns your stuff in the cloud?". Los Angeles Times. Retrieved 2012-12-14.
125. "Security of virtualization, cloud computing divides IT and security pros". Network World. 2010-02-22. Retrieved 2010-08-22.
126. "The Bumpy Road to Private Clouds". 2010-12-20. Retrieved 8 October 2014.
127. "Should Companies Do Most of Their Computing in the Cloud? (Part 1) – Schneier on Security". www.schneier.com. Retrieved 2016-02-28.
128. "Disadvantages of Cloud Computing (Part 1) – Limited control and flexibility". www.cloudacademy.com. Retrieved 2016-11-03.
129. "The real limits of cloud computing". www.itworld.com. 2012-05-14. Retrieved 2016-11-03.
130. Karra, Maria. "Cloud solutions for translation, yes or no?". IAPTI.org. Retrieved 23 February 2017.
131. Seltzer, Larry. "Your infrastructure's in the cloud and the Internet goes down. Now what?". ZDNet. Retrieved 2020-06-01.
132. Smith, David Mitchell. "Hype Cycle for Cloud Computing, 2013". Gartner. Retrieved 3 July 2014.
133. "The evolution of Cloud Computing". Archived from the original on 29 March 2017. Retrieved 22 April 2015.
134. "Microsoft Says to Spend 90% of R&D on Cloud Strategy". Archived from the original on 18 October 2013. Retrieved 22 April 2015.
135. "Roundup of Cloud Computing Forecasts And Market Estimates, 2014". Forbes. Retrieved 2015-11-22.
136. Ruan, Keyun; Carthy, Joe; Kechadi, Tahar; Crosbie, Mark (2011-01-01). Cloud forensics: An overview.
137. R., Adams (2013). The emergence of cloud storage and the need for a new digital forensic process model. researchrepository.murdoch.edu.au. ISBN 9781466626621. Retrieved 2018-03-18.
138. Richard, Adams; Graham, Mann; Valerie, Hobbs (2017). "ISEEK, a tool for high speed, concurrent, distributed forensic data acquisition". Research Online. doi:10.4225/75/5a838d3b1d27f.
139. "Office 365 Advanced eDiscovery". Retrieved 2018-03-18.

Electronic authentication, References

1. The Office of the Government Chief Information Officer. "What is e-Authentication?". The Government of the Hong Kong Special Administrative Region of the People's Republic of China. Archived from the original on 22 December 2015. Retrieved 1 November 2015.
2. Balbas, Luis. "Digital Authentication - Factors, Mechanisms and Schemes". Cryptomathic. Retrieved 9 January 2017.
3. McMahon, Mary. "What is E-Authentication?". wiseGEEK. Retrieved 2 November 2015.
4. Turner, Dawn M. "Digital Authentication - the Basics". Cryptomathic. Retrieved 9 January 2017.
5. Burr, William; Dodson, Donna; Newton, Elaine (2011). "Electronic Authentication Guideline" (PDF). National Institute of Standards and Technology. doi:10.6028/NIST.SP.800-63-1. Retrieved 3 November 2015.
6. Schneier, Bruce. "The Failure of Two-Factor Authentication". Schneier on Security. Retrieved 2 November 2015.
7. Office of the Government Chief Information Officer. "Passwords and PINs based Authentication". The Government of the Hong Kong Special Administrative Region of the People's Republic of China. Archived from the original on May 31, 2015. Retrieved 2 November 2015.
8. Office of the Government Chief Information Officer. "Public-Key Authentication". The Government of the Hong Kong Special Administrative Region of the People's Republic of China. Archived from the original on May 31, 2015. Retrieved 3 November 2015.
9. Office of the Government Chief Information Officer. "Symmetric-key Authentication". The Government of the Hong Kong Special Administrative Region of the People's Republic of China. Archived from the original on July 9, 2015. Retrieved 3 November 2015.
10. Office of the Government Chief Information Officer. "SMS based Authentication". The Government of the Hong Kong Special Administrative Region of the People's Republic of China. Archived from the original on August 27, 2015. Retrieved 3 November 2015.
11. Office of the Government Chief Information Officer. "Biometric Authentication". The Government of the Hong Kong Special Administrative Region of the People's Republic of China. Archived from the original on January 8, 2015. Retrieved 3 November 2015.
12. Burr, William; Dodson, Donna; Polk, W (2006). "INFORMATION SECURITY" (PDF). National Institute of Standards and Technology. doi:10.6028/NIST.SP.800-63v1.0.2. Retrieved 3 November 2015.
13. Turner, Dawn M. "Understanding Non-Repudiation of Origin and Non-Repudiation of Emission". Cryptomathic. Retrieved 9 January 2017.
14. https://pdfs.semanticscholar.org/c3e6/b094d8052137c6e91f9c89cba860d356483a.pdf
15. http://journal.fidis-project.eu/fileadmin/journal/issues/1-2007/Biometric_Implementations_and_the_Implications_for_Security_and_Privacy.pdf
16. "E-Authentication Risk Assessment for Electronic Prescriptions for Controlled Substances" (PDF). Retrieved 3 November 2015.
17. Radack, Shirley. "ELECTRONIC AUTHENTICATION: GUIDANCE FOR SELECTING SECURE TECHNIQUES". Archived from the original on September 15, 2015. Retrieved 3 November 2015.
18. Bolten, Joshua. "Memorandum: E-Authentication Guideline for Federal Agencies" (PDF). Executive Office of the President, Office of Management and Budget (OMB). Retrieved 9 January 2017.
19. Radack, Shirley. "ELECTRONIC AUTHENTICATION: GUIDANCE FOR SELECTING SECURE TECHNIQUES". National Institute of Standards and Technology. Archived from the original on September 15, 2015. Retrieved 3 November 2015.
20. McCarthy, Shawn. "E-authentication: What IT managers will be focusing on over the next 18 months". GCN. Retrieved 2 November 2015.
21. "Whole of Government Information and Communications Technology".
22. Breaking Barriers to eGovernment (Draft Deliverable 1b), eGovernment unit, European Commission, August 2006. See table 1
23. An overview of International Initiatives in the field of Electronic Authentication Archived 2011-07-22 at the Wayback Machine, Japan PKI Forum, June 2, 2005.
24. Australia Archived 2012-02-12 at the Wayback Machine, Canada Archived 2008-03-05 at the Wayback Machine, US (M04-04).
25. "Draft NIST Special Publication 800-63-3: Digital Authentication Guideline". National Institute of Standards and Technology, USA. Retrieved 9 January 2017.
26. Turner, Dawn. "Understanding eIDAS". Cryptomathic. Retrieved 12 April 2016.
27. "Regulation (EU) No 910/2014 of the European Parliament and of the Council of 23 July 2014 on electronic identification and trust services for electronic transactions in the internal market and repealing Directive 1999/93/EC". EUR-Lex. The European Parliament and the Council of the European Union. Retrieved 18 March 2016.
28. "Постановление Правительства РФ от 28 ноября 2011 г. N 977 "О федеральной государственной информационной системе "Единая система идентификации и аутентификации в инфраструктуре, обеспечивающей информационно-технологическое взаимодействие информационных систем, используемых для предоставления государственных и муниципальных услуг в электронной форме"".
29. Margaret, Rouse. "mobile authentication definition". SearchSecurity.com. Retrieved 3 November 2015.
30. Government of India Department of Electronics and Information Technology Ministry of Communications and Information Technology. "e-Pramaan: Framework for e-Authentication" (PDF). Retrieved 3 November 2015.
31. Tolentino, Jamie (16 March 2015). "How to Increase App Security Through Mobile Phone Authentication". TNW news. Retrieved 3 November 2015.
32. Ford, Matthew (23 Feb 2005). "Identity Authentication and 'E-Commerce'". Warwick, Journal of Information Law &Technology. Retrieved 3 November 2015.
33. Sawma, Victor. "A New Methodology for Deriving Effective Countermeasures Design Models". School of Information Technology and Engineering, University of Ottawa. CiteSeerX 10.1.1.100.1216.
34. Walker, Heather. "How eIDAS affects the USA". Cryptomathic. Retrieved 9 January 2017.

Physical security, References

1. "Chapter 1: Physical Security Challenges". Field Manual 3-19.30: Physical Security. Headquarters, United States Department of Army. 2001. Archived from the original on 2013-03-13.
2. Garcia, Mary Lynn (2007). Design and Evaluation of Physical Protection Systems. Butterworth-Heinemann. pp. 1–11. ISBN 9780080554280. Archived from the original on 2013-09-21.
3. "Chapter 2: The Systems Approach". Field Manual 3-19.30: Physical Security. Headquarters, United States Department of Army. 2001. Archived from the original on 2013-09-21.
4. Anderson, Ross (2001). Security Engineering. Wiley. ISBN 978-0-471-38922-4.
5. For a detailed discussion on natural surveillance and CPTED, see Fennelly, Lawrence J. (2012). Effective Physical Security. Butterworth-Heinemann. pp. 4–6. ISBN 9780124158924. Archived from the original on 2018-01-05.
6. Task Committee; Structural Engineering Institute (1999). Structural Design for Physical Security. ASCE. ISBN 978-0-7844-0457-7. Archived from the original on 2018-01-05.
7. Baker, Paul R. (2012). "Security Construction Projects". In Baker, Paul R.; Benny, Daniel J. (eds.). The Complete Guide to Physical Security. CRC Press. ISBN 9781420099638. Archived from the original on 2018-01-05.
8. "Chapter 4: Protective Barriers". Field Manual 3-19.30: Physical Security. Headquarters, United States Department of Army. 2001. Archived from the original on 2013-03-13.
9. Talbot, Julian & Jakeman, Miles (2011). Security Risk Management Body of Knowledge. John Wiley & Sons. pp. 72–73. ISBN 9781118211267. Archived from the original on 2018-01-05.
10. Kovacich, Gerald L. & Halibozek, Edward P. (2003). The Manager's Handbook for Corporate Security: Establishing and Managing a Successful Assets Protection Program. Butterworth-Heinemann. pp. 192–193. ISBN 9780750674874. Archived from the original on 2018-01-05.
11. "Use of LED Lighting for Security Purposes". silvaconsultants.com. Retrieved 2020-10-06.
12. "Chapter 6: Electronic Security Systems". Field Manual 3-19.30: Physical Security. Headquarters, United States Department of Army. 2001. Archived from the original on 2013-03-13.
13. Fennelly, Lawrence J. (2012). Effective Physical Security. Butterworth-Heinemann. pp. 345–346. ISBN 9780124158924. Archived from the original on 2013-09-21.
14. "Evaluation of alternative policies to combat false emergency calls" (PDF). p. 238. Archived from the original (PDF) on 2012-11-01.
15. "Evaluation of alternative policies to combat false emergency calls" (PDF). p. 233. Archived from the original (PDF) on 2012-11-01.
16. "Evaluating the Use of Public Surveillance Cameras for Crime Control and Prevention" (PDF). Archived (PDF) from the original on 2012-12-01.
17. Crowell, William P.; et al. (2011). "Intelligent Video Analytics". In Cole, Eric (ed.). Physical and Logical Security Convergence. Syngress. ISBN 9780080558783. Archived from the original on 2018-01-05.
18. Dufour, Jean-Yves (2012). Intelligent Video Surveillance Systems. John Wiley & Sons. ISBN 9781118577868. Archived from the original on 2018-01-05.
19. Caputo, Anthony C. (2010). Digital Video Surveillance and Security. Butterworth-Heinemann. ISBN 9780080961699. Archived from the original on 2013-09-29.
20. Tyska, Louis A. & Fennelly, Lawrence J. (2000). Physical Security: 150 Things You Should Know. Butterworth-Heinemann. p. 3. ISBN 9780750672559. Archived from the original on 2018-01-05.
21. "Chapter 7: Access Control". Field Manual 3-19.30: Physical Security. Headquarters, United States Department of Army. 2001. Archived from the original on 2007-05-10.

22.   *Pearson, Robert (2011). "Chapter 1: Electronic Access Control". Electronic Security Systems: A Manager's Guide to Evaluating and Selecting System Solutions. Butterworth-Heinemann. ISBN 9780080494708. Archived from the original on 2018-01-05.*
23.   *Reid, Robert N. (2005). "Guards and guard forces". Facility Manager's Guide to Security: Protecting Your Assets. The Fairmont Press. ISBN 9780881734836. Archived from the original on 2018-01-05.*

Cryptography, References

1.   *Liddell, Henry George; Scott, Robert; Jones, Henry Stuart; McKenzie, Roderick (1984). A Greek-English Lexicon. Oxford University Press.*
2.   *Rivest, Ronald L. (1990). "Cryptography". In J. Van Leeuwen (ed.). Handbook of Theoretical Computer Science. 1. Elsevier.*
3.   *Bellare, Mihir; Rogaway, Phillip (21 September 2005). "Introduction". Introduction to Modern Cryptography. p. 10.*
4.   *Menezes, A.J.; van Oorschot, P.C.; Vanstone, S.A. (1997). Handbook of Applied Cryptography. ISBN 978-0-8493-8523-0.*
5.   *Biggs, Norman (2008). Codes: An introduction to Information Communication and Cryptography. Springer. p. 171.*
6.   *"Overview per country". Crypto Law Survey. February 2013. Retrieved 26 March 2015.*
7.   *"UK Data Encryption Disclosure Law Takes Effect". PC World. 1 October 2007. Retrieved 26 March 2015.*
8.   *Ranger, Steve (24 March 2015). "The undercover war on your internet secrets: How online surveillance cracked our trust in the web". TechRepublic. Archived from the original on 12 June 2016. Retrieved 12 June 2016.*
9.   *Doctorow, Cory (2 May 2007). "Digg users revolt over AACS key". Boing Boing. Retrieved 26 March 2015.*
10.   *Whalen, Terence (1994). "The Code for Gold: Edgar Allan Poe and Cryptography". Representations. University of California Press. 46 (46): 35–57. doi:10.2307/2928778. JSTOR 2928778.*
11.   *Rosenheim 1997, p. 20*
12.   *Kahn, David (1967). The Codebreakers. ISBN 978-0-684-83130-5.*
13.   *"An Introduction to Modern Cryptosystems".*
14.   *Sharbaf, M.S. (1 November 2011). "Quantum cryptography: An emerging technology in network security". 2011 IEEE International Conference on Technologies for Homeland Security (HST). pp. 13–19. doi:10.1109/THS.2011.6107841. ISBN 978-1-4577-1376-7. S2CID 17915038. Missing or empty |title= (help)*
15.   *Oded Goldreich, Foundations of Cryptography, Volume 1: Basic Tools, Cambridge University Press, 2001, ISBN 0-521-79172-3*
16.   *"Cryptology (definition)". Merriam-Webster's Collegiate Dictionary (11th ed.). Merriam-Webster. Retrieved 26 March 2015.*
17.   *"Internet Security Glossary". Internet Engineering Task Force. May 2000. RFC 2828. Retrieved 26 March 2015.*
18.   *I︠A︡shchenko, V.V. (2002). Cryptography: an introduction. AMS Bookstore. p. 6. ISBN 978-0-8218-2986-8.*
19.   *electricpulp.com. "CODES – Encyclopaedia Iranica". www.iranicaonline.org.*
20.   *Kahn, David (1996). The Codebreakers: The Comprehensive History of Secret Communication from Ancient Times to the Internet. Simon and Schuster. ISBN 9781439103555.*
21.   *Broemeling, Lyle D. (1 November 2011). "An Account of Early Statistical Inference in Arab Cryptology". The American Statistician. 65 (4): 255–257. doi:10.1198/tas.2011.10191. S2CID 123537702.*
22.   *Singh, Simon (2000). The Code Book. New York: Anchor Books. pp. 14–20. ISBN 978-0-385-49532-5.*
23.   *Leaman, Oliver (16 July 2015). The Biographical Encyclopedia of Islamic Philosophy. Bloomsbury Publishing. ISBN 9781472569455. Retrieved 19 March 2018 – via Google Books.*
24.   *Al-Jubouri, I. M. N. (19 March 2018). History of Islamic Philosophy: With View of Greek Philosophy and Early History of Islam. Authors On Line Ltd. ISBN 9780755210114. Retrieved 19 March 2018 – via Google Books.*
25.   *Al-Kadi, Ibrahim A. (April 1992). "The origins of cryptology: The Arab contributions". Cryptologia. 16 (2): 97–126. doi:10.1080/0161-119291866801.*
26.   *Simon Singh, The Code Book, pp. 14–20*
27.   *Lennon, Brian (2018). Passwords: Philology, Security, Authentication. Harvard University Press. p. 26. ISBN 9780674985377.*
28.   *Schrödel, Tobias (October 2008). "Breaking Short Vigenère Ciphers". Cryptologia. 32 (4): 334–337. doi:10.1080/01611190802336097. S2CID 21812933.*
29.   *Hakim, Joy (1995). A History of US: War, Peace and all that Jazz. New York: Oxford University Press. ISBN 978-0-19-509514-2.*
30.   *Gannon, James (2001). Stealing Secrets, Telling Lies: How Spies and Codebreakers Helped Shape the Twentieth Century. Washington, D.C.: Brassey's. ISBN 978-1-57488-367-1.*
31.   *Diffie, Whitfield; Hellman, Martin (November 1976). "New Directions in Cryptography" (PDF). IEEE Transactions on Information Theory. IT-22 (6): 644–654. CiteSeerX 10.1.1.37.9720. doi:10.1109/tit.1976.1055638.*
32.   *Wolfram, Stephen (2002). A New Kind of Science. Wolfram Media, Inc. p. 1089. ISBN 978-1-57955-008-0.*
33.   *Cryptography: Theory and Practice, Third Edition (Discrete Mathematics and Its Applications), 2005, by Douglas R. Stinson, Chapman and Hall/CRC*
34.   *Blaze, Matt; Diffie, Whitefield; Rivest, Ronald L.; Schneier, Bruce; Shimomura, Tsutomu; Thompson, Eric; Wiener, Michael (January 1996). "Minimal key lengths for symmetric ciphers to provide adequate commercial security". Fortify. Retrieved 26 March 2015.*
35.   *"FIPS PUB 197: The official Advanced Encryption Standard" (PDF). Computer Security Resource Center. National Institute of Standards and Technology. Archived from the original (PDF) on 7 April 2015. Retrieved 26 March 2015.*
36.   *"NCUA letter to credit unions" (PDF). National Credit Union Administration. July 2004. Retrieved 26 March 2015.*
37.   *"Open PGP Message Format". Internet Engineering Task Force. November 1998. RFC 2440. Retrieved 26 March 2015.*
38.   *Golen, Pawel (19 July 2002). "SSH". WindowSecurity. Retrieved 26 March 2015.*
39.   *Schneier, Bruce (1996). Applied Cryptography (2nd ed.). Wiley. ISBN 978-0-471-11709-4.*
40.   *"Notices". Federal Register. 72 (212). 2 November 2007.*
       "Archived copy" (PDF). Archived from the original on 28 February 2008. Retrieved 27 January 2009.
41.   *"NIST Selects Winner of Secure Hash Algorithm (SHA-3) Competition". Tech Beat. National Institute of Standards and Technology. 2 October 2012. Retrieved 26 March 2015.*
42.   *Diffie, Whitfield; Hellman, Martin (8 June 1976). "Multi-user cryptographic techniques". AFIPS Proceedings. 45: 109–112. doi:10.1145/1499799.1499815. S2CID 13210741.*
43.   Ralph Merkle was working on similar ideas at the time and encountered publication delays, and Hellman has suggested that the term used should be Diffie–Hellman–Merkle aysmmetric key cryptography.
44.   *Kahn, David (Fall 1979). "Cryptology Goes Public". Foreign Affairs. 58 (1): 141–159. doi:10.2307/20040343. JSTOR 20040343.*
45.   *"Using Client-Certificate based authentication with NGINX on Ubuntu - SSLTrust". SSLTrust. Retrieved 13 June 2019.*
46.   *Rivest, Ronald L.; Shamir, A.; Adleman, L. (1978). "A Method for Obtaining Digital Signatures and Public-Key Cryptosystems". Communications of the ACM. 21 (2): 120–126. CiteSeerX 10.1.1.607.2677. doi:10.1145/359340.359342. S2CID 2873616.*
       "Archived copy" (PDF). Archived from the original (PDF) on 16 November 2001. Retrieved 20 April 2006.
       Previously released as an MIT "Technical Memo" in April 1977, and published in Martin Gardner's *Scientific American* Mathematical recreations column
47.   *Wayner, Peter (24 December 1997). "British Document Outlines Early Encryption Discovery". The New York Times. Retrieved 26 March 2015.*
48.   *Cocks, Clifford (20 November 1973). "A Note on 'Non-Secret Encryption'" (PDF). CESG Research Report.*
49.   *Singh, Simon (1999). The Code Book. Doubleday. pp. 279–292.*
50.   *Shannon, Claude; Weaver, Warren (1963). The Mathematical Theory of Communication. University of Illinois Press. ISBN 978-0-252-72548-7.*
51.   *"An Example of a Man-in-the-middle Attack Against Server Authenticated SSL-sessions" (PDF).*
52.   *Junod, Pascal (2001). On the Complexity of Matsui's Attack (PDF). Selected Areas in Cryptography. Lecture Notes in Computer Science. 2259. pp. 199–211. doi:10.1007/3-540-45537-X_16. ISBN 978-3-540-43066-7.*
53.   *Song, Dawn; Wagner, David A.; Tian, Xuqing (2001). "Timing Analysis of Keystrokes and Timing Attacks on SSH" (PDF). Tenth USENIX Security Symposium.*
54.   *Brands, S. (1994). "Untraceable Off-line Cash in Wallet with Observers". Untraceable Off-line Cash in Wallets with Observers. Advances in Cryptology—Proceedings of CRYPTO. Lecture Notes in Computer Science. 773. pp. 302–318. doi:10.1007/3-540-48329-2_26. ISBN 978-3-540-57766-9. Archived from the original on 26 July 2011.*
55.   *Babai, László (1985). "Trading group theory for randomness". Proceedings of the seventeenth annual ACM symposium on Theory of computing - STOC '85. Proceedings of the Seventeenth Annual Symposium on the Theory of Computing. Stoc '85. pp. 421–429. CiteSeerX 10.1.1.130.3397. doi:10.1145/22145.22192. ISBN 978-0-89791-151-1. S2CID 17981195.*
56.   *Goldwasser, S.; Micali, S.; Rackoff, C. (1989). "The Knowledge Complexity of Interactive Proof Systems". SIAM Journal on Computing. 18 (1): 186–208. CiteSeerX 10.1.1.397.4002. doi:10.1137/0218012.*
57.   *Blakley, G. (June 1979). "Safeguarding cryptographic keys". Proceedings of AFIPS 1979. 48: 313–317.*
58.   *Shamir, A. (1979). "How to share a secret". Communications of the ACM. 22 (11): 612–613. doi:10.1145/359168.359176. S2CID 16321225.*
59.   *"6.5.1 What Are the Cryptographic Policies of Some Countries?". RSA Laboratories. Retrieved 26 March 2015.*
60.   *Rosenoer, Jonathan (1995). "Cryptography & Speech". CyberLaw. Missing or empty |url= (help)*
       "Archived copy". Archived from the original on 1 December 2005. Retrieved 23 June 2006.
61.   *"Case Closed on Zimmermann PGP Investigation". IEEE Computer Society's Technical Committee on Security and Privacy. 14 February 1996. Retrieved 26 March 2015.*
62.   *Levy, Steven (2001). Crypto: How the Code Rebels Beat the Government—Saving Privacy in the Digital Age. Penguin Books. p. 56. ISBN 978-0-14-024432-8. OCLC 244148644.*
63.   *"Bernstein v USDOJ". Electronic Privacy Information Center. United States Court of Appeals for the Ninth Circuit. 6 May 1999. Retrieved 26 March 2015.*
64.   *"Dual-use List – Category 5 – Part 2 – "Information Security"" (PDF). Wassenaar Arrangement. Retrieved 26 March 2015.*
65.   *".4 United States Cryptography Export/Import Laws". RSA Laboratories. Retrieved 26 March 2015.*
66.   *Schneier, Bruce (15 June 2000). "The Data Encryption Standard (DES)". Crypto-Gram. Retrieved 26 March 2015.*
67.   *Coppersmith, D. (May 1994). "The Data Encryption Standard (DES) and its strength against attacks" (PDF). IBM Journal of Research and Development. 38 (3): 243–250. doi:10.1147/rd.383.0243. Retrieved 26 March 2015.*
68.   *Biham, E.; Shamir, A. (1991). "Differential cryptanalysis of DES-like cryptosystems". Journal of Cryptology. 4 (1): 3–72. doi:10.1007/bf00630563. S2CID 206783462.*
69.   *"The Digital Millennium Copyright Act of 1998" (PDF). United States Copyright Office. Retrieved 26 March 2015.*
70.   *Ferguson, Niels (15 August 2001). "Censorship in action: why I don't publish my HDCP results". Missing or empty |url= (help)*
       "Archived copy". Archived from the original on 1 December 2001. Retrieved 16 February 2009.
71.   *Schneier, Bruce (6 August 2001). "Arrest of Computer Researcher Is Arrest of First Amendment Rights". InternetWeek. Retrieved 7 March 2017.*
72.   *Williams, Christopher (11 August 2009). "Two convicted for refusal to decrypt data". The Register. Retrieved 26 March 2015.*
73.   *Williams, Christopher (24 November 2009). "UK jails schizophrenic for refusal to decrypt files". The Register. Retrieved 26 March 2015.*
74.   *Ingold, John (4 January 2012). "Password case reframes Fifth Amendment rights in context of digital world". The Denver Post. Retrieved 26 March 2015.*
75.   *Leyden, John (13 July 2011). "US court test for rights not to hand over crypto keys". The Register. Retrieved 26 March 2015.*
76.   *"Order Granting Application under the All Writs Act Requiring Defendant Fricosu to Assist in the Execution of Previously Issued Search Warrants" (PDF). United States District Court for the District of Colorado. Retrieved 26 March 2015.*

Computer network, References

1. F. J. Corbató, et al., *The Compatible Time-Sharing System A Programmer's Guide* (MIT Press, 1963) ISBN 978-0-262-03008-3. "Shortly after the first paper on time-shared computers by C. Strachey at the June 1959 UNESCO Information Processing conference, H. M. Teager and J. McCarthy at MIT delivered an unpublished paper "Time-shared Program Testing" at the August 1959 ACM Meeting."
2. *"Computer Pioneers - Christopher Strachey". history.computer.org. Retrieved 2020-01-23.*
3. *"Reminiscences on the Theory of Time-Sharing". jmc.stanford.edu. Retrieved 2020-01-23.*
4. *"Computer - Time-sharing and minicomputers". Encyclopedia Britannica. Retrieved 2020-01-23.*
5. *Gillies, James M.; Gillies, James; Gillies, James and Cailliau Robert; Cailliau, R. (2000). How the Web was Born: The Story of the World Wide Web. Oxford University Press. pp. 13. ISBN 978-0-19-286207-5.*
6. *"История о том, как пионер кибернетики оказался не нужен СССР" [The story of how a cybernetics pioneer became unnecessary to the USSR]. ria.ru (in Russian). МИА «Россия сегодня». 2010-08-09. Retrieved 2015-03-04.* Главным делом жизни Китова, увы, не доведенным до практического воплощения, можно считать разработку плана создания компьютерной сети (Единой государственной сети вычислительных центров – ЕГСВЦ) для управления народным хозяйством и одновременно для решения военных задач. Этот план Анатолий Иванович предложил сразу в высшую инстанцию, направив в январе 1959 года письмо генсеку КПСС Никите Хрущеву. Не получив ответа (хотя начинание на словах было поддержано в различных кругах), осенью того же года он заново направляет на самый верх письмо, приложив к нему 200-страничный детальный проект, получивший название 'Красной книги'. [One can regard the magnum opus of Kitov's career as his elaboration of the plan – unfortunately never brought into practical form – for the establishment of a computer network (the Unified State Network of Computer Centres – EGSVTs) for the control of the national economy and simultaneously for the resolution of military tasks. Anatolii Ivanovich presented this plan directly to the highest levels, sending a letter in January 1959 to the General Secretary of the Communist Party of the Soviet Union Nikita Khrushchev. Not receiving a reply (although supported in various circles), in the autumn of the same year he again sent a letter to the very top, appending a 200-page detailed project plan, called the 'Red Book']
7. *"1960 - Metal Oxide Semiconductor (MOS) Transistor Demonstrated". The Silicon Engine. Computer History Museum.*
8. *Raymer, Michael G. (2009). The Silicon Web: Physics for the Internet Age. CRC Press. p. 365. ISBN 9781439803127.*
9. *Isaacson, Walter (2014). The Innovators: How a Group of Hackers, Geniuses, and Geeks Created the Digital Revolution. Simon and Schuster. pp. 237–246. ISBN 9781476708690.*
10. *"Inductee Details – Paul Baran". National Inventors Hall of Fame. Archived from the original on 2017-09-06. Retrieved 2017-09-06.*
11. *"Inductee Details – Donald Watts Davies". National Inventors Hall of Fame. Archived from the original on 2017-09-06. Retrieved 2017-09-06.*
12. *Chris Sutton. "Internet Began 35 Years Ago at UCLA with First Message Ever Sent Between Two Computers". UCLA. Archived from the original on 2008-03-08.*
13. *Gillies, James; Cailliau, Robert (2000). How the Web was Born: The Story of the World Wide Web. Oxford University Press. p. 25. ISBN 0192862073.*
14. *C. Hempstead; W. Worthington (2005). Encyclopedia of 20th-Century Technology. Routledge. ISBN 9781135455514.*
15. *Bennett, Richard (September 2009). "Designed for Change: End-to-End Arguments, Internet Innovation, and the Net Neutrality Debate" (PDF). Information Technology and Innovation Foundation. p. 11. Retrieved 2017-09-11.*
16. *Robert M. Metcalfe; David R. Boggs (July 1976). "Ethernet: Distributed Packet Switching for Local Computer Networks". Communications of the ACM. 19 (5): 395–404. doi:10.1145/360248.360253. S2CID 429216. Archived from the original on 2007-08-07.*
17. *Cerf, Vinton; Dalal, Yogen; Sunshine, Carl (December 1974), RFC 675, Specification of Internet Transmission Control Protocol*
18. *Pelkey, James L. (2007). "6.9 – Metcalfe Joins the Systems Development Division of Xerox 1975-1978". Entrepreneurial Capitalism and Innovation: A History of Computer Communications, 1968-1988. Retrieved 2019-09-05.*
19. *Spurgeon, Charles E. (2000). Ethernet The Definitive Guide. O'Reilly & Associates. ISBN 1-56592-660-9.*
20. *"Introduction to Ethernet Technologies". www.wband.com. WideBand Products. Retrieved 2018-04-09.*
21. *Pelkey, James L. (2007). "Yogen Dalal". Entrepreneurial Capitalism and Innovation: A History of Computer Communications, 1968-1988. Retrieved 2019-09-05.*
22. *D. Andersen; H. Balakrishnan; M. Kaashoek; R. Morris (October 2001), Resilient Overlay Networks, Association for Computing Machinery, retrieved 2011-11-12*
23. *"End System Multicast". project web site. Carnegie Mellon University. Archived from the original on 2005-02-21. Retrieved 2013-05-25.*
24. *Meyers, Mike (2012). CompTIA Network+ exam guide : (exam N10-005) (5th ed.). New York: McGraw-Hill. ISBN 9780071789226. OCLC 748332969.*
25. *"Bergen Linux User Group's CPIP Implementation". Blug.linux.no. Retrieved 2014-03-01.*
26. *A. Hooke (September 2000), Interplanetary Internet (PDF), Third Annual International Symposium on Advanced Radio Technologies, archived from the original (PDF) on 2012-01-13, retrieved 2011-11-12*
27. *"Define switch". webopedia. Retrieved 2008-04-08.*
28. *Bradley Mitchell. "bridge – network bridges". About.com. Archived from the original on 2008-03-28.*
29. *Andrew S. Tannenbaum, Computer Networks, 4th Edition, Prentice Hall (2003)*
30. For an interesting write-up of the technologies involved, including the deep stacking of communication protocols used, see.*Martin, Thomas. "Design Principles for DSL-Based Access Solutions" (PDF). Retrieved 2011-06-18.*
31. *Paetsch, Michael (1993). The evolution of mobile communications in the US and Europe: Regulation, technology, and markets. Boston, London: Artech House. ISBN 978-0-8900-6688-1.*
32. *Bush, S. F. (2010). Nanoscale Communication Networks. Artech House. ISBN 978-1-60807-003-9.*
33. *Margaret Rouse. "personal area network (PAN)". TechTarget. Retrieved 2011-01-29.*
34. *"New global standard for fully networked home". ITU-T Newslog. ITU. Archived from the original on 2009-02-21. Retrieved 2011-11-12.*
35. *"IEEE P802.3ba 40Gb/s and 100Gb/s Ethernet Task Force". IEEE 802.3 ETHERNET WORKING GROUP. Retrieved 2011-11-12.*
36. *"IEEE 802.20 Mission and Project Scope". IEEE 802.20 — Mobile Broadband Wireless Access (MBWA). Retrieved 2011-11-12.*
37. *Mansfield-Devine, Steve (December 2009). "Darknets". Computer Fraud & Security. 2009 (12): 4–6. doi:10.1016/S1361-3723(09)70150-2.*
38. *Wood, Jessica (2010). "The Darknet: A Digital Copyright Revolution" (PDF). Richmond Journal of Law and Technology. 16 (4). Retrieved 2011-10-25.*
39. RFC 5321, "Simple Mail Transfer Protocol", J. Klensin (October 2008)
40. RFC 1035, "Domain names – Implementation and Specification", P. Mockapetris (November 1987)
41. *Peterson, L.L.; Davie, B.S. (2011). Computer Networks: A Systems Approach (5th ed.). Elsevier. p. 372. ISBN 978-0-1238-5060-7.*
42. *ITU-D Study Group 2 (June 2006). Teletraffic Engineering Handbook (PDF). Archived from the original (PDF) on 2007-01-11.*
43. Telecommunications Magazine Online, Americas January 2003, Issue Highlights, Online Exclusive: Broadband Access Maximum Performance, Retrieved on February 13, 2005.
44. *"State Transition Diagrams". Archived from the original on 2003-10-15. Retrieved 2003-07-13.*
45. *"Definitions: Resilience". ResiliNets Research Initiative. Retrieved 2011-11-12.*
46. *Simmonds, A; Sandilands, P; van Ekert, L (2004). An Ontology for Network Security Attack. Lecture Notes in Computer Science. 3285. pp. 317–323. doi:10.1007/978-3-540-30176-9_41. ISBN 978-3-540-23659-7. S2CID 2204780.*
47. *"Is the U.S. Turning Into a Surveillance Society?". American Civil Liberties Union. Retrieved 2009-03-13.*
48. *Jay Stanley; Barry Steinhardt (January 2003). "Bigger Monster, Weaker Chains: The Growth of an American Surveillance Society" (PDF). American Civil Liberties Union. Retrieved 2009-03-13.*
49. *Emil Protalinski (2012-04-07). "Anonymous hacks UK government sites over 'draconian surveillance'". ZDNet. Retrieved 12 March 2013.*
50. *James Ball (2012-04-20). "Hacktivists in the frontline battle for the internet". The Guardian. Retrieved 2012-06-17.*
51. RFC 2547, "BGP/MPLS VPNs", E. Rosen; Y. Rekhter (March 1999)

Wireless security, References

1. *IEEE ñ 802.11-1997 Information Technology- telecommunications And Information exchange Between Systems-Local And Metropolitan Area Networks-specific Requirements-part 11: Wireless Lan Medium Access Control (MAC) And Physical Layer (PHY) Specifications. 1997. doi:10.1109/IEEESTD.1997.85951. ISBN 978-0-7381-3044-6.*
2. *"How to: Define Wireless Network Security Policies". Retrieved 2008-10-09.*
3. *"Wireless Security Primer (Part II)". windowsecurity.com. 2003-04-23. Retrieved 2008-04-27.*
4. *"Fitting the WLAN Security pieces together". pcworld.com. 2008-10-30. Retrieved 2008-10-30.*
5. *"SECURITY VULNERABILITIES AND RISKS IN INDUSTRIAL USAGE OF WIRELESS COMMUNICATION". IEEE ETFA 2014 – 19th IEEE International Conference on Emerging Technology and Factory Automation. Retrieved 2014-08-04.*
6. *"Network Security Tips". Cisco. Retrieved 2011-04-19.*
7. *"The Hidden Downside Of Wireless Networking". Retrieved 2010-10-28.*
8. *"Top reasons why corporate WiFi clients connect to unauthorized networks". InfoSecurity. 2010-02-17. Retrieved 2010-03-22.*
9. *Margaret Rouse. "Encryption". TechTarget. Retrieved 26 May 2015.*
10. *Bradely Mitchell. "What is Ad-Hoc Mode in Wireless Networking?". about tech. Retrieved 26 May 2015.*
11. *"SMAC 2.0 MAC Address Changer". klcconsulting.com. Retrieved 2008-03-17.*
12. *Lisa Phifer. "The Caffe Latte Attack: How It Works—and How to Block It". wi-fiplanet.com. Retrieved 2008-03-21.*
13. *"Caffe Latte with a Free Topping of Cracked WEP: Retrieving WEP Keys from Road-Warriors". Retrieved 2008-03-21.*
14. *"Official PCI Security Standards Council Site – Verify PCI Compliance, Download Data Security and Credit Card Security Standards".*
15. *"PCI DSS Wireless Guidelines" (PDF). Retrieved 2009-07-16.*
16. "The six dumbest ways to secure a wireless LAN", George Ou, March 2005, ZDNet
17. *"What is a WEP key?". lirent.net. Retrieved 2008-03-11.*
18. [e.g. "Weaknesses in the Key Scheduling Algorithm of RC4" by Fluhrer, Mantin and Shamir
19. "FBI Teaches Lesson In How To Break Into Wi-Fi Networks", informationweek.com
20. "Analyzing the TJ Maxx Data Security Fiasco", New York State Society of CPAs
21. "PCI DSS 1.2".
22. Hacking Wireless Networks for Dummies
23. *Robert McMillan. "Once thought safe, WPA Wi-Fi encryption is cracked". IDG. Retrieved 2008-11-06.*
24. *Nate Anderson (2009). "One-minute WiFi crack puts further pressure on WPA". Ars Technica. Retrieved 2010-06-05.*
25. *Kevin Beaver; Peter T. Davis; Devin K. Akin (2011-05-09). Hacking Wireless Networks For Dummies. p. 295. ISBN 978-1-118-08492-2.*
26. *"Extensible Authentication Protocol Overview". TechNet. Retrieved 26 May 2015.*
27. *"Extensible Authentication Protocol Overview". Microsoft TechNet. Retrieved 2008-10-02.*
28. *Joshua Bardwell; Devin Akin (2005). CWNA Official Study Guide (Third ed.). McGraw-Hill. p. 435. ISBN 978-0-07-225538-6.*
29. *George Ou. "Ultimate wireless security guide: A primer on Cisco EAP-FAST authentication". TechRepublic. Archived from the original on 2012-07-07. Retrieved 2008-10-02.*

30. *"Wi-Fi Protected Access". Wi-Fi Alliance. Archived from the original on May 21, 2007. Retrieved 2008-02-06.*
31. *"WiGLE – Wireless Geographic Logging Engine – Stats".*
32. *"WPA2 Hole196 Vulnerability". 2019-01-28.*
33. *"How to: Improve Wireless Security with Shielding". Retrieved 2008-10-09.*
34. *"What is Kismet?". kismetwireless.net. Retrieved 2008-02-06.*
35. *"End Point Wireless Security Solution Provides IT Control With User Flexibility". newsblaze.com. Retrieved 2008-03-03.*
36. *Khamish Malhotra; Stephen Gardner; Will Mepham. "A novel implementation of signature, encryption and authentication (SEA) protocol on mobile patient monitoring devices". IOS Press. Retrieved 2010-03-11.*
37. Wireless Networks, Hacks and Mods for Dummies
38. *"Offene Netzwerke auch für Deutschland!". netzpolitik.org. 2006-09-15.*

Computer access control, References

1. Dieter Gollmann. *Computer Security*, 3rd ed. Wiley Publishing, 2011, p. 387, bottom
2. Marcon, A. L.; Olivo Santin, A.; Stihler, M.; Bachtold, J., "A UCONabc Resilient Authorization Evaluation for Cloud Computing," *Parallel and Distributed Systems, IEEE Transactions on*, vol. 25, no. 2, pp. 457–467, Feb. 2014 doi:10.1109/TPDS.2013.113, bottom
3. *"Definition of: clipping level". PC Magazine.*
4. Jin, Xin, Ram Krishnan, and Ravi Sandhu "A unified attribute-based access control model covering dac, mac and rbac." *Data and Applications Security and Privacy* XXVI. Springer Berlin Heidelberg, 2012. 41–55.
5. *Hu, Vincent C.; Ferraiolo, David; Kuhn, Rick; Schnitzer, Adam; Sandlin, Kenneth; Miller, Robert; Scarfone, Karen. "Guide to Attribute Based Access Control (ABAC) Definition and Considerations" (PDF).*
6. eXtensible Access Control Markup Language (XACML) V3.0 approved as an OASIS Standard, eXtensible Access Control Markup Language (XACML) V3.0 approved as an OASIS Standard.
7. *Ferreira, Ana; Chadwick, David; Farinha, Pedro; Correia, Ricardo; Zao, Gansen; Chiro, Rui; Antunes, Luis (2009). "How to Securely Break into RBAC: The BTG-RBAC Model". Computer Security Applications Conference (ACSAC). IEEE. pp. 23–31. doi:10.1109/ACSAC.2009.12.*
8. *Brucker, Achim D.; Petritsch, Helmut (2009). "Extending Access Control Models with Break-glass.". ACM symposium on access control models and technologies (SACMAT). ACM Press. pp. 197–206. doi:10.1145/1542207.1542239.*
9. *Feltus C. (2014). Aligning Access Rights to Governance Needs with the Responsibility MetaModel (ReMMo) in the Frame of Enterprise Architecture. Archived from the original (PDF) on 2014-07-24.*
10. *Ballard, Ella Deon (2013). "Identity Management Guide: Managing Identity and Authorization Policies for Linux-Based Infrastructures". Red Hat. Retrieved 2014-01-06.* Any PAM service can be identified as to the host-based access control (HBAC) system in IdM.

Public key infrastructure, References

1. *"An Overview of Public Key Infrastructures (PKI)". Techotopia. Retrieved March 26, 2015.*
2. *"Internet X.509 Public Key Infrastructure Certificate Policy and Certification Practices Framework". IETF. Retrieved August 26, 2020.*
3. *"Public Key Infrastructure". MSDN. Retrieved March 26, 2015.*
4. *"Using Client-Certificate based authentication with NGINX on Ubuntu - SSLTrust". SSLTrust. Retrieved June 13, 2019.*
5. *Adams, Carlisle; Lloyd, Steve (2003). Understanding PKI: concepts, standards, and deployment considerations. Addison-Wesley Professional. pp. 11–15. ISBN 978-0-672-32391-1.*
6. *Trček, Denis (2006). Managing information systems security and privacy. Birkhauser. p. 69. ISBN 978-3-540-28103-0.*
7. *Vacca, Jhn R. (2004). Public key infrastructure: building trusted applications and Web services. CRC Press. p. 8. ISBN 978-0-8493-0822-2.*
8. *Viega, John; et al. (2002). Network Security with OpenSSL. O'Reilly Media. pp. 61–62. ISBN 978-0-596-00270-1.*
9. *McKinley, Barton (January 17, 2001). "The ABCs of PKI: Decrypting the complex task of setting up a public key infrastructure". Network World. Archived from the original on May 29, 2012.*
10. *Al-Janabi, Sufyan T. Faraj; et al. (2012). "Combining Mediated and Identity-Based Cryptography for Securing Email". In Ariwa, Ezendu; et al. (eds.). Digital Enterprise and Information Systems: International Conference, Deis, [...] Proceedings. Springer. pp. 2–3.*
11. "Mike Meyers CompTIA Security+ Certification Passport", by T. J. Samuelle, p. 137.
12. *Henry, William (March 4, 2016). "Trusted Third Party Service".*
13. http://news.netcraft.com/archives/2015/05/13/counting-ssl-certificates.html
14. *"CA:Symantec Issues". Mozilla Wiki. Retrieved January 10, 2020.*
15. *"Chrome's Plan to Distrust Symantec Certificates". Google security blog. Retrieved January 10, 2020.*
16. *"JDK-8215012 : Release Note: Distrust TLS Server Certificates Anchored by Symantec Root CAs". Java Bug Database. Retrieved January 10, 2020.*
17. Single Sign-On Technology for SAP Enterprises: What does SAP have to say? *"Archived copy". Archived from the original on July 16, 2011. Retrieved May 25, 2010.*
18. Ed Gerck, Overview of Certification Systems: x.509, CA, PGP and SKIP, in The Black Hat Briefings '99, http://www.securitytechnet.com/resource/rsc-center/presentation/black/vegas99/certover.pdf and http://mcwg.org/mcg-mirror/cert.htm Archived 2008-09-05 at the Wayback Machine
19. *"Decentralized Identifiers (DIDs)". World Wide Web Consortium. December 9, 2019. Archived from the original on May 14, 2020. Retrieved June 16, 2020.*
20. *"Decentralized Public Key Infrastructure" (PDF). weboftrust.info. December 23, 2015. Retrieved June 23, 2020.*
21. *Allen, Christopher (November 2015). "Decentralized Public Key Infrastructure" (PDF). Rebooting the Web of Trust design workshop.*
22. *Huang, Yahsin (May 14, 2019). "Decentralized Public Key Infrastructure (DPKI): What is it and why does it matter?". Hacker Noon. Retrieved May 22, 2019.*
23. *Fromknecht, Conner (November 2014). "A Decentralized Public Key Infrastructure with Identity Retention" (PDF). IACR Cryptology ePrint Archive.*
24. *Bünz, Benedikt (February 2019). "FlyClient: Super-Light Clients for Cryptocurrencies" (PDF). IACR Cryptology ePrint Archive.*
25. *Letz, Dominic (May 2019). "BlockQuick: Super-Light Client Protocol for Blockchain Validation on Constrained Devices" (PDF). IACR Cryptology ePrint Archive.*

14. Ran Canetti: Universally Composable Signature, Certification, and Authentication. CSFW 2004, http://eprint.iacr.org/2003/239

15. Ben Laurie, Ian Goldberg (18 January 2014). "Replacing passwords on the Internet AKA post-Snowden Opportunistic Encryption" (PDF).

16. "NIST Computer Security Publications – NIST Special Publications (SPs)". csrc.nist.gov. Retrieved 2016-06-19.

17. "SP 800-32 Introduction to Public Key Technology and the Federal PKI Infrastructure" (PDF). National Institute of Standards and Technology.

18. "SP 800-25 Federal Agency Use of Public Key Technology for Digital Signatures and Authentication" (PDF). National Institute of Standards and Technology.